WITHDRAWN

KING PHILIP'S WAR

A VOLUME IN THE SERIES

Native Americans of the Northeast
Culture, History, and the Contemporary

EDITED BY

COLIN G. CALLOWAY AND
BARRY O'CONNELL

KING
PHILIP'S
WAR

*Civil War
in New England,
1675–1676*

❦

JAMES D. DRAKE

University of Massachusetts Press

AMHERST

Copyright © 1999 by
The University of Massachusetts Press
All rights reserved
Printed in the United States of America
LC 99-35539
ISBN 1-55849-223-2 (cloth); 224-0 (pbk.)

Designed by Dennis Anderson
Set in Dante by Graphic Composition, Inc.
Printed and bound by Sheridan Books

Library of Congress Cataloging-in-Publication Data
Drake, James David, 1968–
King Philip's War : civil war in New England, 1675–1676 / James D. Drake.
p.   cm. — (Native Americans of the Northeast)
Includes bibliographical references (p.   ) and index.
ISBN 1-55849-223-2 (cloth : alk. paper). — ISBN 1-55849-224-0 (pbk. : alk. paper)
1. King Philip's War, 1675–1676.   I. Title.   II. Series.
E83.67.D74   1999
973.2′4—dc21
99-35539
CIP

British Library Cataloguing in Publication data are available.

CONTENTS

NOTE ON THE TEXT

To AVOID confusion, dates in this study have been rendered in the modern Gregorian calendar. The days from January 1 to March 25 have been cited as part of the new year. For example, what would have appeared as February 15, 1675/6 in a document has been changed to February 15, 1676.

Quotations for the most part follow the spelling and usage of the sources cited. Exceptions include the transliteration of "ye" and "yt" to "the" and "that." In many cases I have also changed *i* to *j* and *u* to *v* to make reading easier while maintaining the character and flavor of the original sources.

KING PHILIP'S WAR

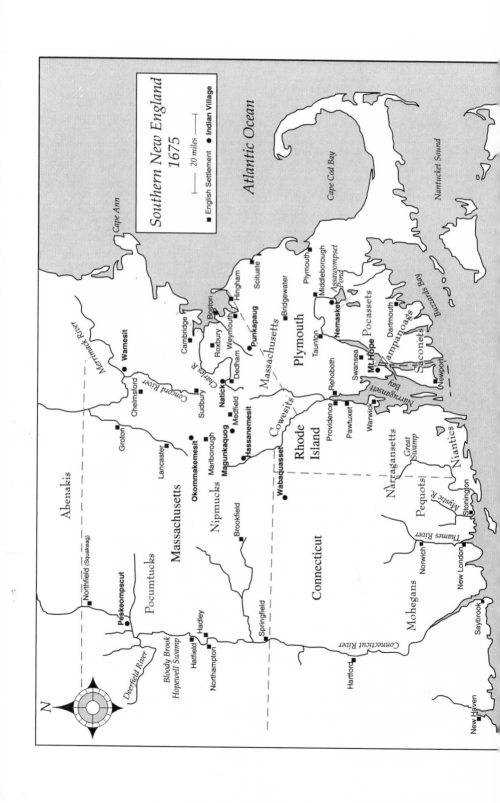

Southern New England
1675

—— 20 miles

■ English Settlement ● Indian Village

Atlantic Ocean

Cape Ann

Cape Cod Bay

Nantucket Sound

Buzzards Bay

Saconets

Pocassets

Wampanoags

Narragansett Bay

Newport

Mt. Hope

Swansea

Rehoboth

Providence

Pawtuxet

Warwick

Rhode Island

Niantics

Pequots

Mohegans

Narragansetts

Great Swamp

Mystic R.

Stonington

New London

Norwich

Thames River

Saybrook

New Haven

Hartford

Connecticut

Connecticut River

Springfield

Northampton

Hadley

Hatfield

Bloody Brook
Hopewell Swamp

Peskeompscut

Northfield (Squakeag)

Deerfield River

Pocumtucks

Abenakis

Merrimack River

Concord River

Wamesit

Chelmsford

Groton

Lancaster

Massachusetts

Nipmucks

Brookfield

Marlborough

Okommakemesit

Magunkaquog

Hassanemesit

Wabaquasset

Cowesits

Medfield

Sudbury

Natick

Dedham

Charles R.

Roxbury

Cambridge

Boston

Weymouth

Hingham

Scituate

Bridgewater

Punkapaug

Massachusetts

Plymouth

Plymouth

Middleborough

Assawompset
Pond

Nemasket

Taunton

Dartmouth

N

INTRODUCTION

WHAT MANY consider the deadliest war in American history began in June 1675 when some Wampanoag Indians under the leader Philip, pressured by the loss of land and political autonomy, rebelled against Plymouth Colony in New England. Philip and his followers, like many Indian groups in seventeenth-century New England, had submitted to a colony in an arrangement of mutual obligation. Philip's supporters believed that in exchange for their loyalty they could rely on Plymouth as a kind of protectorate. Events of the 1660s and 1670s, however, made it clear to the Wampanoags that their relationship with the colony had failed to protect them from English expansion. They had lost land while rival Christian Indians appeared to be gaining it. The Wampanoags felt they had to break off their political ties to Plymouth. They had to rebel.

First they attacked the southwestern Plymouth town of Swansea, killing a handful of colonists. At the time, no one foresaw that this relatively innocuous skirmish would initiate a chain of events leading all of southern New England into a full-scale war. The fault lines for such a conflict developed only over the next six months. Cultural differences, misunderstandings, the twists and turns of the war, and paranoia eventually lured most New England groups—Indian and English—into the contest. Although it involved both Indians and English, the opposing sides did not draw up neatly along ethnic lines. Some Indian groups even contributed more soldiers on a per capita basis than the English colonists to put down the Indian rebellion.

King Philip's War, as it came to be called, violently altered the course of New England history. For most of the fourteen-month contest, rebel forces dominated and threatened to topple the colonies and their Indian allies. The colonists' initial insistence on waging war according to English norms proved detrimental to their cause. As one colonial settlement after another felt the hit-and-run wrath of Philip's supporters, colonists began, at the urging of their Indian allies, to alter their strategy. Only after mimicking the enemy's tactics and relying more heavily on their native supporters were the colonies able to stem the tide of rebel success. Committed to total victory, the colonial forces then began in the spring of 1676 to punish ruthlessly those who refused to surrender. The English and their Indian allies managed to whittle away at the weakened rebel forces, until Philip himself succumbed to a gunshot from another Indian's musket in August 1676.

For most of New England's inhabitants, King Philip's War had devastating results. Yet the indigenous peoples suffered by far the most. Partly because Indians joined both sides, they experienced more casualties than the English; the proportion of Native Americans in the region went from one-fourth to one-tenth. The death and removal of so many Indians from the society shook to the ground the delicate political scaffolding upon which New England had been built. It forced the intervention of English royal authority to rebuild what had been painstakingly created over decades.

Without question, King Philip's War was brutal, vicious, and violent. But its importance does not stem from having the highest casualty rate in America's history. Indeed, the assertion that it was the "deadliest war" is problematic. This study is driven by a more fundamental question: Whose war was it? I proceed from the assumption that seventeenth-century New England is a foreign place for twentieth-century inhabitants of the United States. To view Philip's War as the deadliest in "our" history involves gerrymandering very narrowly across time the definition of "we." It entails a teleological view of seventeenth-century New England as America's origin, at the expense of the rest of the continent. Instead of viewing the English colonists living three hundred years ago as the seeds of a history that inevitably sprouted or progressed into the nation as we know it, I argue that the natives and the colonists of New England had enough in common to form their own unique society. Fought among various groups of these Indians and the English, King Philip's War was a civil war that destroyed that incarnation of New England.

Although the conflict sifted huge numbers of Indians out of the region and left English colonists at a new pinnacle of power, it should not be assumed that the English and the Indians had invariably been headed toward a dramatic confrontation. Attributing inevitability precludes the possibility of morally judging inhabitants of the past or seeing the past through their cultural filters. This becomes clear when one ponders a simple question: If a historical event was inevitable, who caused it to happen? The answer, of course, is "no one," if you truly believe it was inevitable. The event was beyond human control and its participants were not responsible for its outcome. Impersonal forces control human actions: physical factors, environment, custom, or even, in the words of Isaiah Berlin, "the 'natural' growth of some larger unit—a race, a nation."[1]

In writing this book I have assumed that the conflict's path and outcome depended more upon human choices and motives than upon vast impersonal forces. Yet many historians have made English (using the term loosely, given that huge numbers of Indians allied with the colonists) victory seem inevitable by pointing to factors such as numbers, technology, access to supplies, and culture. In a standard history of the war, *Flintlock and Tomahawk,* historian Douglas Leach trumpeted the theme of inevitability in the first sentence: "From the day when the first English settlers landed on New England shores and built permanent homes there, King Philip's War became virtually inevitable. Here in the wilderness two mutually incompatible ways of life confronted each other, and one of the two would have to prevail."[2] Later Leach explained that Indians, "in their primitive ignorance, failed to realize the size and strength of the invading force." He described Philip as the leader of the native rebellion, a "proud man embittered by the humiliations imposed upon him through superior strength."[3] Yet some of the most celebrated victories and infamous defeats in American military history prove that neither the size of an army nor its access to technology and supplies necessarily determines its success. In the American Revolution, patriots faced the highly regarded British army; they lost the vast majority of the battles but still won the war. Conversely, in Vietnam American forces ostensibly had superior weaponry and finances and won the majority of the battles, yet ultimately they suffered defeat. Such examples raise doubts about the common perception that the English inevitably defeated the Indians because of their military superiority.

The carnage and destruction suffered by both sides in King Philip's War should also make suspect any notion that the war's path was predetermined. As late as May 1676, many colonists feared defeat. New England's English settlers had to abandon about a third of their towns. At one point the English leadership, having to accept that they and their Indian allies were not destined to win the war but might very well lose it, desperately considered surrendering vast amounts of land and withdrawing behind a lengthy string of fortifications. An agent of the English Crown, Edmund Randolph, estimated that the English had lost houses and livestock valued at £150,000. English colonial officials added to this total by claiming that they had spent more than £100,000 prosecuting the war. If the English did indeed suffer £150,000 in property damage and spent £100,000 prosecuting the war, their total expense would have amounted to approximately £21 per household—more than the annual salary of the treasurer or the deputy governor of Connecticut in 1676. In making these expenditures the English certainly acted as if they had some control over the war's outcome. Precious little is known of Indian property losses in the war, but their actions suggest that they too felt they could influence the course of history. Indians rebelling against the English and their Indian allies boasted of their will to win. A group of them, believing they might eliminate the English presence in the region, noted that they would "war this twenty one years if you will; there are many Indians yet."[4]

Convictions such as these led to calamitous casualties for both sides. The region torn apart by the war was inhabited by approximately sixty thousand English settlers and eighteen thousand Indians. Contemporary casualty estimates varied widely, yet they all pointed to a sizable percentage of this population. Depending upon whose figures are used, English deaths amounted to anywhere from less than 1 percent to 5 percent of their population. Indians suffered much more, losing about 40 percent of their population.[5] Such estimates have led to the familiar refrain over the last forty years that King Philip's War, relative to population, was the bloodiest in American history.

THE DEADLIEST war in "our" history. The assertion has been made many times over the years, but authors never elaborate. Although King Philip's War was certainly no less violent than America's other wars, the notion that it fell within "American" or "our" history is problematic. It should spark an obvious question, one asked by humans throughout the ages, How wide is the circle of we?[6] By presenting King Philip's as the deadliest war in "our" or "American" history, scholars have implicitly posited a close relationship between late-twentieth-century U.S. citizens, on one hand, and English colonists and Native Americans living more than three hundred years ago, on the other; they have defined a society—a "we"—across time. But setting aside the disjunctions of time, there are further questions. Were communities of English colonists in the Chesapeake, with their unique governments, a part of the same society as their New England counterparts? Is it just the English colonists who are part of our history, or are Indians included as well, even though many of them resisted colonial authority? If New England's Indians are included, should not all the other Indians within what is now the United States be construed as part of "our" or "American" history? How about the French in the Mississippi Valley or the Spanish in the Southwest? Raising such questions makes it clear that defining a society—especially one that spans three hundred years of history and includes widely varying Indian cultures and groups of English colonists with divergent purposes, all in the context of the emerging and maturing United States—is no easy matter.[7]

Failure to address this issue explicitly has kept historians from comparing the death rate of King Philip's War to those of other conflicts in North America that did not involve English combatants. The Beaver Wars between the Iroquois and various Great Lakes Indians in the mid-seventeenth century, for example, had horrific effects on the populations of the participating Indian nations, prompting historian Richard White to write, "Never again in North America would Indians fight each other on this scale or with this ferocity." The French colonization of Louisiana led to the Natchez War, in which the Natchez were virtually exterminated. And the Pueblo Revolt of 1680 produced casualty estimates of nearly 20 percent for settlers of European descent in New Mexico. All of these took place, at least partially, in regions that eventually became part of the United States.[8]

Yet King Philip's War is rarely, if ever, compared to conflicts such as the Beaver Wars, the Natchez War, or the Pueblo Revolt; instead, it is measured against the Civil War, World War II, and the Vietnam War. In making these comparisons and foisting the label of "most deadly war in American history" on King Philip's War, historians have implicitly defined a society and anachronistically imposed its boundaries on people in the past. Worshiping, in the words of historian Marc Bloch, the "idol of origins," these scholars point to New England as the site where American history began. Bloch might warn this cohort of scholars that "[g]reat oaks from little acorns grow. But only if they meet favorable conditions of soil and climate."[9] Never mind the possibility that the "great oak" of the United States might actually be a forest that grew out of many "acorns."

How is it, then, that for at least forty years historians have managed so casually to make seventeenth-century New Englanders past members of our society—within the circle of "we"—and to exclude the continent's other inhabitants, by calling King Philip's War the deadliest in American history? In answering this question, we ought to take a cue from Jill Lepore's insightful study of the conflict, *The Name of War,* and recognize that "wars generate acts of narration" that work toward "defining the geographical, political, cultural, and sometimes racial and national boundaries between peoples."[10] While the war was still raging in the forests and towns of New England, English men and women from throughout the region started fighting for control of its written history (contemporary Indians did not write any histories of the war). They set out to memorialize the conflict for posterity, hoping that ink would outlast any physical scars New Englanders had suffered. Although they may have harbored doubts about their civility and moral conduct when they were fighting with muskets, when fighting with words they absolved themselves of guilt. In this respect the battle for control of the meaning of the war differed much from the conduct of the actual conflict.

Many have argued that wars can make life psychologically simpler; they focus attention. There are good guys and bad guys. Internal problems may seem trite compared to an external threat. Suicide rates go down. Economic hardship that would be intolerable during peace can appear logical and maybe even as a kind of sacrifice to a good cause. But war does not just clarify life's complexities or make them seem less important; sometimes people have to oversimplify issues in order to wage war. The chaos of King Philip's War challenged the identities of both the Indians and the English. Individuals and groups could not easily be categorized as friend or foe. Ethnicity was no litmus test of alliance. Such confusion made people grope for clear dividing lines, which did not exist. In a letter to the governor of Connecticut just a few months into the conflict, Rhode Islander Samuel Gorton observed, "People are apt in these dayes to give credit to every flying and false report; and not only so, but they will report it again, as it is said of old, report and we will report; and by that means they become deceivers and tormentors one of another, by feares and jelousies." The result was "a rumour as though all the Indians were in combination . . . as though God brought his people hither to destroy them by delivering them into the hands of such Barbarians."[11]

Indians, too, struggled to distinguish ally from enemy. They agonized because often they had overlapping identities, and sometimes they belonged only ambivalently to a community. Even Englishmen recognized vacillation on the part of Indians. William Hubbard noted after the outbreak of violence that "many of the Indians were in a kind of Maze, not knowing well what to do; sometimes ready to stand for the English, as formerly they were wont to do, sometimes inclining to strike in with Philip."[12] When asked why they attacked those English who had been "kind Neighbours," a group of Narragansetts admitted that they "were in A Strang Way."[13] And many Indians' loyalty to the English waned when they were asked to attack other Indians with whom they were on good terms.[14] Both sides suffered from muddled convictions and uncertainties about the war's boundaries and divisions.

In this confusion the English turned to writing, almost as therapy, to render the conflict comprehensible and justifiable. Their texts simplified the war by bifurcating the society along ethnic lines and invoking the idea of inevitable progress. Of course, most histories of the conflict were written with the benefit of hindsight and failed to capture the confusion and uncertainty felt by colonists and their Indian allies when rebel attacks struck like hammer blows for months on end. In his *Brief History of the War with the Indians of New England,* one of the more prolific Puritan writers on the war, Increase Mather, interpreted the events of the 1675 uprising as indicators of either Puritan impiety or moral advancement. Mather blamed his fellow settlers for bringing the conflict upon Massachusetts Colony, but he showed little doubt that victory would be realized once God had taught Massachusetts a lesson. In his history, the Puritans were "God's chosen people," whereas the Indians were "heathens." God had destined the Puritans and the Indians to be separate communities. Because Mather believed that God omnipotently imposed a sacred teleology on all events, his account, although written while Massachusetts was still reeling from the destruction of the war, left little doubt as to who would be the victor. On the settlers' narrow failure to capture the Indian leader Philip early in the war, for example, Mather concluded, "God saw it not good for us as yet," implying that God would eventually bring victory.[15] Mather's Indians could never be ready for deliverance, because he did not see them as a part of God's chosen people. Yet God appeared so powerful to Mather that his hand controlled even some "heathen" Indians. When Puritan piety reached a certain threshold in May 1676, "God had let loose the Mohawks upon our Enemies," and victory was right around the corner.[16] God's constant control of human events shaped the war experience, and military setbacks appeared as temporary deviations that would eventually self-correct: God would undoubtedly lead his chosen people to victory.

Many other ministers in New England agreed. Even Mather's arch rival, William Hubbard, spoke in similar terms about the role of divine providence in shaping the course of the war. Like Mather, Hubbard viewed the region's English colonists as God's chosen people, stacking the deck heavily against their Indian opposition. In his history of the war, Hubbard wrote, "[A]lthough the Almighty hath made use of them to be a scourge to his People, he hath now turned his hand against them, to their utter destruction and extirpation from off the face of the earth, peradventure to make room for others of his People to come in their room, and in their stead."[17] Believing they were God's chosen, New England's Puritans looked to divine forces as the root of the conflict and its resolution instead of the human choices and motives of the Indians they fought.

However, the community of God's chosen people that Mather and Hubbard constructed did not correspond to the sense of community perceived by other English settlers in the conflict-ridden region. The composition of the English population was far from homogeneous, and within it various groups contested the meaning of the war. They debated whether war should be waged, and some colonists even withheld support. The Quakers of Rhode Island most vocally condemned the war, not only because of their pacifist beliefs but also because of their ostracization and persecution at the hands of the Puritans. Yet, for all of the differences the Quakers had with the Massachusetts Puritans, they shared with them, especially as the war progressed, a broader sense of English identity. They felt closer to the Puritans than to the Indians, and, like Mather, most Quakers interpreted the war as a sign of God's wrath against the English. In Quaker accounts of the war, the Indians had little historical agency; they were relegated to the role of reacting to the machinations of English settlers. So although Puritans and Quakers offered conflicting interpretations of the war, their accounts shared a dismissal and a lack of understanding of Indian culture. They both robbed the Indians of the power to alter the course of history. They indirectly wove inevitability into their narratives.

In this war of words, many Quakers interpreted the conflict as God's retribution against Massachusetts for the executions of Quakers between 1659 and 1661. A Quaker fisherman from Marblehead claimed that "The Cause of the Judgments of God upon us by Reason of the Wars was theire murthering of Quakers." During the war, Edward Wharton, a Quaker resident of Salem, built a monument in honor of the executed Quakers that also offered his view of the war: "Though here our Innocent Bodyes in silent Earth do lie, Yet are our Righteous Souls at Rest, our Blood for Vengance Cry." Though it is noteworthy that these men saw the Indians in part as avenging the Puritans' persecution of Quakers, it is even more important to recognize that none saw the Indians as being on their side or of their own kind. The Marblehead fisherman saw the war as "Judgments of God upon *us*," meaning English settlers, including both Quakers and Puritans. And Edward Wharton described his monument in a pamphlet entitled *New England's Present Sufferings under their cruel Neighboring Indians,* implying that Indians were outside of both the Quaker and the New England—as they tended to narrowly define it—society. Ironically, the entire community had to suffer at the hand of the "other," to avenge the wrongs committed within the community. In memorializing the war, they narrowly defined and oversimplified the circle of "we."[18]

These early attempts to control the memory of King Philip's War, with God guiding events in favor of the English community or avenging wrongs within it, helped to set the tone for future writers, regardless of ethnicity. The "we" that subsequent writers constructed mirrored the simplistic bifurcation of races found in seventeenth-century texts. Even Indian authors constructed a dichotomous conflict, pitting the English against the Indians. They anachronistically projected their postwar world—where Anglo-Americans were the overwhelmingly dominant cultural group—onto the prewar and wartime society. William Apess, a Methodist minister, a Pequot, and probably the most famous Native American writer of the nineteenth century, exemplified the revising of history to create a cultural identity. His writings served to preserve an Indian identity opposing an English one. In them he simultaneously displayed loyalty to the Pequots—who constituted one of the Indian groups most closely allied with the English during King Philip's War—and to a pan-Indian cultural heritage and resistance movement. Philip, in Apess's memory, was "King of the Pequot," even though he was a Wampanoag, and "the greatest man that ever lived upon American shores."[19] Apess's work reflected the reconstitution of Pequot identity in the postwar world. As a Christian and a believer in a shared origin for all peoples, he could not rely on an origin myth to posit a distinct communal identity for the Pequots and Native Americans as a whole; rather, he had to refer to a revised account of the past in which his people had actively opposed the English—a narrative that Pequots who fought in the war might not have recognized.

The legend of the surviving Indians within New England also often posits an oppositional relationship between themselves and the English. Most of New England's present-day Indians, even those most directly descended from groups that allied with the English, trace their ancestry back to those who fought against the colonists. They believe Philip's ghost is still in New England and that he contacts them periodically.[20] A selective amnesia or disavowal of their past assistance in putting down Philip characterizes their memory of the war. Mashpee Indians, under the influence of missionary Richard Bourne, fought alongside the English. Yet, in a recent Indian-produced history of the Mashpees, the author describes the group as "under Philip" at the outbreak of conflict. The work's description of seventeenth-century Indian-English relations bifurcates the two ethnicities much as the writings of Increase Mather and his Quaker rivals do.[21] Like Quakers and Puritans, descendants of the Indians who allied with the English have written accounts of the past that render it comprehensible to them, revising as necessary to do so.

The partisan disputes of Quakers and Puritans and the writings of William Apess may seem distant to many twentieth-century Americans, but some of their core assumptions have clearly survived. Fast forwarding to the second half of the twentieth century, the United States has attained a pinnacle of power unprecedented in world history. In this environment Douglas Leach published his *Flintlock and Tomahawk*, which to this day remains a standard account of the war. Much of Leach's analysis hinges upon a dichotomy between the "civilized" English and the "savage" Indians. Whereas Mather held a strong belief in divine providence, Leach clings to an equally powerful guiding force—progress. Primitive societies naturally evolved into advanced ones—or became extinct. Within this framework the Indians and the English could not coexist. Leach thus portrays the English and the Indians as groups that had nothing in common.

Their interaction could not result in mutual adaptation or produce anything new akin to what happens when different cultures combine in a
"melting pot." One society had to survive at the other's expense.

As primarily a military history, *Flintlock and Tomahawk* should seemingly allow for a tremendous amount of contingency. Of all forms of human interaction, war arguably most defies the predictability of social science theory. Yet a closer examination of Leach's language reveals a
conflict following a formula wherein the Indians fight the English and the
outcome is easily predicted. Leach adopts the language handed down to
him from the war's English contemporaries and early historians. He re-
serves disparaging remarks for Indians and favorable ones for colonists.
Thus he shows the similarities between a seventeenth- and a twentieth-
century historian.

Like Leach, Increase Mather used different terms to describe the actions of the Indians and the colonists. Mather's Indians "lurked," "slaugh-
tered," and were capable of "treachery"—pejoratives never used against
the English. In Leach, the colonists also faced "lurking" Indians; they accepted a "danger of treachery" when dealing with Christian Indians;
Philip could not control the "ardor of his hot-blooded braves;" and when
war broke out, his "warriors either were unleashed at this time, or managed to slip their leash."[22] Likewise, two tactically similar offensives, one
undertaken by Indians and the other by colonists, receive drastically
different descriptions in Leach's account. In both cases, combatants set
fire to their opponent's settlements. Yet Leach's terminology is just as
dichotomous as Mather's: "[T]he savages indulged in an orgy of destruction," whereas in the English offensive the "officers had demonstrated a
bold and spirited leadership" by giving orders "to set the wigwams on
fire as the safest means of routing the enemy within the walls."[23] Like
Increase Mather, Leach favors the side to which he feels a stronger sense
of attachment. A belief in Euramerican progress gave him a Whiggish
view of the past and reinforced his sense of social identity with the winning side in American history.

KING PHILIP'S War generated narratives that fostered the development
of racial and eventually national identities—identities that have allowed
historians to label the conflict the "deadliest in our history" without elaboration or qualms. Granted, a line of ancestry can be drawn from seventeenth-century New England colonists to the American Revolution. But

many in the present-day United States trace their ancestry to other times
and places. For the large mestizo population of the American Southwest,
the dichotomous portrayal of Indian-white relations in the Northeast
offers little to explain the beginnings of their diverse heritage. Historians
must act more cautiously around the "idol of origins," impersonal forces
of inevitability, and the definition of "we." The powerful lures of these
concepts stem from narratives, generated by the war, that served partisan
purposes and reduced its complexity. Such texts describe a reality or a
context that many of the war's participants did not experience. They have,
however, helped define some of the contours of modern debates surrounding American identity.

Race, culture wars, identity politics: our society is brimming with tension and antagonism on the issue of who we are. This historical study
enters the debate on national identity with the belief that shedding light
on the past helps people find meaning in the present. Today's generation
is not the first to struggle over how to keep a society from unraveling.
Yet historian David Hollinger suggests that Americans now face the opportunity to create a *"postethnic* future" in which existing tensions are reduced. He envisions the possibility of a type of multiculturalism that he
terms *"cosmopolitanism"* guiding individuals in shaping their identity.
Cosmopolitanism allows the individual freedom to trace his or her ethnic
descent in ways other than those prescribed by social conventions.[24]

As an example of prescribed racial affiliation despite a mixed heritage,
Hollinger points out that the African American author Alex Haley felt
compelled in his book *Roots* to trace his heritage to Gambia rather than
to Ireland, the home of his white grandfather. In a similar vein, historian
Barbara Fields notes how arbitrarily a white woman can give birth to a
black child but a black woman cannot give birth to a white child. Abandoning such conventions and recognizing a more complex reality, children who have one black and one white parent could voluntarily trace
their ancestry along either parent's lineage and appreciate themselves as
a part of that culture. In Hollinger's words, cosmopolitanism or postethnicity "reacts against the nation's invidiously ethnic history, builds upon
the current generation's unprecedented appreciation of previously ignored cultures, and supports on the basis of revokable consent those
affiliations of shared descent that were previously taken to be primordial."
In a nutshell, postethnicity complicates our racial categories and recog-
nizes that people have multiple identities and are often ethnic hybrids.[25]

What if we were to apply such aspirations to the broader notion of a national descent? The myth portraying English colonists in the Northeast as the origins of U.S. history would certainly have less holding power, and Americans would feel more free to look upon other groups as part of the national genealogy. We could conceive of the United States as having grown into a forest of oaks originating from many acorns. We would recognize, as did the many Algonquians who fought against Philip's forces in 1675 and the English who opposed the conflict, that ethnicity is not necessarily a primordial shaper of one's identity. Although many of our laws, customs, and even language have English origins, recognizing the hybrid nature of past American societies highlights the importance of non-English peoples in sowing the seeds of our republic.

This study approaches King Philip's War with an inclusive spirit and embraces the hybridity of colonial New England. Ever since the conflict ceased, scores of writers have told powerful stories about it that have resonated well among their readers. These readers, however, have been far from representative of those who actually participated in the conflict. Indian voices are scarce, and we must compensate for that in order to achieve a narrative that takes in the experiences of a broad segment of New England's wartime population. No single overview of the war can completely capture its events precisely as experienced by any one of its individual participants. Yet narrative history is more than an artificial order imposed on a chaotic series of events after the fact. The events of King Philip's War had at the time, as they do now, multiple narratives woven into them.[26] Many of these narrative strands cannot be recovered from the war of words to memorialize the conflict; the actions of contemporaries, archaeological evidence, and the language of Indians must sometimes be allowed to speak louder than the many texts produced by Englishmen. I make no claim that this work is comprehensive, but it is synthetic. Drawing heavily on the work of other scholars, it emphasizes an inclusive analytical thread for the war. It is an effort to render the conflict comprehensible to today's readers without violating the worldviews of the majority of its participants.

None have had their worldview more abused in the war's histories than those Indians who allied with the English. In the words of historian Richard R. Johnson, "The enduring characterization that pits white man against Indian has a satisfying simplicity that has too often obscured a more complex reality." This has manifested itself in histories of seventeenth-century New England in an overemphasis on King Philip's War as a conflict *between* Indians and English rather than *among* various groups of them. This distortion is attributable largely, Johnson says, to "the widespread assumption that such stereotyped rivalries were a prompt and inevitable consequence of a meeting of the races." The rhetoric of historians from Mather to the present, polarizing English and Indian, has masked the complex reality that historical actors faced. Relative to population, many New England Indian groups provided more combatants to the "English" side of the conflict than did their neighboring colonists (see chapter 4). Moreover, Indians tortured and killed Indians on the opposing side, suggesting that relations between some groups of Indians were as strained as those between some of the English and some of the Indians, who were pitted against one another.[27] It is not enough merely to pay lip service to these facts; historians must rethink their view of the conflict as an unavoidable contest between bifurcated Indian and English cultures.

Rather than positing seventeenth-century English colonists as the seed of our "we," the twentieth-century United States, and overemphasizing the English-versus-Indian aspect of King Philip's War, I argue that seventeenth-century colonists and natives created their own unique "we" and together constituted a society. The New England that erupted into violent conflict in 1675 had been built by the conscious interweaving of English and Indian polities by individuals hoping to preserve their identities in a rapidly changing world. This entailed creating strong links between peoples of diverse backgrounds. By 1675 many Indians and English people had tried to merge their futures and needed one another for their communities to persist.

An analogy from chemistry might help illustrate this point, keeping in mind, of course, that this is a study of people and not a physical science. Like the atoms in a covalent chemical bond, wherein distinct atoms bond together by sharing electrons, the Indians and the English became one society by virtue of their shared social space and economy, as well as by their overlapping legal and political systems. Just as the nuclei of atoms in a covalent bond remain intact, Indian and English communities to a large extent retained their distinct cultural identities, but they concurrently merged together to form a new form of matter, a "covalent society." For this reason King Philip's War, from the perspective of many contemporaries, took on aspects of a civil war, severing the ties that bound the region's various Indian and English groups together. King Philip's War destroyed a society that comprised both English and Indians. This is not to say that the conflict was not one of conquest or a race war; those facets of King Philip's War have been documented elsewhere, but those histories give the civil component minimal consideration.

The postwar incarnation of New England society differed so much from its prewar version that it must be considered a new one. Its form had fundamentally changed, just as removing the oxygen atom from a water molecule leaves behind hydrogen rather than a smaller water molecule. After the war Indians lacked the political clout to significantly shape the region's future. New England society, its "we," had to be rebuilt. In this respect, although King Philip's War might not have been inevitable or the most deadly war in American history, it is certainly difficult to imagine American history taking the path that it did had the conflict been avoided. It was a necessary but far from sufficient cause to create the society we live in. Seventeenth-century New England was not simply a less developed version of our society. The past, after all, is a foreign country.[28]

1

CHIEFS AND FOLLOWERS

IF WE COULD have seen it, New England in the years before King Philip's War would have been nearly unrecognizable. The harbors and streams were cleaner, the forests thicker in spots, and temperatures a little cooler. The largest town, Boston, consisted of a few thousand people clustered on a patch of land that, depending upon the tide, had been an island at times.[1] One out of four of the region's seventy-eight thousand inhabitants in 1675 was Indian. And if we could get into the heads of all of those people, we would undoubtedly be struck by their mindset. One of the hardest tasks that faces a historian is placing the reader into the perspective and context looming before the historical participants under discussion. When a person studies seventeenth-century New England, it is difficult to set aside the knowledge that its English and Indians were going to become embroiled in a climactic war in 1675. Although historians have gone so far as to explain the 1675 conflict as "virtually inevitable" once English settlers arrived in the region, colonists and Indians in previous years did not operate with the assumption that a tremendous war lay ahead in 1675.[2] Rather, groups more often than not worked energetically to prevent the conflict that eventually ensued.

The emphasis on conflict rather than accommodation has stemmed partly from the concerns reflected in the writings of the English. As historian Jill Lepore has demonstrated, in the midst of hostilities colonists wrote more than they did when there were peaceful relations among the different English and Indian groups.[3] To be sure, there was more tension in the region than its inhabitants would have liked. But widening the angle of vision and putting New England into a hemispheric context reveals relative peace and even remarkable parallels between English and Indian polities. The colonists and the Indians had the necessary mutual cultural traits to facilitate the intermeshing of their previously distinct societies. Understanding the extent to which various groups fused together is essential to understanding how they subsequently came apart.

Connecticut, Massachusetts, Rhode Island, and Plymouth—the English colonies—had intricate ties to the Nipmucks, the Mohegans, the Narragansetts, the Pequots, and the Wampanoags—the largest Indian ethnic and political entities in the region.[4] Although most of these designations are modern-day political units, they were not nearly so important or rigid in the seventeenth century. Then they constituted just a handful of the region's complex overlapping political entities. On one hand, both English and Indians drew their primary political identity from their local village or band rather than from any regional polity. On the other, regional leaders of both colonial governments and Indian confederations struggled against these centrifugal, localistic forces in efforts to reinforce the power of their regional polities. Within this context, both regional and local leaders entered their communities into voluntary, and sometimes overlapping, coalitions of perceived common political interests. It was both local communities and these voluntary coalitions that formed the true warp and woof of seventeenth-century political life in the Northeast.[5] Recognition of the overlap among Indian and English polities sheds light on the linkages that led to the relatively peaceful coexistence of New England's inhabitants between 1620 and 1675, a covalent society.

A CENTURY earlier and thousands of miles removed from the arrival of Pilgrims in New England, the Spaniard Hernando Cortés led an expedition into central Mexico. By 1521, two years after first arriving, his party, numbering in the hundreds, had conquered Indians numbering in the millions. A decade later, a Spanish party under the leadership of Francisco Pizarro accomplished a similar feat when it made short work of the Inca empire. Remarkably, neither Spanish expedition had professional soldiers in it, and 90 percent of the men involved had no formal military training.[6] In subsequent expeditions, adventurers from Spain and other European countries, fueled by visions of wealth and the relative ease with which Cortés and Pizarro had defeated the densest populations in the Americas, tried to replicate their results against other Indians in locations throughout North America. For most of these men, the past did not repeat itself.

The conquests of Cortés and Pizarro were largely ones of Indian labor, and it was the nature of the Indian societies they met that made conquest possible. Their actions were profitable because they gained access to Indian wealth in the form of *encomiendas*—most simply, the legal title to tribute that would have been due an Indian leader in preconquest society. In both central Mexico and Peru, the conquerors found social structures and tribute mechanisms upon which they could capitalize. Rather than try to destroy these, the Spanish found they could base the jurisdictions of their encomiendas on those of indigenous sovereign entities. In the early phases of postconquest society, Spaniards simply replaced the local leaders at the head of the social hierarchy. For Indian commoners, life went on much as it had in the past, the main difference being that the product of their labor ended up in the hands of a European. Since they lived sedentary lives, they did not consider fleeing or resisting Spanish invasion as an option, because it would have constituted a wholesale change in their way of life. Thus, submission to new rulers seemed the more palatable alternative; they had relatively little will to fight, so they surrendered even though they vastly outnumbered the invaders.[7]

In contrast to the conquests of central Mexico and the Incan empire, most subsequent European forays into the Americas dealt with less sedentary Indians. The results differed dramatically. When the Spanish headed north from central Mexico, they met the Chichimecs—nonsedentary Indians. To render these Indians profitable or even nominally Christian, Spaniards tried to institute wholesale changes in their way of life, imposing sedentariness to make them like their southern counterparts. They failed. Because they were nomadic, the Chichimecs viewed Spanish efforts to colonize their labor as fundamental challenges to their way of life. Their will to fight was strong. Facing inspired opposition, the Spanish had to adapt their techniques to the new circumstances. Efforts to conquer the nonsedentary Indians of northern Mexico led to paying European soldiers for their services—for the first time in the Americas. Since nomadic Indians did not have the same permanent infrastructure as the Nahuas of central Mexico, the Spanish had to build it (or force Indian slaves to do so). Hence, the presidio and the mission were born. Despite such measures, the Spanish were unable to replicate their feats in central Mexico and Peru; the Indians persistently rebelled against Spanish authority.[8]

The Spanish example highlights the ability of indigenous cultures and institutions to shape the contact experience. A provocative synthesis of early Latin American history by James Lockhart and Stuart B. Schwartz has gone so far as to argue that "Indian peoples and the resources of their lands were the primary determinants of regional differentiation." In broad brush strokes, Lockhart and Schwartz divide Indians of the Americas into three categories: sedentary, nonsedentary, and, somewhere between the two, semisedentary. They are admittedly arbitrary in breaking a continuum of lifeways down into three categories. Nevertheless, the categories do have predictive power when it comes to Indian-European contact. Sedentary Indians, usually with vast wealth recognized by Europeans, attracted the first colonists. These Indians lived in the societies that looked most familiar to Europeans, and they had populations in which Europeans saw the labor necessary to extract wealth from the Americas. Only in areas like central Mexico and Peru did the Spanish find people who lived lives relatively similar to those of Europeans, enabling them to establish lucrative encomiendas, Indian parishes, and functioning Indian municipalities. As Lockhart writes, "the Europeans and indigenous peoples of the central areas had more in common than either did with the other peoples of the hemisphere."[9]

The most different from Europeans, regardless of nationality, were the nomadic peoples of the Americas. In places like northern Mexico, the Argentine Pampas, the American Great Plains, and the American Southwest, small numbers of indigenous peoples fought European and Euramerican domination well into the nineteenth century. In an instance known to most Americans, a small band of Apaches, including Geronimo, refused to succumb to a well-armed U.S. military force numbering in the thousands. These Indians gained a reputation as the "fightingest" of the United States.[10] Nonsedentary Indians usually had the smallest and most mobile societal units, inhabited the lands least attractive to Europeans, and were the least willing to accept the changes that Euramericans tried to foist on them. When Euramericans and nomadic indigenous peoples met, relatively little accommodation occurred and conflict was the norm.[11] The two groups had little cultural overlap and did not recognize much usefulness in one another.

Northern New England, what is now Maine, New Hampshire, and Vermont, was inhabited by relatively nonsedentary Indians. As might be expected, seventeenth-century English colonists never established much more than a minimal foothold in this region. Southern New England,

what is now Massachusetts, Rhode Island, and Connecticut, was a different matter; natives there had semisedentary lifestyles. To be sure, there
were local variations in the economies and political structures of southern
New England's Indian groups, with Indians along the coasts and in the
river valleys tending to be slightly more sedentary and living in more
densely populated settlements than those in upland areas. But most of
them subsisted on agriculture in combination with hunting or fishing, in
contrast to northern New England's Indians, who relied much less on
agriculture.[12] It was the coastal and river Indians that the English colonists
first met and had their most extended, intimate contact with. Like semisedentary Indians throughout the Americas, these Indians had an ability
and a desire to resist European domination somewhere between that of
sedentary and nonsedentary Indians. Rather than being easily conquered
or resisting initially and indefinitely, southern New England's Indians explored the many areas of cultural overlap they had with the European
newcomers. They tested the English political system, and many groups
found that they could use it to their advantage. In some respects the arrival of the English "magnified" internal social and political trends that
were in place before their arrival. For the English, in keeping with patterns demonstrated throughout the Americas, southern New England's
Indians, as semisedentary peoples, could appear valuable, even familiar.
The colonists, in Lockhart and Schwartz's words again, might "use the
social structure of the semi-sedentary groups to their advantage to the
extent that they were willing and able to become a part of it themselves."[13]
And so they did. Southern New England Indians and English colonists
had social structures and lifestyles that enabled them to intermingle with
relative peace—at least temporarily.

ARCHAEOLOGICAL EVIDENCE shows that before they met the English, Indian communities in southern New England had been in flux. In the centuries just before European arrival, they had developed more densely
populated, complex societies. This change was especially pronounced in
coastal regions, where population growth stressed the supply of shellfish
around 1300. Facing food shortages, coastal Indians put more resources
into agriculture. By the time the Europeans arrived, maize cultivation
had been adopted by most of southern New England's indigenous
peoples. Intensification of agriculture had led to competition for land
even before English colonization. Historically, growing population and

competition for resources has been a catalyst for political centralization and stratification across cultures, and New England's native peoples were no exception. Increasingly powerful leaders rose to authority through competition based on the ability to provide their group with productive land. Others rose to prominence by controlling the supply or production of wampum, beads made of shells that became more economically and spiritually important during this period. The result of political centralization and consolidation was the crystallization of many of the sovereign Indian entities in New England that we are familiar with today, such as the Wampanoags, the Narragansetts, and the Mohegans. In the seventeenth century, these units functioned as chiefdoms.[14]

Anthropologists and archaeologists concur that a chiefdom is a centrally organized regional polity with a population in the thousands. These societies contain a certain amount of heritable social status and stratification based on access to strategic resources. They usually evolve out of more simply organized community groupings and sometimes form an intermediate step toward what might be recognized as a state. Chiefdoms, however, do not always unilinearly evolve out of simpler societies. Rather, as the Danish archaeologist Kristian Kristiansen has argued, "[m]any 'autonomous' chiefdoms and tribes may simply be devolved societies, temporarily cut off from the larger system of which they had historically been a part. . . . Within such a world system, the regional systems maintain a degree of autonomy, despite their dependency on remote regions for supplies of metal, prestige goods, and ritual information."[15] Within such a world system and societal evolutionary or devolutionary framework, the New England colonies, like the region's Indians, also demonstrated the political dynamics of chiefdoms. This meant that the two could see similarity in their political cultures.

The most vexing problem facing students of chiefdoms is explaining why individuals cast their loyalty with a regional polity. Why should the subjects of a chiefdom allow others to have power over them? What prevents these subjects from "voting with their feet" against the society's leadership? The English migration of the 1630s largely represented resentment against the encroachment of centralized rule. The historian Timothy Breen notes that migrants to Massachusetts "departed England determined to maintain their local attachments against outside interference, and to a large extent the Congregational churches and self-contained towns of Massachusetts Bay stood as visible evidence of the founders' decision to preserve in America what had been threatened in the mother country." Breen argues that village localism persisted in North America and that freemen—individuals who could vote—usually resisted centralized control such as the efforts of Gov. John Winthrop, Sr., and the General Court of Massachusetts to impose on the towns colonywide taxes, militias, and religions. Although the colonial legislature developed a town-based system for the distribution of land, ordinary colonists within the towns implemented it. Rarely did colonial governments meddle in the affairs of townspeople. Winthrop walked a delicate balance trying to maintain authority over ten thousand to fifteen thousand subjects with a government much weaker than the one they had already defied. In several cases he failed; subjects voted against him with their feet and created factional offshoots. Thus, "New England was not a single, monolithic 'fragment' separating off from the mother country. It was a body of loosely joined fragments, and some of the disputes that developed in the New World grew out of differences that existed in the Old."[16]

In the Northeast, these fragments found Indians eager to use them for their own political purposes. Shortly before the establishment of permanent English settlements, epidemics scoured the region, their devastation distributed unevenly. By 1620 the Pequots and the Narragansetts, left virtually unscathed by disease, had a newfound power relative to other Indians in the region. From their lands in what are now Connecticut and Rhode Island, respectively, these two groups exerted a strong influence throughout southern New England and even into Iroquois territory in New York. Central to Narragansett and Pequot influence was the control of wampum, beads made of shells found predominantly along Long Island sound. Since the Narragansetts and the Pequots had a nearly exclusive access to these shell beads that were highly valued by the Iroquois and the Algonquians for ceremonial purposes and as a medium of exchange, they were powers to reckon with.[17] The Pequots exacted tribute from Indians along the Connecticut River to the north of them in exchange for military protection. Similarly, the Narragansetts expanded their authority over smaller Indian groups such as the Cowesits, the Shawomets, the Pawtuxets, and some Nipmucks to their north and the Eastern Niantics to their east in the 1620s and early 1630s. In many instances, smaller groups looked to the political leaders of these relatively powerful groups for military protection and access to trade goods and land; in others they felt threatened by them.

Into this context of political fluidity, consolidation, and rivalry among Indians, came Dutch and English colonists. The Dutch arrived first and established a fairly successful trade along the southern coast of New England, taking advantage of the competition between the Narragansetts and the Pequots. After landing at Plymouth in 1620 and at Boston in 1630, English colonists tried to replicate the economic aspects of earlier European colonization efforts while improving upon them morally. Like the Spanish, they hoped to take care of their material needs by tapping into the existing local economy; unlike the Spanish—at least the Spanish of their perceptions—they hoped to avoid atrocities. More than simply imitating Spanish actions in the Americas, New England's settlers strove to be superior colonizers. The Black Legend, propaganda condemning Spanish conquistadors for barbarous cruelty and spread by the likes of the Spanish friar Bartolomé de Las Casas, shaped the English colonists' treatment of Indians throughout the hemisphere. The Puritan settlers of Providence Island in the Caribbean, for example, expected the nearby Indians to seek solace from Spanish brutality by submitting to English rule.[18] Spanish atrocities, although undoubtedly exaggerated at times in the Black Legend, led the English colonists to try to demonstrate the righteousness of their cause.

In addition to trying to avoid the atrocities that they perceived the Spanish had committed against Indians, the migrants to New England hoped not to repeat the mistakes they felt had been made by their brethren in the Chesapeake. John Winthrop believed that efforts at Jamestown had been strife-riven because "their mayne end which was proposed was carnal and not religious." The colonizers of Virginia included "a multitude of rude and misgoverned persons the very scumme of the land," who aimed for "profitt and not the propagation of religion."[19] Those who migrated to New England felt that their venture offered hope for a fresh attempt at colonization in which the mistakes of the Spaniards and even fellow Englishmen would not be repeated.

Initially, the political flux among Indian groups worked to their advantage in this endeavor. Unlike the Chesapeake in 1607, where Indians had not seen an epidemic in decades, New England Indians had been dying in droves just the year before the Pilgrims landed at Plymouth. This led some Indians to seek English assistance. In 1620, Squanto linked his fate to the survival of Plymouth in order to cope with the reduced strength of his Patuxet band, which had been decimated by disease, and carve out

a measure of autonomy under the shadow of the more powerful Wampanoags, led by Massasoit. Similarly, in March 1621 Massasoit submitted to
the English at Plymouth Colony to prevent Narragansett expansion, resulting in the famous treaty.[20] Following suit, the Massachusetts leader
Chickataubut also established a relationship with the English to stem the
tide of the Narragansetts. In 1631 an Indian leader in the Connecticut River
Valley invited Bostonians to settle in the region, probably in an effort to
bolster Algonquian defenses against attacks from the Iroquois to the west
and, more importantly, to restore a balance of power in his relations with
the Pequots, to whom he owed tribute.[21] The Indians, jockeying for political position in the aftermath of the intensification of agriculture and the
devastation caused by disease, looked upon the Europeans as being similar to themselves and, in many cases, as being valuable trade partners and
political allies. The Europeans saw the Indians as valuable trade partners
whose support was necessary if they were to establish a foothold in the
region.

With time, colonists flocked to those parts of southern New England
that they found most desirable, largely avoiding the north. The first map
of New England produced in the Americas supplemented one of the first
histories of King Philip's War, and English perceptions of the differences
between southern and northern New England are carved into its wood-
cut. Only a few English settlements appear in the north, and those hug
the coast at the mouths of rivers, on which they usually ran sawmills. A
wilderness pins the small settlements against the coast on the map. Unlike
southern New England, the northern sections include strange-looking
animals. There are also two figures between the coastal settlements and
the forest beyond. The people lack permanent residence and carry muskets on their shoulders. Perhaps hunters, trappers, or traders—but definitely not farmers—the two appear isolated in the wilderness as either
Indians or Indianized Englishmen. Unlike the south, where Indians have
been thoroughly marginalized, the north seems to be under native control. The sparseness of settlement, the wild animals, and the nomadic
character of the people all suggest that for the map's maker, John Foster
of Cambridge, the north was a fearful, untamed frontier.[22]

Mid-seventeenth-century Maine has been described by one of its historians as "A World on the Edge." Another asserts that in the second half of
the seventeenth century it was a "rural backwater, an economic hinter-
land of Puritan Massachusetts . . . a frontier war zone, a buffer between

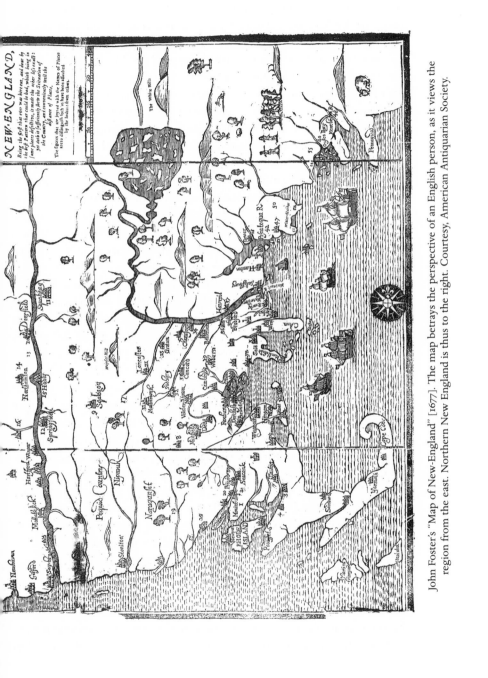

John Foster's "Map of New-England" [1677]. The map betrays the perspective of an English person, as it views the region from the east. Northern New England is thus to the right. Courtesy, American Antiquarian Society.

New England and its enemies, the native people of northern New England and their French allies." Puritan minister and contemporary historian of King Philip's War William Hubbard saw the north as "a barren and rocky Country . . . that whole Tract of Land, being of little worth." Accordingly, growing crops proved difficult for seventeenth-century Englishmen and native inhabitants in the north. The soil was far less fertile and more acidic, and the growing season was shorter than in southern New England.[23] These conditions meant that farmers needed more land in order to subsist; therefore, when they settled they did so even farther from their neighbors than their southern counterparts.

Not surprisingly, the development of English settlement patterns was a far cry from the Puritan ideal of a "city on a hill." A number of writers observed the lack of community among Maine's colonists. The town of Kittery was to William Hubbard "a long scattering Plantation made up of several Hamlets." John Josselyn noted that Blackpoint was "scatteringly built." And Samuel Maverick reported in Casco Bay and along the Kennebec River "many scattering Families settled."[24] For orthodox Puritans, especially in Massachusetts and Plymouth colonies, these observations had deep meaning. The necessity to live scattered or isolated and not belong to a community meant that inhabitants became a part of the very wilderness that the English were trying to tame. Puritans believed their culture would best expand only through the establishment of coherent communities. To be sure, the reality never quite matched the Puritan ideal in either north or south, and settlements were far more scattered than the English leadership desired. On numerous occasions in the seventeenth century, New England colonies tried to legislate tight settlement patterns. Although these efforts can be seen as failures, they appear to have done better in the south, based on southerners' perceptions of northerners.[25] Southern New Englanders saw northern individuals as even more lacking in community ties than themselves.

The same environmental conditions that sparked the colonists' sparse settlement patterns had influenced the culture of northern New England's Indians for centuries. The Eastern and Western Abenakis relied less on horticulture than the Indians to the south did. Also, the farther north Indians lived, the less important agriculture became; beyond the Kennebec River subsistence was based solely on hunting, gathering, and fishing. Northern New England's Indians thus had smaller social units and more mobile settlement patterns. Small family bands were the primary social unit, and the larger chiefdoms found in the south were absent.[26]

Based on larger patterns in the history of American colonization, wherein less sedentary groups are usually more hostile toward Europeans than the more sedentary, it is not surprising that the English had their most troubled relations with northern New England's native inhabitants. Because the northern Indians were not organized into chiefdoms, colonists found fewer parallels in their political culture. They did not find groups organized under the "monarchies" that they interpreted in southern political culture. Indian social structures in the north were "fundamentally egalitarian," according to historian Harald E. L. Prins.[27] To the colonists this must have appeared as relative chaos. The fragmentation of the population into family bands without higher-level chiefs made achieving the formal submission of most of the people impractical if not impossible, especially since the English lacked centralized settlement in the region. Northern New England Indians, in turn, viewed the colonists' political culture as more foreign than did the southern Indians. To intermesh their communities with those of the English would have required a fundamental change in their lifestyles. For this reason they resisted both conquest and the formation of a covalent society. When they fought against the English and their Indian allies during and after King Philip's War, it did not represent the dissolution of a single society but an effort to prevent becoming a part of one. It was frontier war, not civil war.

ALTHOUGH THE English found the land and the Indians in the southern part of the region to be most compatible with their desires, relations there were not always peaceful. Intercultural trade led to tragedy, at least for some. In 1637 the Pequot War served as a clarion call to Indians throughout the region, announcing that European-style warfare was very different from their own. The conflict centered on the Dutch and English efforts to take advantage of the trade rivalry between the two tribes that, because of their control of wampum, were dominant economic players, the Narragansetts and the Pequots. The Dutch were the premier European power in the region in the 1620s, with ties to both the Pequots and the Narragansetts. As the English expanded into the region in the 1630s, the Dutch tried to solidify their claim to its commerce by building a trading post and purchasing land in the lower Connecticut River Valley. The

Dutch could not, however, ease discontent within those Indian groups with which they traded. Some of the communities that had tributary relations with the Pequots looked to cooperation with the English as a way of breaking these ties. Some signed separate trade agreements with the English or even ceded them land. Others, such as the Narragansetts, partially under the influence of English religious dissenter Roger Williams, eventually allied with the Massachusetts Bay Colony.

Hostilities broke out when the Pequots sought revenge against a Dutchman who, against their wishes, had traded with some of their tributaries. But instead, probably by accident, they killed an English ship captain, John Oldham. The English set out with Narragansett and Mohegan allies to subdue the Pequots, who, not coincidentally, occupied some of the most valuable land in New England. The conflict climaxed in May 1637 after the English and their Indian allies surrounded a palisaded Pequot village on the Mystic River. They attacked one morning before dawn, and in the ensuing chaos the village was torched. As for those Pequot men, women, and children who managed to flee the flames, Englishmen, to the horror of their Indian allies, shot them down with their muskets. By the end of the day, six hundred to seven hundred Pequots had died. Most were noncombatants, and most were burned alive.[28]

The English and their Indian allies had contrasting views of the day's events. The English for the most part saw the carnage as a sign of divine favor in their struggle against the "savages." As the English captain John Mason declared, "God was above them, who laughed his Enemies and the Enemies of his People to scorn making them as a fiery Oven. . . . Thus did the Lord judge among the Heathen, filling the Place with dead Bodies." For Indians, even if they had allied with the English, it was a different story. They had never seen warfare of the scope or scale waged by the English at the Pequot village. Their culturally prescribed rules of war had in the past dictated low-casualty conflicts characterized by hit-and-run tactics—often with the aim of acquiring live captives. The torching of the village and shooting of inhabitants as they fled prompted a complaint about "the manner of the Englishmen's fight . . . because it is too furious, and slays too many men."[29] They were not likely to forget the war. Indeed, their lingering memory of it probably made them cautiously avoid conflict in subsequent years.

Although many Indians were shocked at the conduct of the Pequot War, some Indian leaders were highly satisfied with its results. The Mohegan leader Uncas is the quintessential example of a New England native who vied for political power and successfully used the assistance of those from another continent to get it. As relatively new entities, the "tribes" that Uncas and others belonged to were fluid and often lacked rigid boundaries. Moreover, intermarriage across group lines was common, and many Indians freely shifted loyalty from one to another as political conditions changed. Before the Pequot War, Uncas's Mohegans were linked to the Pequots by intermarriage and a tributary status. Uncas himself claimed to be the rightful leader by birth of both the Mohegans and the Pequots. Leadership of the Pequots was not entirely hereditary, however; it was based partially on elections. In the first half of the 1630s, Uncas had tried several times to depose the Pequot leader Sassacus, only to fail repeatedly.[30] When the English arrived looking to avenge John Oldham's death, Uncas found a power that could tilt the political balance in his favor. The aftermath of the Pequot defeat in 1637 saw Uncas's emergence as the grand sachem of the Pequots and the Mohegans.

The Pequot War also helped Uncas establish strong ties of mutual obligation with the English colony of Connecticut. In 1640 Uncas ceded all of the land of his band and its tributaries to Connecticut. This deal benefited both Uncas and Connecticut. Thereafter the colony lent overwhelming support to Uncas's efforts to gain hegemony over smaller bands to the north and east; the main benefit to Connecticut resided in the official deed, which offered some of the same benefits as a royal patent. Like a charter, this document helped legitimate the colony's existence and provided legal protection against the encroachment of other colonies.[31] Connecticut's relationship with Indians solidified its political authority.

Uncas found his relationship with the English to be a potent one. He could and did count on English assistance whenever trouble arose between the Mohegans and the Narragansetts. After the Pequot War, Uncas on numerous occasions made false accusations to Connecticut concerning the Narragansetts. Through these accusations he gained the military assistance of the United Colonies—a military coalition consisting of Massachusetts, Connecticut, Plymouth, and the short-lived New Haven Colony—to defend himself from the Narragansetts in 1645, 1657, and 1658. In 1643, when the Narragansett sachem Miantonomo began calling for an Indian rejection of the English and their ways, Uncas made a call on the English legal system. As a result he got the United Colonies to convict Miantonomo of murder and allow Uncas to personally enforce the death sentence.[32] The relationship of Uncas and the English colonies continued to follow trajectories of this sort, with both increasing in power throughout most of the seventeenth century.

The rise of the Mohegans under Uncas and their close relations with the colonies helped foster a delicate balance of power between some of southern New England's Algonquians and the Iroquois in eastern New York. If this balance had not involved peoples to the west, New England's covalent society could not have developed. The Mohawks, the easternmost group of Iroquois, demanded vast quantities of wampum for use in diplomacy and in rituals to console those who were mourning the loss of relatives to increasing rates of disease and warfare. In the 1640s and 1650s, the Mohawks maintained an alliance with the Indians along the middle and upper Connecticut River and the Narragansetts to ensure the flow of wampum from Narragansett Bay toward Iroquoia. The Mohawks reciprocated with furs obtained in part through wars with neighbors to the north and west. The Narragansett–River Indian–Mohawk alliance had enough power to thwart English efforts to encroach on the Narragansetts. Rhode Island's founder, Roger Williams, warned the Massachusetts General Court that the Mohawks and the Narragansetts "are the two great bodies of Indians in this country, and they are confederates." Williams implied that the colonies should not advance Mohegan or English interests at the expense of the Narragansetts, no matter how much Uncas or land-hungry colonists might have wanted them to do so. So long as the Narragansetts, the River Indians, and the Mohawks maintained their alliance, the power of the Mohegans and their English allies was held in check.[33]

Within this tangled web, Uncas and other Indian leaders like him acted in ways that not only facilitated a temporary peace and the survival of English colonies, but in the long run also laid the groundwork for King Philip's War. Uncas, of course, ceded land directly to the colonies in exchange for political ties. Indians in the Connecticut River Valley similarly offered land as collateral for English goods received on credit with the promise of future payment in furs.[34] As the supply of furs eventually dwindled, they could not make their payments and lost their land. From the English perspective, trade with the Indians had proved inadequate to support their material needs. English colonists therefore increasingly sought Indian land, rather than trade or tribute, as time progressed.[35] This helped stabilize the colonies and at the same time threatened the long-term viability of many Indian communities. Private property in land became one of the institutional arrangements that allowed the New England colonies to thrive. As historian Karen Ordahl Kupperman has shown, the ventures of colonists culturally similar to those of New England in other parts of the world, such as those in the Caribbean's Providence Island in the 1630s, failed in part because they did not institutionalize private landholding.[36] For most Indians, of course, the growth of English landholding intensified preexisting tensions over land allocation.

One of the principal ways the English expanded their landholdings was through the founding of new towns. This process largely involved the entrepreneurialism of a select, skilled few, who, like Uncas, rose in power—as chiefs of sorts, although never called such—through their abilities to allocate lands for their followers' use. Because establishing towns posed tremendous challenges, only prominent individuals who had greater access to resources such as wealth, political power, religious authority, or, perhaps most importantly, the ability to deal with the Indians—either diplomatically or militarily—had the capacity to found a town. These elites oftentimes did not live in the town that they helped to establish, opting instead to reap profits as absentee landowners. Men notable for their colonial leadership such as William Pynchon, Benjamin Church, John Mason, Richard Smith, and Roger Williams epitomized the character of some of New England's early town founders. It is no coincidence that these men also earned reputations for their skill in diplomacy or warfare with Indians. Their skills in dealing with Indians enabled them to become leaders at the colony level. They, like southern New England Indian leaders, functioned as chiefs.[37]

Like chiefs, colonial leaders struggled for the loyalty of their subjects, facing the ever-present threat that their followers might reject their rule. Leaders at the colony level often had residents who challenged their authority, much as Sassacus had to confront Uncas's insurrections. The English who came to the Americas culturally preferred localistic, homogeneous villages and feared the encroachment of centralized power. Working in favor of colonial leaders, however, the environment in which the colonists set up their communities often demanded the external assistance of a centralized power or individual. This need led the English in New England to show some loyalty to their colonies' general courts. Nevertheless, as Timothy Breen has shown, the relationships between towns and general courts were tense: residents struggled to keep the town's power as autonomous as possible without completely severing connections to the central authority. Most legal disputes among colonists, for example, were resolved in local county courts. Rarely did cases arise on appeal to the Court of Assistants or the General Court. Efforts to maintain tight-knit, autonomous communities often succeeded, as is evidenced by Kenneth A. Lockridge's study of seventeenth-century Dedham, Massachusetts. He describes that town as a "coherent social organism."[38]

The regional fragmentation and resulting localism of the English who migrated to New England becomes especially apparent when one examines doctrinal disputes. English differences over separatism, radical spiritualism, anabaptism, millenarianism, and Quakerism shattered the hopes of regional leaders who aspired toward establishing a monolithically orthodox religious and political community. In desperate efforts to maintain homogeneity within their community, leaders of Plymouth and Massachusetts banished perceived heretics, but that only further undermined the attempts to maintain orthodoxy within the region. To the chagrin of those who banished Roger Williams, he did not return to England, as expected, but instead fled to what is now Rhode Island, providing a refuge for subsequent dissenters.[39]

Williams essentially established an independent chiefdom. Rhode Island became a haven for those not loyal to Massachusetts, Plymouth, or Connecticut. To establish the colony, Williams relied on close ties with the resident Indians that legitimated his claims to land. His relationships with them served as a political foundation of the colony, proving that Williams, like Uncas, was willing to use others, regardless of "race" or ethnicity, for his own political purposes. These relationships usually took the form of the submission of a group of Indians to an English colony and, indirectly, to the king of England. Rhode Islanders effectively used the Narragansetts and the closely related Eastern Niantics in 1644 to help protect themselves from the colonies of Plymouth, Massachusetts, Connecticut, and New Haven, which had formed a military alliance in 1643. Both Samuel Gorton and Roger Williams worked hard to gain the loyalty of the Narragansetts and the Niantics, and once they succeeded they immediately took their case that Massachusetts had no right to their lands to the English Parliament. Both men argued that Massachusetts, under its charter, had no right to Indian lands lying outside its predefined jurisdiction. Williams, in particular, sought and acquired a new charter for

Rhode Island that was based on the consent of the region's indigenous inhabitants.

When Williams applied for Rhode Island's charter in 1643 and 1644, he presented two documents supporting his case. The first, *Bloudy Tenent of Persecution*, accused Massachusetts of abusing religious heretics. The second, *A Key into the Language of America*, demonstrated Williams's belief that English settlers needed Eastern Algonquian aid and knowledge for their very survival. Unlike the preceding New England travel narratives and colonial writings about Indians in general that, according to literary critic Mary Louise Pratt, controlled and domesticated Native Americans for a reading population in Europe, Williams crafted his *Key* in a way uniquely suited to aiding actual interactions with Indians. Williams also differed from contemporary English writers in that he did not offer the standard preface stating that the author would draw his authority from either the monarch or the Bible; rather, Williams allowed the Narragansett language to stand as his authority. His text centered on oral, rather than written, exchanges, thus recognizing the power and authority of Narragansett speech. In short, Williams's *Key* provided a means for colonists to meet natives on native terms. By trying to facilitate such cross-cultural interactions, Williams conceded that English settlers, and especially Rhode Island dissenters, depended upon Indians for their very survival.[40]

Like the leaders of Connecticut and Rhode Island, those of Massachusetts and Plymouth also sought Indian "subjects." In the case of Massachusetts it was mainly to legitimate their competing claims to parts of what is now Rhode Island. In this endeavor they had the help of two Narragansett sachems, Pomham and Saconoco, who departed from the majority of the Narragansett confederation and swore allegiance to the colonial government of Massachusetts. Massachusetts claimed that these leaders represented the desires of the majority of the confederation, whereas Rhode Island claimed that only the sachem Miantonomo had the power to speak for the group. Similarly, Plymouth received the loyalty of many Wampanoags in 1639 when Massasoit submitted to that colony and when Metacom, subsequently known as Philip, formally renewed this submission in 1662 and 1671. Plymouth, like other colonies, saw Indian submissions as pivotal factors in land disputes. So powerful were Indians in shaping the jurisdictions of colonies that Roger Williams feared that Wampanoag claims to parts of Rhode Island might lead Plymouth to claim authority over its largest town, Providence.[41]

Thus, colonists did not just come to the Americas and create a "New" England. They had to intermesh their communities with the region's indigenous inhabitants. Southern New England's chiefs and followers—English and Indian—worked hard to advance their interests and avoid war. The fluidity of New England politics and the tensions between regionalism and localism challenged New England's most talented leaders. The covalent society that emerged was based on a fragile interdependence among various New England groups and a balance of power created by the Pequot War and relations with peoples to the west.

2

PEACE

How DID various New England groups perceive their relations with their neighbors? Why did English groups feel the need to have Indians of a region "subject" themselves in order to legitimate their authority over a jurisdiction? Other nations, notably Spain, had simply conquered Indians, at least when dealing with those who were sedentary. New England colonists, of course, strove to do better than these perceived barbarians. Equally if not more important, however, was the nature of the indigenous society with which they were dealing. The semisedentary Indians of New England had a greater ability and desire to resist military conquest than those who were more sedentary. New England colonists feared the Indians whom they encountered.[1] They also needed security against competing English colonies. The leaders of Massachusetts, Connecticut, and Plymouth, in their efforts to maintain tightly controlled, homogeneous polities, could ill afford to have their jurisdictions border on a refuge for dissenters or the territory of Indians with whom formal relations had not been established. This in turn left Rhode Islanders feeling continually threatened by the other English polities.

That threat became especially apparent in 1643 when Connecticut, Massachusetts, Plymouth, and New Haven allied themselves as the United Colonies of New England. Not merely a military alliance formed by English settlers to protect themselves from Indians, the confederation also worked to isolate and even destroy Rhode Island. In 1644 the commissioners of the United Colonies decided that they would accept Rhode Islanders into the alliance only if the majority of them would "without reservation submit" to either Massachusetts or Plymouth. Four years later, a leader of one of Rhode Island's main political factions, William Coddington, sought the assistance of the United Colonies in his local political struggles with factions led by Samuel Gorton and Nicholas Easton. The commissioners of the United Colonies declined, writing to Coddington that "upon the perusall of the antient Patent graunted to New Plymouth they finde Roade Iland upon whic your plantacions are setled to fall within their lines bounds, which the honourable comittie of parlement thinke not fitt to Straighten or infringe."[2] The commissioners would consider Rhode Island for membership in their alliance only if Rhode Islanders would submit and conform to the desires of one of the larger neighboring colonies.

Threatened by the United Colonies, Rhode Islanders tried to go to a perceived higher authority than that body's commissioners—the Parliament of England. The fact that Rhode Islanders sought a charter from England shortly after other English colonies had excluded them from a large alliance was no coincidence. Various Rhode Islanders pursued the strategy of drawing upon a higher political authority outside of New England to validate their claims within it. Unlike William Coddington, men such as Samuel Gorton and Roger Williams resisted the authority of Massachusetts and Plymouth by appealing over their heads. Their appeals argued that they had closer relations with the Indians than their competitors. Gorton, for example, sought protection against the encroachments of the United Colonies, as the subtitle of his major tract indicates: "The Combate of the United Colonies, not onely against some of the Natives and Subjects, but against the authority also of the Kingdome of England . . ." The same subtitle went on to remind its reader that the Indians of the region had "submitted" to Rhode Island, further incriminating the United Colonies of acting beyond the law of their charter.[3] Similarly, Roger Williams, with his *Key into the Language of America,* proved through the demonstration of linguistic and cultural knowledge of the Narragansetts that few if any could match his level of intimacy with native peoples.

But since Rhode Islanders seemingly could have enhanced their security through a simple alliance with the Indians, why was it so crucial that Indians had "submitted" or consented to English rule? The answer has two parts. First, the English settlers believed themselves superior to the Indians—they held that it was only natural for "civilized" Englishmen to rule Indian "savages." It must be emphasized, however, that the colonists did not see Indians as having inborn "racial" traits that made them inferior. Such views were the product of later generations of Euramericans. Englishmen familiar with Indians in the early seventeenth century argued that the Indians shared, in the words of one historian, a "common humanity with Europeans—even common origins." Differences between the Indians and the Europeans stemmed from factors such as environment, generations of isolation, or religion rather than genetics. Thus, most colonists saw the relationship between English and Indian as tutelary. During this period the ideal relationship between Englishman and Indian paralleled that between English husband and wife, older brother and younger, or parent and child of the day. Englishmen viewed Indians as dependents to be instructed in their ways, not as equals.[4] Accordingly, most English colonists felt that it was for the better of the whole that the English rule and the Indians follow. It was inconceivable that the English subject themselves to Indians or ally with them as equals, even though they were thought to be within their "jurisdiction."

Another source of the English desire to rule over Indians as subjects is found in the constraints imposed by their charters. Although the degree to which the English migrants to New England remained loyal to the English government is debatable, they could not completely disregard their charters.[5] A colonial leader who violated a charter risked having his actions challenged by those whom they hurt before the Crown or Parliament. The charters provided a lever by which dissenters could resist what they perceived as the unfair exertion of power. The central limitations of charters were their delineation of jurisdictions and stipulations regarding relations with Indians. Connecticut, Rhode Island, Massachusetts, and Plymouth continually debated the boundaries of their colonies. And they always founded their arguments on the charter granted to them by the government of England—with the exception of Plymouth, which never had a charter and based its legality before England on its functioning as a kind of protectorate over the Wampanoags.[6]

In addition to defining jurisdictions, charters also specified the fate of the native inhabitants within the boundaries of the colonies. The charter of Massachusetts imputed to that colony a strong missionary impulse. "The Principall ende of this plantacion," it stated, was to "wynn and incite the natives of country to the knowledg and obedience of the only true God and Savior of mankinde, and the Christian fayth." The official seal of the colony also captured this motive with its caption of an Indian saying "Come over and help us." These formal statements of policy did not fall on deaf ears: several missionaries, including John Eliot and Daniel Gookin of Massachusetts and Richard Bourne and Thomas Mayhew of Plymouth actively proselytized Indians. Missionary activity took on added urgency for many millenarians who saw the conversions of natives as an indication of the coming of Christ's kingdom in New England.[7]

A few caveats must be noted and terms defined in regard to English conceptions of the Indians' place within English polities. The original charter of Massachusetts defined that colony's "jurisdiction" to include numerous Indian villages. The English defined *jurisdiction,* much as we do today, as the territorial range in which a polity could extend authority and control. Because many Indians lived within what the English defined as their jurisdictions, these Indians were de jure "subjects" of English rule. As subjects, they were technically bound by English laws and no others. An examination of the records of the General Court of Massachusetts bears out this English view. The laws and records show that colonial leaders differentiated between "foreign" and "domestic" Indians of Massachusetts and other colonies.[8] Moreover, the records also indicate that the English referred to Indian groups living outside the boundaries of English jurisdictions, such as the Mohawks, as "nations," just as they referred to England and France as nations. Groups of Indians living within English jurisdictions might receive notice as Narragansetts or Wampanoags, but rarely if ever as nations.[9]

This de jure system of classification that distinguishes between foreign and domestic Indians did not translate into a de facto English ability to rule over Indians within their jurisdiction. The historian Alden Vaughan has recognized that not all Indians living within English jurisdictions were equally subject to the influence of English law.[10] His three-part classification divides Indians into groups that maintained their independence from the English, those that nominally subjected themselves to the English, and those individual Indians who lacked affiliation with any Indian group and lived within English communities, most often as servants or laborers. These categories reflect not only Indian resistance to English rule but also English qualms about the propriety of unilaterally imposing their rule on others without their consent.

Beyond the formalities of General Court records and charters and at a more local level, English town leaders certainly thought of themselves as having Indians under their rule. The correspondence of John Pynchon offers a prime example of the way leaders of localities within particular English colonies viewed their relations with Indians. Pynchon, a major figure in the Connecticut River Valley, consistently referred to the Agawam, Pocumtuck, Pojassic, Wissantinnewag, and Nalwottog Indian communities along the Connecticut River and within the boundaries of Massachusetts as "our Indians." When writing Connecticut governor John Winthrop, Jr., Pynchon referred to the Indians within that colony's boundaries as "your Indians." These designations "our Indians" and "your Indians" did not necessarily mean "Massachusetts's Indians," or "Connecticut's Indians," or even "Indians supporting the English." Rather, Pynchon usually applied the term "our Indians" only to those along the Connecticut River Valley, whereas he might refer to others in Massachusetts such as those under the influence of Massachusetts missionary John Eliot as "Mr. Eliot's Indians."[11] Thus, Pynchon, a man of tremendous importance primarily in the village of Springfield but also in the colony of Massachusetts, which he served as a magistrate, saw strong ties between local English communities and nearby Indians, and not just between the larger provincial government and Indian confederations.

English colonies, although they already viewed themselves as having power over the Indians within their royally defined jurisdictions, nonetheless went to the trouble of garnering oaths of fidelity from the Indians. They sought de facto rather than simply de jure rule over them. And, in the English mind, de facto rule was most legitimate if it was consensual. The English ideal of a political covenant stressed the voluntary nature of political submission and confederation. English colonies required oaths of allegiance of freemen and residents. They sought similar oaths from Indians. The Indian fidelity oaths, like those sworn by the English, explicitly emphasized the voluntary nature of submission. The freeman and the English resident had to "freely & sincerely" acknowledge the power of Massachusetts; likewise, Indians had to present their oaths "volentarily & without any constraint or perswasion."[12]

Consensual rule should not be interpreted as mandating egalitarian treatment. Because the Indians were viewed by the English as being in tutelage, they were considered "other." But for the English, their own kind—that is English men and women—could also be "other." Indians were not the only people that English labeled as "savages" or "Indians": any English person perceived to live outside the bounds of law was susceptible to being called a savage. Even within the technical jurisdiction of

England, English "subjects" living in the forest were "Indians." And within New England, when Roger Williams fled from colonial authorities to Rhode Island after his banishment, he wrote to John Winthrop, Sr., expressing his "belief, that for myself, I am not yet turned Indian." Similarly, in 1641, inhabitants of Providence, Rhode Island, sought the assistance of Massachusetts in restraining the "insolent and Riotous cariages of Samuell Gorton and his Company." They feared that the Gortonites might steal their cattle, "First pleading Necesity, or to maintaine Wife and Family, but afterwards boldy to maintaine licentious lust like Savages." Not only did English settlers perceive themselves as having the capacity to become Indian, but they also allowed for the possibility that Indians might become English. John Pynchon, for example, referred to some Indians living at their village of Nalwottog as "Indian English." He also called the Indians under the missionary pressure of John Eliot "English Indians."[13] Such references support the idea that English settlers believed that Indians could become full-fledged members of English polities. Nevertheless, in the seventeenth century, English settlers in New England came nowhere near treating Indians as their equals.

Some of the main obstacles to egalitarian treatment within the New England polities that Indians faced included legal restrictions imposed on their purchasing of arms and liquor, as well as on their selling of furs and pork. But although such rules might have discriminated against many natives, it is important to note that the colonial governments did not apply such restrictions against them exclusively. In November 1637, as a result of the controversy over Anne Hutchinson, the Massachusetts General Court disarmed 59 Englishmen in Boston, 5 in Salem, 3 in Newbury, 5 in Roxbury, 2 in Ipswich, and 2 in Charlestown, because it perceived these men as internal threats to the security of the colony. By way of comparison, in 1671 Plymouth sought to disarm an estimated 120 Wampanoags under Philip, yet it managed to acquire the arms of only 16 or 17.[14] Disarming served as a punishment for both English and Indian "subjects" who colonial leaders felt had violated the terms of the covenant. Colonial leaders hoped to weaken these subjects, while preserving their own power.

Like disarming, restrictions on trade worked to preserve the power of central governments—both Indian and English. Trade in seventeenth-century New England provided lucrative avenues to both material profit and political power. The Indians and the English provided to one another large markets for goods, and clearly the opportunity to trade could result in the accumulation of wealth for some. Additionally, however, trade ties led to political relationships that could enhance the power of an individual or a local polity. For this reason, English chiefdoms sought to confine trade by strictly limiting the number of individuals who could trade and the amount of goods that could be traded. Many Indian leaders stood to benefit from these restrictions and helped the English to enforce them. Indian leaders could enhance their power over other Indians and with respect to English settlers by demonstrating an ability to affect or control the English. The Indian leader or community that cooperated with English trade policies was often able to acquire more goods than a competing community. And because many Indians highly valued selected European trade goods for either utilitarian or spiritual uses, the leader or group who appeared to have greater access to such trade goods stood to acquire greater respect and power among his followers.[15]

Reading only the formal colonial decrees against trade with Indians—especially of guns, liquor, furs, and foodstuffs—one might think that the natives had an insatiable demand for goods and that the English limited their flow primarily in the interest of security. Delving into sources other than official colonial records, however, reveals instances of Indians' working energetically to enforce English trade laws. Correspondence between John Pynchon and John Winthrop, Jr., contains evidence of such an incident in 1671: a group of Indians in the Connecticut River Valley that was apparently loyal to Massachusetts tried to prevent men from Connecticut from trading with other Indians in the region. The Connecticut men threatened violent revenge against those Indians. This threat worried Pynchon; he wrote that it "tends to the laying of authority low and the discouraging of Indians from acting anything when imployed by authority in one or the other colony." Pynchon did not see the threats against the Indians as merely depredations against "savages"; rather, he viewed the situation as a potential affront to his authority in the region: "they did it in revenge, whether to the Indians or myself I leave."[16] Regardless of whom the Connecticut men sought to intimidate through violence, it remains evident that some Englishmen and Indians worked together to limit trade between their communities, because many groups saw it to be in their self-interest. For prominent colonists and Indians, regulation of trade helped to stabilize their positions in the larger polities.

The English inclusion of Indians in New England polities as subjects did not necessarily stem from a benevolent desire to uplift indigenous peoples or share with them what they perceived as superior political institutions. Rather, their efforts at inclusion had strong utilitarian motives. There was no rigid frontier separating the sixty thousand English from the eighteen thousand Indians living in New England on the eve of the 1675 conflict. Indian and English settlements formed a honeycomb pattern that made frequent social contact impossible to avoid. Early travelers' maps conceptualized "New England" as interspersed with Indian villages. Douglas Leach, in his *Flintlock and Tomahawk,* provided a map of the overland transportation routes between Indian and English villages, showing that the English often had to travel through Indian lands on the way to another English village. Often, however, the English would not even make these journeys themselves, opting instead to engage Indian messengers to relay important information between English settlements; that was usually the case when John Pynchon and John Winthrop corresponded between Springfield, Massachusetts, and Hartford, Connecticut.[17]

Town and colony records also demonstrate the tremendous amount of intimate contact between Indians and the English. Much has been made of periodic English increases in military preparedness because of perceived Indian threats, but perhaps more common were the much more mundane concerns that reveal their frequent interaction. The English enacted prohibitions against Indians' entering English residences without first knocking; the English had to consider policy on Indian-English intermarriage; they had to prohibit Indians from shooting guns or making too much noise near towns on the Sabbath.[18]

Evidence of close contact between the English and Indians comes not only in the form of prohibitive legislation but also from problem-solving agreements. Indians living in English towns were periodically required to serve in local militias. The natives, like the English, received money payments from English towns whenever they killed wolves. And in supposedly tightly knit, homogeneous Dedham, Ephraim, an Indian, paid taxes and assisted with building roads and the meetinghouse. These fairly intimate contacts raise the issue of economic integration. Neal Salisbury has emphasized that between 1638 and 1675 the English and the Indians together formed a single economy. Indians produced wampum (the dominant currency before 1662), furs (the main export), and the foodstuffs, including fish, corn, pork, and venison, upon which colonists relied most heavily in the earlier years of settlement. Large numbers of Indians also

The South part of Nevv-England, as it is Planted this yeare, 1635.

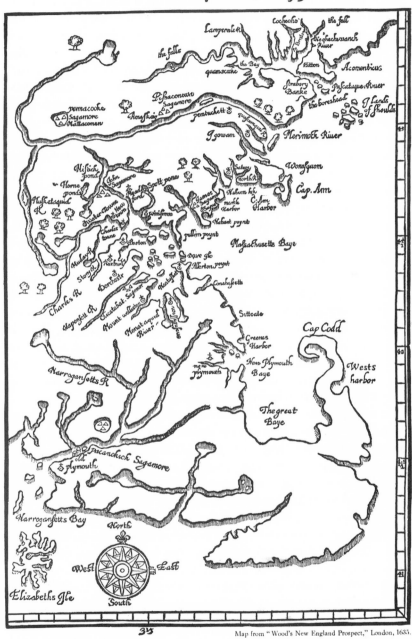

"The South part of New-England, as it is Planted this yeare, 1635," originally printed in William Wood's *New-England's Prospect* (London, 1635). Indian settlements appear as three triangles, and English settlements are represented by a circled dot with a cross at its upper edge. Courtesy, American Antiquarian Society.

worked for the English as either servants or wage laborers.[19] This economic interdependence of the English and the natives facilitated a relatively peaceful coexistence for nearly forty years, during which time Indian confederations and English colonies were intermeshed.

In sum, the close ties between Indians and the English, both geographically and economically, raised questions concerning the formal political and legal ties between the two. English cultural biases—including the civilization-savagery ideology, rivalries among English groups, and pressures imposed by charters and millennial beliefs—led the English to try to incorporate Indians into their polities as subjects. English reactions, once many Indians started a war in 1675, further indicate the considerable extent to which the English saw Indians as subordinate members of their polity. The English referred to the war as an internal "rebellion." Whereas the Pequot War had raised questions about whether or not the "laws of nations" had been violated, the 1675 war provoked questions as to why the Indians were "rising up in hostility" or were in a "condition of rebellion." In correspondence to England, one settler sought to explain why Indians had committed "high treason."[20] Thus, despite seeing the Indians as "savages," the English had created a legal status for New England's natives as subordinate subjects.

How DID Indians view their political relationships—often ones of submission—with the English? And, equally important, did the English and the natives have any common elements in their political cultures? Between 1620 and 1675 Indians had extensive political interaction with colonists. Traditionally, explanations of the causes of the 1675 conflict have focused on the cultural differences among the participants, especially the schism between the Indians and the English. Yet to truly understand the war, it is equally important to probe the cultural similarities the participants had perceived in one another, as well as the schisms within the cultures of the Indians and the colonists. Such an approach follows the lead of anthropologists such as Renato Rosaldo, who has argued against the fallacy of positing cultures as distinct, nonoverlapping entities and has called for the examination of the "borderlands," or elements shared between cultures. Similarly, historian Richard White has awakened historians to the "middle ground" that often existed between Indians and whites.[21] Since war has with justification been called the violent extension of diplomacy, the causes of King Philip's War cannot be comprehended without a comparative understanding of English and Indian political culture. In the second half of the seventeenth century, when Indians and the English examined the workings of each other's polity, each found the other polity similar to their own in important ways. This is not to say by any means that the English and the Indians shared identical political cultures, or even that the similarities outweighed the differences, but merely that neither would have seemed completely foreign to the other. The English were not able to conquer southern New England Algonquians as the Spanish had the Nahuas; nor did they face the same measure of prolonged hostility that most Euramericans faced when they tried to control nomadic peoples. Instead, the Indians and the English entered into a period of cultural accommodation and negotiation. If anything, the two groups perceived more similarity between themselves than there really was, in what functioned as a type of mutual misunderstanding.

Much of what we know about Indian political culture comes through the filter of colonists' reports. English observers in the Northeast consistently described Indian government as "monarchical." Roger Williams noted in his *Key into the Language of America* (1643) that the Narragansett sachems of Rhode Island "have an absolute Monarchie over the people." In Massachusetts, on the eve of King Philip's War, the missionary Daniel Gookin commented that "[t]heir [the Indians within Massachusetts] government is generally monarchical." John Josselyn offered the same characterization of Indian government in 1675, stating unambiguously that "[t]heir government is monarchical."[22]

Such descriptions of northeastern indigenous governments often also defined the limits on Indian rulers' powers. Daniel Gookin and Roger Williams believed that the type of "monarchy" under which Indians lived included bonds of mutual obligation. Followers of a particular leader offered their allegiance only so long as they perceived that ruler to be furthering the group's interest. For example, Williams noted that Narragansett leaders would not act in ways "to which the people are averse, and by gentle perswasion cannot be brought." Likewise, Gookin noticed that "sachems have not their men in such subjection, but that very frequently their men will leave them upon distaste or harsh dealing, and go and live under other sachems that can protect them."[23] When a sachem acted in a way that was contrary to a group's perceived interest, the sachem risked losing his followers' loyalty to another individual.

Many historians have dismissed seventeenth-century Englishmen's observations that Indians lived in a monarchical polity as projections of English biases and preconceptions onto the native peoples. To be sure, seventeenth-century English settlers tried to fit their observations of Indians into their own cultural categories. Yet, to simply dismiss the views of Englishmen such as Williams and Gookin, two men who probably had as much contact and familiarity with Indian political culture as any writers on the subject, fails to address why they chose to categorize the Indian polity as monarchical rather than aristocratic or democratic. The Englishmen's choice of the term *monarchy*, rather than other readily available terms, reveals facets of Indian culture that resonated with the English and highlights areas of Indian and English cultural overlap.

A possible reason why recent historians may have been too quick to dismiss English descriptions as mere cultural projections is that those historians were at the same time projecting their own biases about monarchy onto the early English settlers of New England. Efforts to depict innocent Indians subject to the atrocities of English invaders have led some interpreters to draw on preconceptions of monarchy that emphasize its tyrannical aspects.[24] A closer examination of English political culture shows that English inhabitants of seventeenth-century New England saw the monarchical bond not purely as one of tyranny, but as one of mutual obligations between king and subject. In a thorough study of eighteenth-century political culture in Massachusetts, historian Richard Bushman writes, "The central monarchical principle was the belief that the king was the protector of his people. Protection and allegiance were reciprocal obligations." Moreover, "[k]ings did seek to repress the opposition, of course, but resistance was as integral to monarchical political culture as obedience. . . . Protection obligated people to submit; failure to protect dissolved the obligation."[25]

Although Bushman's study focuses on the period after 1691, English inhabitants of New England held similar conceptions of monarchy and rulership in general in the seventeenth century. In his *Character of a Good Ruler*, Timothy H. Breen argues that English political culture emphasized the voluntary and reciprocal relationship between ruler and subject as early as 1620: "In Massachusetts the covenant idea proliferated far beyond what it had been in the mother country. . . . They [the Massachusetts English] spoke of secular government, for example, as a voluntary agreement existing between the ruler and his subjects. . . . The essential ingredient in this contract was free will." The impact of this belief appears in the colony's correspondence with the king. In 1661 the Massachusetts General Court reaffirmed its "dutjes of alleagiance" to the king but maintained their right to "pleade with theire prince against all such as shall at any time endeavor the violation of theire priviledges." In 1664 and 1665 the Massachusetts General Court sent lengthy letters to the king, containing not only a great deal of humble flattery but also requests for continued protection and patent priviledges.[26] These actions of the Massachusetts General Court do not represent blind submission to a ruler no matter the cost. Instead, they demonstrate that inhabitants of the colony expected a return on their investment of loyalty in the form of protection of patent privileges; they expected reciprocity on the part of the Crown.

Seventeenth-century Rhode Islanders ostensibly gained even more than the English inhabitants of Massachusetts did through their relationship with the king. With the granting of a royal charter in 1663, Rhode Island received from him protection and freedom. Individuals who had been banished from other colonies regained rights to travel and conduct business in the English colonies. The king also forbade the other colonies from invading Rhode Island, allowing its inhabitants, in their words, to "hold forth a lively experiment that a most flourishing civil state may stand and best be maintained, and that among our English subjects, with a full liberty in religious concernments."[27] Rhode Island, like Massachusetts, offered allegiance to the king with the expectation of protection in return.

English monarchical culture contains strong parallels with what has been described for the Algonquians of the Northeast as an "ethos of reciprocity." Both the English and Indians in the region emphasized, although perhaps to varying degrees, the voluntary nature of allegiance to a ruler and the right to withdraw such loyalty when the leader did not fulfill perceived obligations. The most active English missionary in Massachusetts, John Eliot, wrote a treatise in which he explained that he would teach Indians "to imbrace such Government, both Civil and Ecclesiastical, as the Lord hath commanded in the holy Scriptures." Eliot's interpretation of the Scriptures, which his sermons to Indians surely must have reflected, included the notion that subjects must submit to a ruler voluntarily. He argued that "all men are commanded to chuse unto themselves rulers" who are "liable to Political observation." Their decisions are binding only insofar as they are made with the "consent and submission of the party or parties concerned."[28] The English arrangements described by

Eliot were not entirely foreign to the Indians, whose leaders in the past had depended upon a reciprocal arrangement of mutual obligations. Indeed, the English notion of *covenant* emphasized the voluntary nature of civil society. Thus, Indians and the English, rather than representing two fundamentally opposed groups with distinct, nonoverlapping cultures, had common ground on which to meet and negotiate.

Because of these similarities, many Indians perceived a compatibility between their own political culture and that of the English, which allowed them to accommodate English culture without entirely sacrificing Indian autonomy. Contact between Indians and the English consisted of much more than the creation of a foreign "other"; Indian-white relations in New England, regardless of whether the participants had good or bad intentions, were at least as much a search for compatibility and accommodation on the part of both Indians and English. Indians such as Philip and the Wampanoags, Uncas and the Mohegans, and Miantonomo and the Narragansetts faced threats to their land in the form of English population growth and encroachment; yet the perceived compatibility of English political culture with their own allowed the Indians to form a semi-separate "parapolitical" entity within the English polity to protect their own sovereignty.[29]

Beginning in the 1640s, Indian leaders increasingly followed English rules to further their own and their group's cause, even going so far as to submit directly to a colony or to the king of England. After the Massachusetts, Connecticut, Plymouth, and New Haven colonies agreed in 1643 to form the United Colonies, the major Narragansett sachems in Rhode Island sought a way to preserve their independence and to protect themselves. Probably having observed Rhode Island's success in appealing to a distant royal authority for protection, the Narragansett leadership followed suit. In 1644 they decided "freely, voluntarily, and most humbly to submit, subject, and give over ourselves, peoples, lands, rights, inheritances, and possessions . . . unto the protection, care and government of that worthy and royal Prince, Charles, King of Great Britain and Ireland." The written act of submission made it clear what the Narragansetts hoped to gain; it stated that allegiance depended *"upon condition of His Majesties' royal protection,"* including protection against "any of the natives in these parts." More importantly, however, they realized that submission to the king legally protected them from other subjects of the king living in the colonies: *"Nor can we yield over ourselves unto any, that are subjects themselves in any case.*"[30] The sachems understood that encapsulating themselves within the larger political structure of the English empire lent them advantages in their local struggles with various parties of the English and other Indians.

Subsequent records suggest that groups such as the Narragansetts had submitted to the king with the utmost sincerity, yet they did not see such action as conflicting with their own autonomy. In 1669 Rhode Island authorities brought the Niantic sachem Ninigret before them to answer accusations that he had been plotting against the English. In response to this claim, Ninigret stated (through an interpreter) that he

> wondered there should bee any such report raised, considering his owne innocency, and that ever since himselfe heard the words by the Commissioners, spoken as from King Charles his mouth, and hath since laid it up in his heart that the King did looke upon himselfe and Sucquansh and the Indians as his subjects, together with the English; and said hee understood that the English of this Colony were to help them, if any should bee too mighty for them, and they to doe the like to the English if any should invade or make war upon the Colony.[31]

Whether or not Ninigret had plotted against the English, clearly he believed that he could use royal authority to his advantage. Similarly, when several English colonists tried to extract tribute from some Narragansett sachems, the sachems refused, "telling them they would pay King Charles and none else."[32] They shrewdly understood how to protect themselves by using the English political system.

An examination of Massachusett linguistics from the period just after King Philip's War also suggests that Indians did not perceive submission to an English colony as a complete break from traditional political behavior. Wills written by Wampanoags in the last quarter of the seventeenth century demonstrate how natives probably conceived of English colonies. To refer to "Plymouth Colony," these Indians borrowed the English word for "Plymouth" but used a Massachusett term for "colony." The Massachusett word for colony, *nanauwunnumoonkan,* is related to the Massachusett verbs meaning "to protect" and "to look after." That Indians could use a Massachusett word, instead of borrowing the English term *colony,* suggests that the Northeast's Indians saw similarities between their own political structures and those of the English and that it would be possible for them to weave their polities into English ones. Moreover, the relationship between *nanauwunnumoonkan* and the verb "to protect" means that the Indians viewed a colony, like a sachemship, as a type of protectorate. Another indication of overlap between Indian and English culture in the region is that in the surviving Massachusett texts, the Indian authors used the same term, *ketahsoot,* to describe both native and English rulers. These writers applied this same title both to the king of England and to their own sachems. And presumably they believed that they could utilize English rulers to their benefit—gain protection in exchange for allegiance—much as they could their own sachems.[33]

Ninigret and the various Rhode Island Indians were not alone in using the English political system to protect their autonomy from threatened English encroachment. At roughly the same time that the relatively powerful Narragansetts submitted to royal authority, fragments of devastated Indian groups in eastern Massachusetts also began to accede to nominal colonial rule. In June 1643 and in March 1644, different groups of Indians residing in Massachusetts submitted to the colony. On both occasions the records claim that the sachems of these groups came voluntarily, without persuasion. Once the Indians had arrived, it appears that the colonial government prepared a formulaic statement of loyalty, for on separate occasions the statement was worded identically. The Indians agreed "to bee governed & protected by them [Massachusetts], according to their just lawes & order, so farr as wee shalbee made capable of understanding them." Unlike the Indians living in Rhode Island, the Indians in Massachusetts also agreed to "bee willing from time to time to bee instructed in the knowledg & worship of God." This final act paved the way for the missionary efforts that would follow.[34]

Although the Indian submissions in the Massachusetts records appear formulaic, the records also suggest that the Indians had real incentives, aside from coercion, to offer fidelity to the English. The General Court recognized these Indian motives and understood Massachusetts's need to live up to its promise to protect those Indians who had submitted. In May 1644 the court considered "what dangerous consequence it might be unto us if we should altogether neglect them, & leave them to the cruelty and bluddymindednes of the Naragansets, these two sachims haveing sent unto us for ayde, if we faile them we breake our covenant wth them." Clearly the court recognized an obligation toward the Indians who had submitted, and it also saw that continued fidelity depended upon the colony's living up to its promise of protection. Should Massachusetts neglect its duty to provide protection, it would cause "the Indians that have put themselves under our jurisdiction, & consequently protection, to fly of[f] from us, & to fall to our enemies, & set themselves against us." To prevent the Indians from rescinding their allegiance to Massachusetts, the colony provided armed men to help them build a palisade.[35]

This particular incident was not unique. English colonists built several forts for Indian subjects in the period from 1637 to 1675. Indian inhabitants at Natick received one in the 1650s, and the Mohegans under Uncas had tremendous amounts of English help building a fortification at Shantok in the 1670s. More important, English assistance did not end with construction projects. For example, as late as 1662 and 1667 the leader of the Wampanoags, Philip, relied on the assistance of Plymouth, the colony to which he had promised allegiance, in land disputes with his longtime rivals the Narragansetts, who had previously sworn allegiance to Rhode Island. Plymouth responded by siding with the Wampanoags and reprimanding the Narragansetts. In other instances, English colonies would even mobilize militias to assist their Indian subjects. In the 1640s Massachusetts, at the request of Pomham and Sacononoco, sent troops who marched alongside armed Indian allies against the Gortonists at Warwick, Rhode Island.[36] Thus, the English colonies, at the very least, often saw it in their self-interest to back their Indian subjects. Such actions, whether taken out of a sense of obligation toward Indians or out of self-aggrandizement, probably communicated to the Indians in question that the English took their responsibilities as rulers seriously and reinforced the sincerity of those Indians who submitted to English colonies.

THE INDIANS and the English had enough similarities in their political culture and political structures that they would find a degree of compatibility between them. In both Indian and English polities, tensions existed between local and regional communities. Indian and English men and women identified themselves primarily with their local political entity, yet they relied on the aid of regional leaders to assist in town formation or military or trade matters. Both Indians and the English had long traditions of localism, so how did they reconcile the burgeoning need for regional leadership with their contradictory localistic desires?

Ritual space provided at least one avenue for both groups through which they could mediate this discrepancy. Throughout English towns in New England, the meetinghouse was the locus that bound the local community. Several historians have noted this function of the meetinghouse, including most notably Timothy H. Breen and Ola Elizabeth Winslow. According to Breen, "They [the English] gathered here [at the meetinghouse] to pray and sometimes to argue over land divisions or unruly hogs, but the very act of meeting together became in itself a ritual act that reinforced the sense of community." Similarly, Winslow has noted that meetinghouses "embodied fundamental loyalties and created a state of mind in which these loyalties took on reality."[37]

In the early years of English settlement, meetinghouse seats were free and seating was open without regard to social status, except that men and women sat on opposite sides of the room. In the second half of the seventeenth century and as towns farther from the core English community of Boston established meetinghouses, social rank became increasingly important in the ritualized gathering at the meetinghouse. "[A]ll seats would be assigned by an elaborate scheme of privilege and consequent obligation," wrote Winslow. This shift in importance coincided with an increased need for stratified leadership among the English. The establishment of more remote towns west of Boston required leadership with solid political, financial, and military assets. As noted earlier, many of these leaders did not reside in the town they founded, instead remaining in hubs like Boston. But those town founders who actually resided in the town they helped to establish acquired tremendous status.[38] Town residents formally recognized this status whenever they convened at the local meetinghouse by reserving premier seating for town leaders.

The meetinghouse ritual thus served both to recognize status differences and to reinforce the cohesiveness of the community. Though hierarchy and communalism are not necessarily contradictory, in this particular case they were in tension. Almost by definition, important town leaders had strong ties outside of the community that allowed them to become important within it. Ola Winslow has commented on the importance of military titles—assigned largely to deal with Indians—in meetinghouse seating arrangements. In their home town of Dedham, Joshua and Daniel Fisher and Eleazer Lusher all played important roles in arranging meetinghouse seating, while at the same time serving as colonial leaders and shaping policy with the Indians.[39] The meetinghouse ritual served both to reinforce the community's localistic impulse and to reconcile it with an acknowledgment of the community's reliance upon outside aid.

In Indian communities mortuary ritual served some of the same purposes as the English meetinghouse gatherings. Archaeologists have exca-

vated several seventeenth-century Indian cemeteries scattered throughout New England and have found a definite pattern in the sites. First, as
the seventeenth century progressed, Indians paid greater attention to the
boundaries and the spacing of individual plots. The boundaries became
tighter and neater and the individual plots closer together. Most archaeologists have interpreted this change as ritualizing greater local political
consciousness and increased local identity within the community.[40]

Second, like the early meetinghouse rituals, early-seventeenth-century
Indian cemeteries do not show a hierarchical display of wealth; this absence changed with time, however. A large number of nonutilitarian European artifacts have been found interred with Indian bodies during the
third quarter of the seventeenth century. Indians distributed these goods
unequally among the individual internments, marking hierarchical status
differentiation within Indian societies. The ritualized burial of artifacts
with individuals served to validate and legitimate their position within
the community during a period of political flux and restructuring. Moreover, in burying goods with individuals of high status rather than passing
them on to subsequent generations, the Indian community signified that
status was earned as much as it was inherited. Based on this body of data,
archaeologists agree that under the strains induced by European colonization, Indian leaders faced challenges to their authority, which increased
the importance of achieved status relative to ascribed status. The achieved
status came to be reaffirmed and marked through mortuary ritual.

Indian burial sites challenge the traditional stereotype of the egalitarian Indian society by offering evidence of a hierarchically ordered, increasingly individualistic world, where leaders competed for and earned
the loyalty of their communities, ultimately marking their status with material goods. In areas where the English posed an immediate expansion-
ist threat, a leader's apparent ability to control the tide of English expansion and to protect the group's autonomy within such expansion became
a way to achieve and maintain a privileged position within the community.[41]

Control of the English most often did not come through the drawing
of rigid boundaries between themselves and the English; rather, Indian
leaders often subjected groups of Indians to the English and integrated
their polities in order to use the English legal and political system to their
advantage. Mortuary rituals recognized these leaders' accomplishments
and rewarded their ability to integrate Indian polities into those of the

English, yet these rewards coincided with the reinforcement of local political identity. In sum, both English meetinghouse rituals and Indian mortuary rituals served to mediate between their respective communities' contradictory impulses.[42] Both sets of rituals reconciled localistic impulses with the demands for integration into regional polities and helped to facilitate the entry of inward-looking communities into voluntary provincial chiefdoms of perceived common political interests.

As A GLUE holding the region together, ritual obviously had its limits. The intertwining of Indian confederacies and English colonies proved fragile; influences beyond the bounds of New England helped unravel it. Relations between the Indians along the middle and upper Connecticut River and the Mohawks to the west began to deteriorate in the 1660s. The disintegration of peace in western New England threatened a delicate balance of power: it left the Mohegans, allied with the English, in a position to threaten their old Indian rivals to the north and west. The Connecticut River Indians and the Narragansetts would be left looking for allies, English or Indian, to counterbalance the new threat from the Mohawks and the relative rise of the Mohegans. When war broke out between some Wampanoags and English colonists to the east in 1675, their choices were made all the more stark.

Several factors led to the breakdown of relations between the Mohawks and their Indian neighbors in the Connecticut River Valley. The colonists' demand for wampum declined as English overseas trade grew and currency began flowing into the region after 1662. Furs became increasingly scarce and land values rose as more English families moved into western Massachusetts. For the English, real estate became more profitable relative to the fur trade. At the same time the Mohawks, suffering from years of warfare and disease, actually intensified war efforts as a means of replenishing their population with captives. The ties that had bound the Mohawks to the Connecticut River Indians and the Narragansetts—a strong fur trade and access to wampum—had dissolved, and old animosities between the Iroquoian Mohawks and the Algonquians of New England resurfaced.

The effects of the breakdown of Iroquois-Algonquian relations were felt first in what is now northern New England. A cycle of deadly attacks and counterattacks erupted. Algonquian groups, particularly the Sokokis of the upper Connecticut Valley and other Abenakis just to their east, were in disarray as they destroyed Mohawk villages and then suffered equally devastating counterraids. Sokoki and Abenaki refugees began to flow south into the middle Connecticut River Valley and north to New France. As they headed into southern New England, they intensified the Connecticut River Indians' hostility toward the Iroquois. After a Mohawk emissary was killed on a mission to the Pocumtucks, a retaliatory raid annihilated these Algonquians' village, paving the way for English colonists to establish the town Deerfield, Massachusetts, at the same site in 1673. As Pocumtuck refugees scattered, other southern New England Indian groups feared that the Mohawk wrath might reach them. Equally frightening was the prospect that the Iroquois might become allied with the Massachusetts and Connecticut colonies. Many Connecticut River Indians began to seek refuge near the more stable Albany region, as the Mohegans—always politically aligned with Connecticut—established ties with the Mohawks.[43]

In contrast, many of southern New England's other Indians saw increasing violence as yet another incentive to cozy up to the English. Mohawk raids, although most intense in the western parts of New England, began to threaten even those Indians close to Boston by 1665.[44] After a disastrous military foray into Iroquoia in 1669, a number of Massachusetts Indians saw few options other than to rely on ties to the English for protection. The Massachusetts missionary Daniel Gookin touted the benefits that missionized Indians, in particular, reaped under English guidance. In 1674 he wrote:

> [H]ad it not been for relief they had from the English, in compensation for labour, doubtless many of them had suffered famine. For they were driven [by the Mohawk] from their planting fields through fear, and from their fishing and hunting places; yea, they durst not go into the woods, to seek roots and nuts to sustain their lives. But this good effect the war had upon some of them, namely, to turn them from idleness; for now necessity forced them to labour with the English in hoeing, reaping, picking hops, cutting wood, making hay, and making stone fences, and like necessary employments, whereby they got victuals and clothes.[45]

These Indians of southern New England who found sanctuary in English missionary activities expressed the hatred and fear that they felt toward the Mohawks when English colonists captured two Mohawks near Boston.

> The Indians, our neighbours, flocked into Boston, in great numbers not
> only to see those Maquas [Mohawks], but earnestly to solicit the court,
> not to let them escape, but to put them to death, or, at least, to deliver the
> Maquas to them to be put to death. For, said they, these Maquas are unto
> us, as wolves are to your sheep. They secretly seize upon us and our chil-
> dren, wherever they meet us, and destroy us. Now, if we had taken five
> wolves alive, and should let them go again, and not destroy them, you
> Englishmen would be greatly offended with us for such an act: and surely,
> said they, the lives of men are of more worth than beasts.[46]

The Indians expected the English to protect them from the Mohawks in
exchange for their loyalty. They felt that by submitting to the English
and demonstrating their fidelity by killing wolves, they had incurred the
obligation of the English to kill the Mohawks.[47] For many Indians, loyalty
to English polities seemed a small price to pay for protection from external threats. The overlap between Indian and English political cultures
made the price of loyalty manageable. For others, however, especially in
the Connecticut River Valley and the Narragansett territory, the breakdown of relations with the Mohawks left them isolated and vulnerable.

Given this unstable situation, it is little wonder that a large number of
Narragansetts and Connecticut River Indians might sympathize with the
Wampanoags who lashed out at Plymouth Colony in 1675. Cultural overlap and mutual interests had been strong enough to create strong ties
among a sizable number of English and Indians and lead to a relatively
peaceful covalent society after the Pequot War. But in the 1660s a vortex
of forces began to undermine the complex web of relations that had been
created, especially in the west. Closer to the coast, in Plymouth, a roughly
simultaneous series of events would unfold, proving that the Indians and
the English there had misinterpreted one another's motives and desires.
After the conflict broke out, a Narragansett would be left asking Roger
Williams "why the Massachusets and Rode Iland rose, and joynd with
Plymmouth agnst Phillip and left not Phillip and Plymmouth to fight it
out."[48] Apparently, Indians underestimated the latent bond among Englishmen, and their political ties to the English provided, at best, a shaky
foundation of protection.

3

Symbol of a Failed
Strategy

On June 8, 1675, two Wampanoag Indians, Tobias and Mattashunannamo, were hanged on Plymouth Colony's gallows. Just over two weeks
later, on June 24, 1675, some Wampanoags attacked English settlers at
Swansea in Plymouth, beginning King Philip's War. For more than three
hundred years, historians have rightly seen the hangings as the proximate
cause of the cataclysmic conflict. But as many historians have demonstrated, Indians usually received unfair treatment in the colonial courts.
How, then, could these executions in particular, after years of legal inequality, trigger such unprecedented violence?[1] To answer this question,
one must understand exactly what the executions symbolized to various
Indians, especially Philip and the Wampanoags. And to interpret the symbolism of these deaths, one must comprehend the situation that various
Indians believed they had created for themselves and the region's English inhabitants.

Plymouth executed Tobias and Mattashunannamo for killing another
Indian, John Sassamon. Sassamon was no ordinary individual, but a
highly symbolic rival of the Wampanoag sachem Philip. That Wampanoags could be tried in Plymouth for Sassamon's death is crucial, for it
raised issues of land and the legitimacy of Philip's rule. Like all leaders
throughout New England, Philip, as head of the Wampanoags, had to resist currents that might siphon away followers. Many times, like the debates in the English colonies having to do with doctrine, these currents
swirled around issues related to religion. Sassamon was ostensibly Chris-

tian, and Philip was opposed to the spread of Christianity among Indians. But in the second half of the seventeenth century, Indians increasingly flocked to Massachusetts towns that the English had established to convert natives to Christianity. It is questionable whether these "praying Indians" actually converted at these towns, but they certainly received instruction both in religious doctrine and in "civility"—that is, how to live like the English. They also obtained a measure of security in their land tenure that they might not have had otherwise. Thus, both the "praying Indians" of Massachusetts and many of the "nonpraying Indians" of Massachusetts, Plymouth, Connecticut, and Rhode Island had invested heavily in the English political system as a means of preserving their autonomy and, in many cases, a land base.[2]

After 1667 Christian Indians became increasingly common in Philip's Plymouth. By the early 1670s Philip was competing with Christians for followers and often losing. For nonpraying Indians loyal to the sachem Philip, the execution of fellow Indians for the alleged murder of Sassamon, a praying Indian, signaled the failure of their political strategy and the success of the praying Indians. A divine omen of war in the form of a lunar eclipse reinforced this signal and helped lead to a violent rebellion among a large portion of the region's Indian inhabitants.

BECAUSE SEVENTEENTH-CENTURY New England consisted of locally oriented polities that intermeshed with one another, village polities often took precedence over regional entities in shaping the allegiances of individuals. Leaders of local polities had to earn their status by gaining the respect of followers. Within Indian polities, the challenge of colonization was a paramount concern of members. Leadership positions in these groups therefore hinged largely on the perceived ability of the individual to control the impact of English expansion on the polity; leaders from various groups competed for followers by appearing to cope effectively with colonization. A combination of documentary, linguistic, and archaeological evidence shows that voluntary political submission to the English was a very common strategy of natives, who viewed such submissions as establishing bonds of mutual obligation between themselves and the colonists. Both Native American and English groups found enough commonality between their cultures to allow for such bonds, because English monarchical culture and the Algonquian ethos of reciprocity contained strong parallels. Linguistic evidence confirms that natives saw the colonies that they submitted to, like their own sachemship, as a kind of protectorate. The English, in turn, often backed their promises of protection with action, such as when they helped Indians build forts. These political linkages, combined with a shared economy, legal system, and social space, constituted the metaphorical electrons in the covalent society formed by bonds among groups of Indians and the various English colonies in New England.

One of the more significant threats to these bonds lay in the diversity among the Indian groups that had submitted to the English. Seventeenth-century Indians did not try to protect themselves as a monolithic entity; rather, small groups of Indians used a variety of strategies in competition with one another. Two distinct strategies that eventually formed the basis for an intense rivalry took divergent stances on the issues of Christian conversion and literacy. Some groups, such as the praying Indians of Massachusetts, found ties to English missionaries and literacy to be promising avenues to maintaining a measure of autonomy within the English system. Others, such as the Wampanoags in Plymouth, resisted Puritan conversion efforts with the hope that political and legal submission to the English alone would be adequate to protect their culture.

The groups that submitted to Massachusetts, most of which eventually comprised the praying Indians of the colony, were fragments of larger groups that had suffered the most under English colonization and probably succumbed most easily to English influence.[3] Nevertheless, their apparent adoption of Christianity represents more than merely a process of acculturation in which they become more English and less Indian; nor were they even completely "dominated" by the English. In their correspondence with London officials, missionaries such as John Eliot usually emphasized their successes at "civilizing" and converting Indians; yet one should not accept such characterizations at face value, because they were usually directed toward officials upon whom the missionaries depended for funding. Other evidence, moreover, suggests that the Indians closest to the English utilized their relationship to protect and preserve a distinctively Indian identity in a way unavailable to the majority of Indians in the Northeast.[4]

Because the praying Indians consisted of fragments of precontact groups that had been devastated by the process of English colonization, these Indians worked within more powerful constraints than did groups that had been much less affected, such as the Narragansetts.[5] Disease and the pressures of English colonization had caused much suffering among the groups that formed the praying communities. At the same time, the accumulated experience of these Indians, who had known the most intimate contact with the English, offered them avenues of resistance and cultural revitalization. From this perspective, literacy, in particular, became an asset in the competition with other Indians working within the framework of English colonization.

A sound knowledge of English and the ability to use the written word, attributes of 30 percent of the praying Indians in their largest community at Natick, empowered Indians in their relations with the English and with other Indians. Roger Williams reported in his *Key into the Language of America* (1643) that, when asked how the English knew that souls went to heaven or hell, an Indian replied that the English "hath books and writings, and one which God himself made, concerning mens souls, and therefore may well know more than wee that have none, but take all upon trust from our forefathers." That Indians were mystified by literacy or held it in awe became apparent in 1640 when a group of Indians broke into a schoolhouse in Watertown, Massachusetts, and stole sixteen Greek and Latin books.[6] When groups of Indians became literate and gained access to English and the written word, Indian communities underwent an internal transformation and redistribution of power. Such skills offered Indians a way to understand and perhaps even appear to control the English.

Although many Indians displayed an eagerness to become literate, their desire did not arise from a wish to become more like the English per se; rather, the Indians wanted, in the words of anthropologist Kathleen Bragdon, "a source of community strength which helped to preserve their distinctiveness as Indians."[7] Whereas the English saw the establishment of praying towns as a program to civilize and convert the natives, the Indians saw in them an opportunity to encapsulate themselves within the expanding realm of English settlement. Archaeological evidence bolsters this view that English and Indians saw the effects of missionary conversion programs quite differently.

In the 1980s archaeologist Elise Brenner studied the impact of missionary efforts on the material culture of Indians at Natick. Brenner sought, among other objectives, to uncover the extent to which the Indians conformed to one of the primary ambitions of the English missionaries: to get the Indians to live more "sedentarily," in a "civilized" fashion. To this end, a group of archaeologists systematically examined the area where the Indians at Natick had supposedly lived in the English manner. Because they found no material remains at that location—where, had the Indians lived as the missionaries desired, there should have been many—Brenner concluded that the Indians in all probability continued to live in their more "traditional" ways rather than conforming to Puritan norms.[8]

Not only did the Natick site lack material remains indicating a sedentary lifestyle, but burial sites of praying Indians excavated earlier had shown patterns similar to those at burial grounds used by nonpraying Indians. Like the nonpraying burial grounds in what were the colonies of Rhode Island and Plymouth, the praying town cemetery challenged Puritan dogma by associating material objects with the dead. Moreover, the goods contained in the grave sites for Natick were of the same type as those buried in the graves of nonmissionized Indians and differed from those supplied by missionaries for use in a sedentary life. The Indians at Natick maintained contact with nonmissionized Indians and continued to perform non-Christian burial rituals. Documentary evidence corroborates the archaeological. In 1675, after King Philip's War had begun, the Massachusetts Council ordered the praying Indians to arrange "their wigwams that they may stand compact in one place of their plantations respectively."[9] Apparently, praying towns such as Natick, Punquapog, Nashobah, Wamesit, and Hassanemesit had not reached the Puritan ideal of a "city on a hill" comprised of tightly clustered permanent buildings. The praying Indians, although undoubtedly culturally different from nonpraying Indians, had taken a trajectory of change different from that suggested by the English: they lived in wigwams and migrated to take advantage of seasonal means of subsistence.[10]

Although both praying and nonpraying Indians followed strategies that they felt offered the greatest opportunity for ethnic preservation, the paths the two groups chose altered their respective relationships with English colonists. This difference, in turn, heightened tensions among Indians that appeared most strikingly in the contest for control of land among various natives and colonists. Missionized and nonmissionized Indians followed diverse paths in their efforts to protect their land base from English encroachment. The Wampanoags under the sachem Philip increasingly took their land grievances to Plymouth Colony courts. Bounded by either water or other tribes on all sides, the Wampanoags could not migrate to escape the pressures of colonization. Within this

framework, the Wampanoags adapted to the English legal system to defend their rights to the land. The court records of Plymouth Colony demonstrate a dramatic rise in the number of disputes over fraudulent sales,
trespassing, and boundaries between the 1640s and the 1670s.[11] Though
colonial courts may not have treated Indians as well as the English, Indians did enjoy some success before the bench, enough to make the strategy worth pursuing.

The missionized Indians, however, with allies such as John Eliot, could
circumvent the limited avenues available to the Wampanoags. Indeed, the
incentives to join a praying community included, perhaps most importantly, the protection of land. Daniel Gookin made this incentive explicit
when he outlined some key reasons for establishing praying towns: "First,
to prevent differences and contention among the English and Indians in
future times about the propriety of land. Secondly, to secure unto them
and their posterity places of habitation; this being a provision in all those
grants, that they shall not sell or alienate any part of those lands unto any
Englishman, without the general court's consent: for the Indians being
poor, as well as improvident, are very prone to sell their land to the English, and thereby leave themselves destitute."[12] Although putting themselves under the influence of missionaries might have constituted a sacrifice, in doing so the praying Indians strengthened their claims to land.

An example in which both the Wampanoags and the Indians at Natick
had land claims illustrates that the praying Indians had more power to
protect their land than their nonmissionized counterparts. As the population of Natick grew in the 1650s, it required more high-quality land to
supply the Indian inhabitants with a sufficient land base. The only adja-
cent section of land with fertile soil lay along the Charles River, and legal
right to it had already been granted by the Massachusetts General Court
to the English town of Dedham. The interests of local colonists collided
with the proselytizing mission of the colony and the desire among the
praying Indians for secure land tenure. Challenging the interests of local
English residents, John Eliot petitioned the colony on behalf of the Indians for the expansion of Indian land at Natick, and he won. Eliot appealed
to a higher law than did the leaders of Dedham. He made the moral argument that the Lord's work of converting Indians depended upon Natick's acquiring neighboring land from English towns. To this end, he requested in 1651 that the "honord Court would please to treate wth the
othr townes bordering upon them, that as they yeild up much to the

Lords use on the one side, so theire neighbours would be helpfull to them by yeilding up somewhat to them on the other. & thus beging the good blessing of heaven on all your holy counsels & labours, & beging of you, your prayres for me." Responding to Eliot's request, the General Court rescinded Dedham's title to the land and granted the Natick Indians an additional two thousand acres of prime land along the Charles River. In compensation, the court granted Dedham two thousand acres in the Connecticut River Valley at what later became Deerfield.[13] Disputes over the land continued into the 1660s, and Eliot again pleaded with the General Court. The court sided again with the Indians, even though it admitted that "the legall right of Dedham thereto cannot in justice be denied."[14] Eliot had succeeded in strengthening the position of the praying Indians at Natick by appealing to morality and God's desire to convert Indians to Christianity. Meanwhile, the inhabitants of Dedham, relying solely on their legal title to the land, lost a bitter dispute with the General Court of their own colony. In this contest between Dedham and Eliot, Eliot was not the only winner. The Indians at Natick reaped perhaps the greatest gains, successfully protecting themselves from the rapid English encroachment.[15]

This victory for the Natick Indians did not represent a victory for all Indians living within the colony of Massachusetts. The English inhabitants of Dedham who lost land to Natick often sought title in another part of Dedham's grant. Beginning in 1660, Dedham's leaders began to allow individuals to settle a part of Dedham's grant in Massachusetts known as Wollomonuppoag in compensation for their loss at Natick. In December 1662, for example, town leaders offered a parcel of land at Wollomonuppoag "unto Anthon Fisher Juner to take up sattisfaction for his Fathers devident and his owne that was takin away by Naticke." The movement of English settlers into this part of Dedham's grant sparked tensions with the Indians who were using this land. In November 1667, the town council fielded a "[c]omplaint being made that the Indians. emprve [improve] more Land and Timber at Wollomonuppoag much to the damage of the Towne."[16] Responding to this complaint and the many similar ones that followed it, the town began a concerted strategy of consolidating its claims to the Wollomonuppoag area and excluding Indians from its use.

The Indians in question were none other than Wampanoags loyal to King Philip. The town sent a request to Philip to remove all Indians from

the area. The currency-poor Philip shrewdly realized that he might receive payment in return for a release of Indian claims to the area and
offered to sell the land in 1669. He lacked formal ties to Massachusetts,
and he may have even seen his political authority in tension with that of
the Bay Colony. Plymouth, after all, had long disputed its boundary with
Massachusetts, and Philip's father, Massasoit, had engaged in a treaty of
subordination to Plymouth in 1621 and renewed it in 1639. When Philip
became sachem in 1662, he renewed Wampanoag loyalty to Plymouth,
making it his *nanauwunnumoonkan,* his protectorate.[17] Therefore, since he
was dealing with Massachusetts, Philip made the best of a situation in
which he had little political leverage. By selling the land, he put pressure
on his followers at Wollomonuppoag to relocate, preferably away from
Massachusetts, away from the influence of praying Indians and English
missionaries, and closer to his dominion. He also acquired scarce currency that could be used to obtain trade goods.[18] It was not a bad deal,
given that he was dealing with a colony that disputed its very boundary
with his own protectorate, Plymouth.

Although Philip might have perceived the deal he made with Dedham
as the most equitable he could hope for, it may have served warning that
his strategy of submitting to Plymouth to protect his authority was endangered. His success with Wollomonuppoag appeared minuscule in relation to that enjoyed by the Natick Indians in their relations with Dedham. Philip made the most of Dedham's desires and the English system
of land ownership by extracting what he perceived to be a fair price, but
his situation limited his actions to those of an outsider in the Bay Colony's
legal system. This strategy contrasted strikingly with that of the Natick
Indians, who fifteen years earlier had managed through the morality arguments of John Eliot to acquire land legally owned by Dedham. Whereas
the Natick Indians did not have to give up any material resources for their
increased land holdings, Philip had to sell land in exchange for needed
currency to buy trade goods.

As a backdrop to his problems with Massachusetts, Philip also faced
difficulties to his west in Rhode Island. In the months before the Wollomonuppoag controversy erupted, Narragansetts in that colony tested
Philip's power. The Narragansetts had experienced firsthand the machinations of the Mohegan leader Uncas, and they, in turn, tried some of his
techniques against Philip. Uncas had used his strong ties with the English
of Connecticut to advance his interests with regard to the Narragansetts.

On a number of occasions, he fed Connecticut authorities false claims that the Narragansetts were preparing for war. In response, his English allies readily defended him militarily in 1643, 1645, 1657, and 1658. In 1643 Uncas even got the English to convict the Narragansett leader Miantonomo of murder and allow him to carry out the execution. The Narragansetts for years had felt they were on the wrong end of these episodes, and thus they tried to use some of the same methods against their longtime rivals to the east, Philip's Wampanoags. As early as 1662 Philip had found threatening Narragansetts living within Plymouth, even among some of his own people who, it seems, were less than completely loyal. He was able to deal with these Narragansetts by appealing to Plymouth, his protectorate, to have them removed. Such results reaffirmed his belief in his strategies of submission; his relationship with Plymouth had paid dividends and his power was bolstered. He therefore immediately renewed his covenant with the colony.[19]

Five years later, however, the Narragansetts—more specifically, a subgroup of Eastern Niantics—raised the ante. In July 1667 Philip found himself summoned by Plymouth to answer accusations that he was secretly planning an insurrection against the colony. In front of the Plymouth court, he learned that one of his own Wampanoags had told the court that the sachem was making plans for war. To anyone who knew that Philip had had problems five years earlier with disloyal Wampanoags courting Narragansetts in the colony and who was aware that the Narragansetts knew all too well through their experiences with Uncas the power of misinformation, Philip's response to the court would have been entirely believable. He told the court that the Wampanoag who had accused him of plotting against the English had been paid to do so by the Eastern Niantic sachem Ninigret (keep in mind that Ninigret had also been successfully using a colony—Rhode Island—to his political advantage). To convince the English he was telling the truth, he reminded them that in the past it was Plymouth "by whom himself and progenitors had bine preserved from being rewined [ruined] by the Narragansetts."[20] In the end Plymouth believed Philip but decided to keep a watchful eye on him. For Philip, the incident must have served as a grave reminder of just how tenuous his position was and just how much he needed Plymouth Colony.

In the fluid sociopolitical Indian communities of the 1660s, where leaders constantly had to demonstrate their leadership ability in order to legitimate their status, the Wampanoags' respect for Philip's ability to control the English must have been tinged with doubt because of his relative inability to take advantage of the English system the way their brethren at Natick had done in the 1650s. Just as the Narragansetts had successfully used the king of England to protect themselves from the various colonies beginning in the 1640s, the praying Indians of Massachusetts had manipulated the missionary aims of Massachusetts to preserve a land base. Philip and his people, in contrast, struggled in their relations with the English. Although they had experienced some success before the courts in preventing Plymouth from taking their land, they felt relentless pressure at the hands of the English—pressure that would prove too much for the Wampanoags to withstand when, in the first half of the 1670s, they appeared more than ever to lack control of the English relative to many neighboring Indian groups.

Philip's troubles resurfaced in April 1671 when Plymouth Colony again summoned him to answer accusations that he had been plotting an uprising against the English. A number of Philip's followers had flaunted their arms before English settlers at Swansea. The town was fairly new, established by the colony in 1667 through the purchase of some of the prime land in the region from Indians.[21] It was also the town closest to Philip's own village. The Indians in the region were openly angry with their English neighbors, probably because livestock owned by the English were allowed to trespass on native land.[22] However, whether Philip had conspired against the English or, instead, this claim merely reflected Plymouth's paranoia or Narragansett accusations against him is impossible to tell. Philip later claimed to have complied with Plymouth's demands "that thereby Jelosy might be removed." Whatever the case, Plymouth forced Philip to acknowledge a plot, apologize, pay a fine, and surrender his arms.[23]

Five months later, in September 1671, Plymouth summoned Philip once again, this time for having "broken his covenant made with our collonie." Apparently, Philip had surrendered his arms with the understanding that the colony would return them shortly, whereas Plymouth officials believed they had confiscated them permanently. During this third appearance before the General Court of Plymouth, the court also accused Philip of having "entertained, harboured, and abetted divers Indians, not of his owne men, which were vagabonds, our professed enimies."[24] Whether or not the accusation was true, in the eyes of the Plymouth officials Philip had not lived up to his reciprocal obligation of loyalty. The scrutiny of Plymouth made Philip nervous. He explored alternatives to his long-held strategy of encapsulating his people within the colony of Plymouth. Before appearing before the court, he journeyed to Massachusetts hoping to find forceful backing for his grievances against Plymouth. Massachusetts was cordial but offered only a delicately phrased letter. Its leaders wrote Plymouth's governor urging the colony to "a complyance" with Philip. They reminded Plymouth that its relationship with the sachem should be a "naighborly and frindly correspondency." Hemmed in by an unhelpful Massachusetts to the north and hostile Narragansetts to the west, Philip resigned himself to his old strategy. On September 29, 1671, he once again swore an oath of fidelity to Plymouth.[25]

Philip tried to continue the strategy that Indians throughout the region had followed with varying degrees of success for the previous fifty years. He reinforced his band's reciprocal bonds with Plymouth in an effort both to acquire assistance in his rivalries with other Indians and to play the various English colonies off one another. To this end, he agreed to a document once again acknowledging the Wampanoags as "subjects to his majesty the Kinge of England, &c, and the gouvernent of New Plymouth, and to theire lawes."[26] Facing the Plymouth court under these adverse circumstances, Philip decided, perhaps under some pressure, that an oath of fidelity warranted a final chance. After all, he could turn neither to Rhode Island nor to Massachusetts, because they favored Wampanoag rivals: the Narragansetts and the praying Indians, respectively. Moreover, the relative success that the Narragansetts and the praying Indians had experienced by encapsulating themselves within the English political system posed a threat to Philip's leadership status, in that he may have appeared incapable of controlling the English. Reaffirming his loyalty to Plymouth appeared to him to be the best option.

Yet Philip's submission this time was far different from earlier ones. In the past, Christian Indians had made few inroads into Plymouth; most of the praying towns were in Massachusetts. So long as missionary pressures were weak in Plymouth, Philip's authority could remain strong. Starting in 1667, however, the English minister John Cotton began preaching the Gospel to Plymouth's Indians. His efforts were persistent: he preached an average of twenty-five sermons a year to Indians between 1667 and 1675. Indian leaders complained that missionaries undermined their authority. One rejected Cotton "because many of his Indians would forsake him and he should lose much tribute." Nevertheless, by 1671 Christian Indians were on the rise in the colony, and their ascendance was seemingly at Philip's expense. The same year that Philip renewed his oath of fidelity with the colony, a sizable number of Christian Indians did so as well.[27] The colony now had formal obligations to both Philip and Christian Indians who competed for the same resources. Should a conflict arise between praying and nonpraying Indians, Philip undoubtedly worried that the colony would resolve it in favor of the latter. He also feared that Indians loyal to him might join Christian communities.

The praying town at Nemasket, near Assawompset Pond in Plymouth, emerged in Philip's mind as the most serious threat. The site became a scene of controversy at least as early as 1671, when natives loyal to Philip from the region were forced to surrender their arms for allegedly "being in complyance with Phillipe in his late plott," wherein armed Indians were seen around Swansea.[28] After this confrontation, there was a series of contentious deals concerning land near the pond over a period of years. At least once a year for three consecutive years, the Plymouth General Court was needed to arbitrate transactions. In each case, the question arose as to exactly how much land a non-Christian Indian leader, usually Philip or Tuspaquin, had deeded to Englishmen or Christian Indians. Philip, like Uncas in Connecticut, often sold land if it helped his own status. But in these exchanges, the land he was parting with often ended up in the hands of rival praying Indians. Memories of Natick and Wollomonuppoag must have haunted Philip. One deed in particular stands out. In 1673 Tuspaquin granted twenty-seven acres to an Indian named John Sassamon, who, shortly thereafter, began a ministry among the natives at Nemasket.

John Sassamon has to be one of the slipperiest characters in seventeenth-century New England history. An orphan raised by English parents, he grew to be a literate, Christian Indian who was near the center of some of the more important land deals in Plymouth and Massachusetts. For the first forty or fifty years of his life, he was a textbook example of what the English wanted Indians to be. He served with the English-Indian alliance that subdued the Pequots in 1637, taught school at Natick, and attended Harvard College. In 1662, the year Philip's father Massasoit died, Sassamon left Natick to be closer to the Wampanaog transition in leadership. He could not have gotten much closer. In the words of the contemporary English minister William Hubbard, Sassamon "upon some Misdemeanour fled from his Place [at Natick] to Philip, by whom he was entertained in the Room and Office of Secretary, and his Chief Councel-lor." In 1662 Sassamon served as the witness when Philip offered his oath of fidelity to Plymouth. He served as witness to at least three of Philip's land transactions in 1664, 1665, and 1666.[29]

Philip had obvious reasons for wanting Sassamon at his side. He prob-ably hoped that Sassamon, as one of Natick's elites, could ensure the Wampanoags of the same kinds of successes that the Natick Indians had had in preserving their land base. This, in turn, would help Philip legiti-mate his sachemship. But the strategy had obvious risks. Sassamon had strong historical ties to both the English and the praying Indians. He was a capable mediator between the missionized Indians and the English, the Wampanoags and the English, and the Wampanoags and the missionized Indians. Because various groups of Indians competed for advantage in their relations with the English, Sassamon's relations involved a conflict of interest. Philip must have always suspected his loyalty. Would Sassa-mon use his skills to promote his own interests rather than those of Philip?

The answer became a definitive yes. While Philip floundered in his relationships with Plymouth in the early 1670s, Sassamon acquired his own foothold in the region at Nemasket. In 1673 Tuspaquin, a non-Christian Wampanoag leader loyal to Philip, deeded to Sassamon twenty-seven acres, "as my gift given to him." Perhaps Tuspaquin did so to assure Sassamon's loyalty, following a strategy pursued by so many sachems in the past who worried about the support of their followers. Or perhaps Tuspaquin did not really grant him the land and the deed was a fake. In another context two years later, Sassamon was accused of creating fraud-ulent documents. Talking to John Easton of Rhode Island, some Wampa-noags said that Sassamon "was a bad man that king Philop got him to write his will and he made the writing for a gret part of the land to be his but read as if it had bine as Philop wold, but it Came to be knone and then he rund away from him."[30] Unfortunately, we will probably never know why or whether Tuspaquin, who became one of Philip's staunchest allies in the war, deeded land to Sassamon. But we do know, perhaps more importantly, what Sassamon did once he had property in the region. He assumed the ministry at Nemasket's Indian church.[31] The man upon whom Philip had placed his hopes was now an avowed enemy.

At the end of 1674, Sassamon approached Plymouth officials and impli-cated Philip in a plot against the English.[32] Plymouth paid little attention to this warning, because "it had an Indian origin, and one can hardly believe them." Sassamon's report was not, after all, the first report of war presented to the colony by an Indian; false rumors of Indian uprisings circulated frequently and intentionally during the seventeenth century. When Sassamon left Plymouth, he expressed fear that Philip might try to have him killed for exposing his plans. At this point, Sassamon disappeared from the written record, until some Indians reported him missing a month or two later. A search eventually uncovered Sassamon's body under the ice at Assawompset Pond near Nemasket. After his burial, an Indian named Patuckson stepped forward and claimed that he had seen three Wampanoags loyal to Philip—Tobias, Wampapaquan, and Mattashunannamo—murder Sassamon and then try to conceal his body and make it appear as if he had drowned. Based on Patuckson's testimony, Plymouth ordered the three Indians under Philip to appear before the court in June 1675.[33]

The riddle of who killed John Sassamon—indeed, the question whether he was even murdered or perhaps drowned accidentally—is one that historians will probably never conclusively solve.[34] Contemporary accounts conflict. Equally debilitating is our limited understanding of Philip's relationship to his followers. Even if Tobias, Wampapaquan, and Mattashunannamo killed Sassamon, was it at Philip's urging or was it an overt expression of frustration and disillusionment with his rule? Colonists feared organized Indian conspiracies and probably attributed greater unity to the Wampanoags than the circumstances warranted. The label "King Philip's War" suggests an organization and structure for the conflict that is unsupported by evidence. Rather than being the grand conspirator, Philip had quite possibly lost control in 1675. After years of Philip's appearing relatively ineffectual in controlling the English, some Wampanoags, especially male youths, undoubtedly would have been tempted to take matters into their own hands. After war erupted and spread, forcing Indian groups to choose a side, many divided along generational lines (see chapter 4). Was Sassamon's murder a desperate, even last-ditch effort on Philip's part to preserve his authority or the first step on the part of those who had finally given up on him? We will never know, but we should not let the name "King Philip's War" blind us. Even if the Wampanoag sachem backed Sassamon's murder, much of what ensued over the next fourteen months was out of his control.

Whatever the case, Plymouth, trying to appear impartial, allowed the jury of twelve Englishmen to consult with and seek the advice of six of the "most indifferentest, gravest, and sage Indians."[35] Although the record does not say so explicitly, it is highly probable that only literate, Christian Indians qualified as "sage." Upon deliberation, the jury, as well as the Indians involved, unanimously agreed upon a guilty verdict and ordered the alleged murderers executed. On June 8, 1675, the colony hanged Tobias and Mattashunannamo. One month later it had Wampapaquan shot.

WHY DID these executions, among all of the indignities suffered by Indians at the hands of English colonists over the preceding half-century, spawn a war? The answer lies largely in the rivalries among Indians at the time, for the trial was as much the playing out of tensions among groups of Indians in the theater of Plymouth's court as it was a contest between the English and the Indians. The execution of Philip's Indians symbolized the relative success of the praying Indian's strategy—including the adoption of literacy and certain elements of Christianity—of encapsulation within the English political system and the failure of the nonmissionized Indians' variant thereof. After assuming leadership of the Wampanoags in 1662, Philip learned in steps that he could not trust the Narragansetts in Rhode Island, Massachusetts, and now, finally, Plymouth if the colony was going to favor Christian Indians. Following the trial, and on the eve of the outbreak of war, Philip explained that the Christianization of Indians posed a direct threat to his power. He and his entourage demanded that no more Indians be "[c]aled or forsed to be Christian indians. thay saied that such wer in everi thing more mischivous, only disemblers, and then the English made them not subject to ther [Indian] kings, and by ther lying to rong their kings."[36] Similarly, in September 1674 Daniel Gookin encountered, approximately seventy miles west of Boston, at the fledgling praying-Indian community of Wabquissit, an "agent for Unkas, sachem of Mohegan, who challenged right to, and dominion over, this people of Wabquissit. And said he, Unkas is not well pleased, that the English should pass over Mohegan river, to call his Indians to pray to God."[37] Gookin realized that the missionizing of increasing numbers of Indians posed a tremendous threat to traditional Indian leaders. He noted that sachems such as Uncas were usually receptive to Christianity "until at length the sachems did discern, that religion would not consist with a mere receiving of the word; and that practical religion will throw down their heathenish idols, and the sachem's tyrannical monarchy." Gookin even attributed the slow spread of Christianity among some groups of Indians in part to "the averseness of their sachems."[38]

In the fluid sociopolitical situation of seventeenth-century New England, where Indian leaders derived their positions of power from their demonstrated ability to act in their followers' behalf, incidents that revealed a leader's weakness directly threatened his status. In the past, certain incidents had suggested that Philip lacked ability to control the English in comparison to the praying Indians. This was the case when the Natick Indians received land at Dedham whereas Philip sold his tribe's share of this land. When the Natick Indians acquired Dedham land, they did so with the aid of Massachusetts, the colony to which they had submitted themselves for protection. Because Plymouth made no jurisdictional claims to the land in question, Philip could not and did not seek that colony's assistance. However, the Sassamon trial differed dramatically in that it involved Plymouth, the colony to which Philip had submitted for protection, rather than Massachusetts. The trial for Sassamon's alleged murder occurred within Plymouth's court; it involved Indians whom, Philip believed, the colony had promised to protect; and it depended upon evidence submitted by rival Christian Indians. For Philip's followers, the trial of Sassamon signified that they could not depend upon any English colony in North America for protection. On the eve of the war, he lamented to John Easton of Rhode Island that "all English agred against them [the Wampanoags]."[39] The colony of Plymouth had not fulfilled its reciprocal political relationship with the Wampanoags. The world that Philip believed he had created had disintegrated.

After the trial, in a discussion with Easton, who sought to avert war, Philip and a group of Wampanoags indicated how sincerely they had invested in the English political system and how willing they were to let it work the way they believed it should. Easton wrote of the conversation, saying that he had told the Wampanoags that, "thay having submited to our king to protect them others dared not otherwise to molest them, so thay expressed thay tooke that to be well, that we had litell Case to doute but that to us under the king thay wold have yelded to our determenations in what ani should have Cumplained to us against them."[40] Unfortunately for many Indians, communication with the king came only through the channels offered by local colonies. And in June 1675 the Indians perceived these colonies, with the exception of the relatively weak Rhode Island, to be in alliance against nonmissionized Indians. At this time the Wampanoags knew that they had to draw on other resources besides political encapsulation to protect their autonomy.

The Sassamon trial alone probably did not cause the Wampanoags to take the violent actions that they did starting in June 1675, although the trial served the necessary function of steering the Wampanoags away from the policy of playing English colonies off one another through reciprocal relations of allegiance and protection. But whether the Wampanoags had a clear idea of what to replace their old strategy with is unclear. Like the contemporaneous Bacon's Rebellion in Virginia, King Philip's was a war "with abundant causes but without a cause: it produced no real program of reform, no revolutionary manifesto, not even any revolutionary slogan."[41] There is nothing to suggest that when Wampanoags killed nine English colonists at Swansea on June 24, 1675, they intended those deaths to start a war, the scale of which New England had never seen. Their interpretation of the events of the subsequent week pushed them in that direction.

An anthropologist who has collected the folklore of Algonquian tribes in the Northeast has suggested that "[i]f the Indians had written their history of King Philip's War, they might have emphasized the importance of shamanistic divination in the formulation of strategy." This is especially true given that the Sassamon trial had brought the Wampanoags to a crossroads and made them realize the need for a change of course. On June 26, 1675, the Wampanoags witnessed a sign that strengthened their conviction that they must sever relations with the English through violent means. Less than one week after the first and highly tentative skirmishes between Wampanoags and Plymouth colonists at Swansea, a total lunar eclipse manifested itself throughout the region. Colonial almanacs had forecast this event, but whether the region's Indians were aware of its coming in advance will probably never be known.[42] The often haphazard manner in which the rebellion unfolded suggests little in the way of a predetermined strategy. This is not to say that the Indians did not fight well; their destruction speaks for itself. But it seems likely that the eclipse caught most, if not all, of the Indians off guard. It surprised them and fueled a desire to wage war. The movements of the heavenly bodies altered the Northeast's political landscape.

On two separate occasions in the first half of the seventeenth century, Jesuit missionaries had the opportunity to record the meaning of lunar eclipses to natives in the Northeast and the Great Lakes regions. For the

Montagnais, an Algonquian people, eclipses represented the son of the sun and moon, who "comes now and then upon earth; and, when he walks about in their country, many people die."[43] Similarly, a French missionary wrote of the Hurons, an Iroquoian people, that "[t]hey consider Eclipses as omens of mortality, of war, or of sickness; but this augury does not always precede the evil that it predicts. Sometimes it follows it, for the Savages who saw the Eclipse of the Moon that appeared this year, 1642, said that they were no longer astonished at the massacre of their people by the Hiroquois during the winter. They had before them the token and the sign of it, but a little too late to put them on their guard."[44] Some groups nearby and culturally similar to those of southern New England associated eclipses with war, indicating that the June 26 phenomenon did more than simply coincide with the escalation of relatively minor skirmishes into King Philip's War. These observations prompt the question of whether the Sassamon trial alone was the proximate cause of the war, for even if the eclipse did not necessarily and proximately cause the war, it almost certainly intensified the war after it began, given the constant Puritan search for omens of divine providence or disfavor.[45] Once the Sassamon trial had prompted the destruction of the political world that the Indians believed they had created, the eclipse revealed to them that the means by which they should attempt to create a new one—even if they did not have a clear vision of it—would be violent. Furthermore, the eclipse heightened the Puritan reaction against this Indian violence.

New England's inhabitants found themselves on a treacherous path. Warfare among the Indians and the English in southern New England entailed grave risks. It threatened the very bonds that held their society together, since groups of Indians and of the English had intermeshed their polities. Once war broke out, the fabric of their society had the potential to unravel. And, sure enough, conflict quickly expanded beyond the narrow confines of southwestern Plymouth. When Wampanoags attacked Swansea on June 24, 1675, the nine colonists killed were far from the conflict's last.

4

FAULT LINES

NEAR WORDEN POND, in what is now South Kingston, Rhode Island, a group of Narragansett leaders met with Roger Williams in late June 1675 and gingerly discussed the incipient hostilities between Plymouth and the Wampanoags who were loyal to Philip. Williams hoped to learn that the Narragansetts, the largest group of Indians in the region, were not in cahoots with Philip. He must have felt great relief upon hearing them speak. He urgently wrote Connecticut governor John Winthrop, Jr., having been told that the Narragansetts had "prohibited all their people from going on that side: that those of their people, who had made Mariages with them should returne or perish there: That if Phillip or his men fled to them yet they would not receave them but deliver them up unto the English." The Narragansetts expressed no intentions of getting involved.[1]

They also nervously explored how a war might expand and how various English groups would react. They asked Williams "why Plymmouth pursued Phillip." He responded, "He [Philip] broke all Laws and was in Armes of Rebellion agst that Colony his ancient friends and protectours." Apparently satisfied, the Narragansetts then raised what was to them a far more confusing issue: "why the Massachusets and Rode Iland rose, and joynd with Plymmouth agnst Phillip and left not Phillip and Plymmouth to fight it out." The Narragansetts wanted to know why other colonies felt any compulsion to join the fray, because it did not fit within their understanding of the English political system. Living in Rhode Island, their view of the colonies was one of stark rivalry, disharmony, and conflict. Williams's response was the beginning of an educational process for the Narragansetts: "All the Colonies were subject to one K. Charls

[King Charles] and it was his plesure and our Dutie and Engagemnt for one English man to stand to the Death by Each other in all parts of the World." The Narragansetts, like Philip before them, had just taken the first step in learning how greatly they had misinterpreted the English political system. Other incremental steps followed, and by the end of 1675, after what has come to be known as the Great Swamp Fight, it was clear to them that they would have to sever the ties that bound them to the English.[2]

During a month filled with a politicized trial, attacks at Swansea, and an ominous lunar eclipse, similar conversations unfolded throughout New England's forests, in its towns and villages, and on its shores and riverbanks. The region's sixty thousand English colonists and eighteen thousand Indians had to decide what role, if any, they would play in a conflict that had the potential to spread, even though they were not certain that it would do so.[3] We know only in hindsight that King Philip's War tested New England society as no other event in the seventeenth century did. When some Wampanoags decided to break their ties to Plymouth by attacking the English town of Swansea on June 24, 1675, most New Englanders—both English and Indian—did not see such trying times on the horizon. Yet the month surrounding the Swansea skirmish was a period of tremendous caution and uncertainty. The Indians and the English colonists interpreted the armed skirmishes at Swansea in different but parallel ways. Their varied experiences together over the previous fifty-five years had shaped their political allegiances and expectations of the future. The English and the Indians had formed localized webs of social relations that had interlinked and sometimes even united them. In New England's covalent society, though, ambivalent and fluid political allegiances were the norm, not the exception. Not surprisingly, many Indians and many of the English felt their allegiances pulled in a multitude of directions. Deciding which side, if any, to join depended upon numerous variables underpinned by temporal and localized contingencies. All of these variables, of course, showed a strong relationship to regional variations in the demographic, economic, and ecological conditions that affected relations among the English and Indians.

This chapter will illuminate the parameters within which various groups and individuals defined their allegiance after the outbreak of rebellion, from a midsummer month of confusion and uncertainty to the time when the leaves had fallen and inhabitants throughout New England were embroiled in the conflict. Attributing precise motives to each group or individual during the war is nearly impossible: there were almost as many impulses to fight as there were combatants.[4] Moreover, initial motives often differed from those that sustained the will to fight through the ebb and flow of the war. Nevertheless, having acknowledged the variety of situations the inhabitants of the Northeast faced, it is possible to generalize about the interplay of variables in their decision-making processes. The decision to join or fight against Philip's forces hinged largely upon the extent to which an individual or group—Indian or English—felt marginalized by the colonial political structure. Each group's particular position within New England's social web was unique, so perceptions of the conflict that erupted in 1675 varied tremendously. Although the war certainly had an ethnic dimension, allegiance to the colonial polity, or the decision to fight against it, did not derive solely from ethnicity. Allegiance or marginalization could stem from a combination of factors, economic, religious, geographic, familial, or historic. No one of these realms was primary, autonomous, or determinative in shaping actions; they were all interrelated and mutually influential.

THE LOCALISTIC and diverse nature of New England society meant that various groups had constructed the region's collective identity differently. Political identity was not based simply on the construction of a binary, collective self and an other. As political theorist Anne Norton has argued, those who belong ambivalently to a polity serve a critical role in defining it. Such was the case for many in New England chiefdoms, whether they were English or Indian. Norton, drawing on the work of anthropologist Victor Turner, uses the concept of "liminality" to describe those who are only partially absorbed within a political order. Liminality "is a threshold state 'betwixt and between' existing orders," and "liminars" are those individuals or groups who have ambivalent political allegiances. In seventeenth-century New England, a covalent society in which local groups—English and Indian—established ties of mutual obligation and reciprocity, liminality typified large numbers of inhabitants. When members of this society confronted liminars, they were forced to delineate the traits that defined the polity's boundaries. As Norton states, "The people on the boundaries—territorial, cultural, ideological—thus serve to mark the boundaries they prompt the polity to draw."[5]

Although the sides of the conflict did not draw up neatly along ethnic lines, ethnicity affected how one fit into New England's political system and the degree to which one was marginalized by it. Accordingly, the Indians and the English were torn differently as they contemplated their actions. Their polities operated similarly and had intermeshed significantly, but definite cultural differences distinguished the two. For this reason it makes sense to analyze them separately. And since English colonists, as the first to shed blood, immediately confronted the dilemma of what to do, we turn to them first.

RELATIVE TO Indians, the colonists displayed greater homogeneity in their reactions to the burgeoning conflict, though they were far from being decisive or united. To be sure, no English polities actively supported the Wampanoag uprising with military assistance. Some even viewed all Indians as completely alien. Such cases provided the seeds of danger and destruction. In the words of Anne Norton, "Those who identify the liminal as wholly foreign exhibit the same symptoms: fear of conspiracy and a sense of omnipresent danger." Often the Puritans who had perceived no utilitarian or spiritual benefit in recognizing Indians as members of their society rejected them completely. Those men and women were the most outspokenly anti-Indian members of the community; they also held the most paranoid fears of attacks from all Indians, regardless of the relationship of those Indians to other English colonists. And even for those English who did not see Indians as totally alien, their hierarchical view of New England society, with the English occupying a higher rung than the Indians, presented a natural fault line along which the two sides of the war could be drawn.[6]

Just a few months before the attacks on Swansea, few, if any, of the English anticipated widespread violence. When Christian Indians tried to warn the English of possible trouble in April and May, their words fell on deaf ears.[7] In June, however, Benjamin Church paid a visit to Awashunkes, the leader of the Saconet band of the Wampanoags, where he learned of rumors of a darkening horizon. Church used the moment to try to persuade his friend Awashunkes to stay out of any possible conflict, tossing in a stern warning that her band would be crushed should they join the fray on the rebels' behalf. Church promptly relayed his intelligence to Plymouth governor Josiah Winslow, who shortly thereafter sought assurances from Massachusetts governor John Leverett that he could count on that colony's support.

Plymouth, Massachusetts, and Rhode Island all managed to mobilize troops and stepped up efforts to gain Indian allies in the three days immediately following the attacks at Swansea. Massachusetts started preparing for the war after it became clear that the Sassamon trial had disturbed the Wampanoags. Governor Leverett, alert to a possible skirmish at Swansea, assured Plymouth's Governor Winslow that the Bay Colony would provide troops and munitions if they were needed. His promise represented a much stronger commitment than Rhode Island made. That colony's governor offered the more modest patrol of waters between Plymouth and Rhode Island to watch for any attempts by Philip to flee Swansea by water. This was Rhode Island's most extensive involvement in the war. In subsequent months, many may have even wondered if it was too much.

Massachusetts, on the other hand, was just getting started. Once blood had been shed and colonists slain, Massachusetts gave Plymouth the assistance it had promised. Three companies of men were in the field, two headed toward Swansea, by June 26. Massachusetts also rallied the more distant member of the United Colonies military confederation. Leverett sent a letter to John Winthrop, urging Connecticut to mobilize forces, which it did, for a war that to him seemed destined to expand. By July 1, 1675, the United Colonies had, at least on the surface, a consensus: its members, Plymouth, Massachusetts, and Connecticut, all had troops in place to suppress a Wampanoag rebellion.

Yet the colonies were neither confident in their convictions nor uniform in their intentions. Gov. Josiah Winslow of Plymouth, in directing the armed response to the attacks, initially worked to solve what he perceived to be a local problem. He was not even certain how many Indians living within Plymouth would ally with the Wampanoags who did the killing at Swansea. Further complicating matters, the same rivalries among the colonies that the Indians had long used to political advantage refused to die. The most intense disputes occurred between Rhode Island and the loosely organized United Colonies. For the preceding thirty-eight years, Rhode Island had quarreled with its neighbors over religious persecution and boundary lines. Straddling New England's best harbor and some of its most fertile farmland, it feared an outright invasion by the United Colonies into the Narragansett territory. On July 21, 1675, Rhode Island governor William Coddington wrote New York's Governor Andros that Massachusetts aimed "to bring the Indians there to their owne termes, and to call that part of Rhode Island theirs. . . . Wee doubt not

but wee could have prevailed to have brought the Indyans to greater con-
formity than they have done by their Armes."[8] Rhode Island had relied
on its close relationship with the Narragansetts residing in the colony to
help stave off encroachments by other colonies. When war broke out
between the Wampanoags and Plymouth, Rhode Island expressed nearly
as much fear of other English colonists as of Indians.

Although Connecticut agreed to support the United Colonies against
the Wampanoags, that colony, too, had misgivings about the war. Its leadership realized that war with Indian rebels might make their lands vulnerable to the designs of other English colonies. Connecticut's growth since
1637 had gone hand in hand with the rise of the Mohegan leader Uncas.
Thus, when Connecticut finally put troops in the field, they included a
high proportion of Indian troops fighting alongside Englishmen. But Connecticut joined the fray reluctantly for fear it would leave its western border with New York unattended. Connecticut correctly made no assumption that New York's Governor Andros, if he were to intervene in New
England's conflict, would do so on the side of the United Colonies. Connecticut had long disputed its border with New York, and when Philip's
rebellion broke out, New York tried to capitalize on the situation. After
the skirmishes at Swansea in June 1675, Andros sent armed men toward
Saybrook on Connecticut's southern coast. Fearing that Andros intended
to "invade" Connecticut, the General Court of Connecticut felt that his
"actions in this juncture tend to the incouraging of the heathen to proceed in the effusion of Christian blood." The court prioritized defending
the colony's borders from New York's encroachments over helping the
other New England colonies suppress a civil insurrection located primarily in Plymouth and Massachusetts.[9] Such fears proved warranted when
on July 8, 1675, Andros, taking advantage of the situation in New England,
dispatched troops in an unsuccessful bid to seize Saybrook.

The same factionalism that had allowed Indians to use the English and
enter into covalent political relationships with them in the first place subsequently shaped the course and conduct of King Philip's War. Connecticut even found itself at odds with its fellow United Colonies members—
Massachusetts and Plymouth—over its commitment to the war. These
differences would prove long-lived. By October Connecticut and Massachusetts were embargoing each other's trade goods. Although no English
combatants formally engaged one another in the field during the war,
from its commencement they argued over its morality, with some colo-

nists, especially in Rhode Island, condemning outright their fellow colonists' prosecution of the conflict.

As they spearheaded the mobilization of the United Colonies, Massachusetts and Plymouth feared the worst, but like the others they really had no idea what to expect. For those who became most zealously anti-Indian, paranoia and fear compounded this confusion and made the need to act seem all the more urgent. The Puritan conscience, although it encouraged English peoples to enter into covenants with Indian neighbors, had also to varying degrees been shaped by decades of jeremiads that made many of them suspicious of Indians as a whole. In these political sermons many New England ministers denounced the sins of the region's English people and warned of God's imminent and punitive wrath. Those Puritans most under the spell of the jeremiad, conformants to the general orthodoxy of eastern Massachusetts and Plymouth, usually displayed the greatest fear and paranoia of impending doom at the hands of the Indians.[10]

These Puritans' fears stemmed partially from their inability to see Indian grievances as the cause for the war. Instead, with their providential worldview, in seeking to explain the war they looked to what might have made God, rather than the Indians, unhappy. They expected God to use the Indians as tools of retribution for Puritan sins. The minister Thomas Walley wrote John Cotton early in the war arguing that the main breach was between the Puritans and God rather than the Puritans and the Indians: "I fear God's controversy with us is for breach of covenant with him. . . . [A] Quaker told me it was for my saying in my sermon they were blasphemers and Idolaters and for the persecution they have had from us." Such views persisted throughout the conflict. When the prominent Boston minister Increase Mather began writing a history in May 1676, he saw the cause of the war in God's grievances with the Puritans and blamed the war on the pride and flashy dress of many wayward English colonists. Because of the war, Mather resolved to "walk more closely" with God and preached to his congregation "so as to cause Reformation of those things which are displeasing to him." Moreover, Mather actively lobbied the General Court "to consider about Reformation of those evils which provoke [the] Lord against New England."[11]

Opinions such as these became codified in the rules and rituals of the United Colonies. Through officially declared days of fasting and humiliation, they tried to improve their relationship with God. Plymouth declared June 24, the day fighting began, its first official day of public atonement, and Massachusetts did the same four days later. Beginning in September, Connecticut held weekly fasts. As if public declarations were not enough, the Massachusetts General Court codified in law the providential explanation of the war as a breach of the Puritan covenant with God. On November 3, 1675, the court declared that God had "given commission to the barbarous heathen to rise up against us . . . heereby speaking aloud to us to search and try our wayes, and turne againe unto the Lord our God, from whom wee have departed with a great backsliding." To remedy the problem, the General Court allowed county courts to take action against such ills as children's misbehaving in church, men's sporting long hair, "excesse in apparrell," and "swearing and cursing."[12] This jeremiad mentality that led the Puritans to examine their piety rather than their treatment of Indians hindered their analysis of which Indians would become their enemy and which would be their ally. It tended to polarize Indian and English.

Despite the fault lines between the Indians and the English caused by the jeremiad psychology and the hierarchical views of New England society, support for the war varied dramatically among different groups of the English; some wanted to turn the conflict into a zealous anti-Indian campaign, whereas others disapproved of the way that the conflict expanded and the means by which it was put down. The jeremiad was largely a partisan sermon. In eastern Massachusetts it attacked those who did not subscribe to a narrow "orthodoxy," and it displayed a blanket hostility toward Indians. Those English colonists who were removed from the Bay Colony's prevailing drive showed less fear and paranoia toward Indians. Indeed, since many of these English men and women—especially in Rhode Island, Connecticut, and western Massachusetts—had utilized Indians to legitimate their political autonomy from the Bay Colony, they had a much more benevolent view of Indians and even feared threats from other English colonies. Rhode Island's sizable number of Quakers, for example, opposed any armed resistance to Indian violence, even once it had spread beyond the confines of Plymouth.[13] Moreover, the fear and paranoia toward Indians created by decades of "orthodox" jeremiads were countered in part by a utilitarian need for Indian allies and to limit the scope of the war.

Some of the English who displayed less blanket hysteria toward Indians lived in areas that made them more vulnerable to Indian attack. Because they tended to live in smaller, scattered towns that were more susceptible to attack than those to the east, these English expressed the greatest trepidation about the expansion of the war and worked hard to placate potential Indian allies and even English enemies. On July 2, 1675, with the war still confined to Plymouth, John Pynchon wrote from Springfield, Massachusetts, to Connecticut governor John Winthrop on the desirability of having both Indians and God as allies: "It is absolutely necessary to engage some Indians with us . . . I hope you will have the Pequots true to you, but it is best having God on our side."[14]

The recipient of those words expressed similar feelings in the coming days. Winthrop advised military officers of the United Colonies to take a conciliatory approach in their dealings with the Narragansetts because of the past cordial relations and military assistance they had experienced: "The Narragansetts have hitherto continued in amity with the English, and were voluntarily very helpfull to them in those warrs with the Pequott." If reciprocity for past aid were not enough, Winthrop reminded his officers of the utilitarian benefits of Narragansett fidelity. The Narragansetts were "the greatest body of all the heathen neere us: That it were very good & necessary to have that friendship continued." Finally, Winthrop warned against upsetting the Narragansetts by demanding hostages to guarantee their loyalty. He told the officers that, should the Narragansetts hesitate to provide hostages, they ought to "consider whether it be not far better to take up with such an engagement of amity, as can be attained freely & willingly, than that the potentest of all our neighbouring heathen should be made open professed enemies because we have suspicion of them or cannot be so confident or certain of their continued fidelity."[15] Winthrop, like other leaders and inhabitants of regions removed from Plymouth and eastern Massachusetts, proved willing to accommodate and negotiate with Indians. He also recognized the importance of distinguishing among the various Indians when assessing their loyalties.

Diverging motives among colonists did not prevent militias from Plymouth and Massachusetts, including a sizable number of praying Indians, from quickly responding to the attacks at Swansea. Both colonies saw Philip's incipient rebellion as an opportunity to advance their claims to Indian lands—lands claimed by Rhode Island or Connecticut in some cases. Some in Plymouth hoped to establish a fort at Mount Hope to protect lands allegedly forfeited by Philip through his traitorous actions rather than to pursue him into land inhabited by the Pocasset band of

Wampanoags to the east. Similarly, Massachusetts forces hoped to seize Narragansett lands claimed both by Narragansetts and Rhode Island. Connecticut had aims that conflicted with Massachusetts, in that it hoped primarily for peace with its Narragansett neighbors while its troops faced the Andros threat.

As English troops marched south to counter Philip on the night of June 26, 1675, they, as well as all other inhabitants of New England, suddenly received warning that the conflict that would follow might be more than a simple police action against a handful of rebellious Indians. The unfolding eclipse not only made for an especially dark night, but, since English men and women of the seventeenth century looked to signals in nature to decipher God's intentions, it undoubtedly gave them the chills. At first it may have even seemed that divine forces favored Philip. His forces attacked Rehoboth and Taunton, avoided capture, and successfully fled east to the swampy Pocasset territory, where they persuaded that band's leader, Wetamoo, to join their cause. The Plymouth and Massachusetts militias, unsure of Philip's exact whereabouts and unable to quickly adapt their military culture to the hit-and-run tactics they faced, adopted a siege mentality, building a fort in Pocasset. Colonists' efforts to confine the war in its first month did little to stem its tide. The English, of course, had only limited influence on Indian decisions during the summer and fall of 1675. Many natives eagerly threw in their lots with the rebels, and it became apparent that they had successfully fled Pocasset. The Wampanoags expanded their attacks on Plymouth towns to include Middleborough and Dartmouth in late June and early July. Success bred success, as Indians in the region who sat on the sidelines unsure whether they should get involved jumped into the fray.

AFTER PHILIP'S followers made these early strikes, the war moved into a new phase, spreading throughout Massachusetts. When the Wampanoags traveled northwest from Plymouth through central and western Massachusetts to the Connecticut River Valley, they found fertile ground for rebellion. Indians in central Massachusetts had become relatively alienated by the colony as its population had grown and settlements had expanded, especially after 1660. In central Massachusetts the Wampanoags found the support of some of the Nipmucks, who attacked Mendon in mid-July and Brookfield and Lancaster in August. Massachusetts at the same time sent envoys to these Indians in a partially successful effort to ensure either their neutrality or their support. Capt. Ephraim Curtis made some progress with the Nipmucks who had not aided in the attack at Mendon. Even then, these Indians broke into factions, some opting to join the English, others remaining neutral. Meanwhile, forces from Connecticut and Massachusetts, including a sizable numbers of Indians, forayed into central Massachusetts in search of rebel Wampanoags and Nipmucks. Under Capt. Daniel Henchman, they managed some minor skirmishes but had little success finding the elusive enemy. The results were discouraging for the English as many Nipmucks joined the fray in July and began systematically striking sites in central Massachusetts. In this region the English settlements of Mendon, Brookfield, and Lancaster would all feel the rage of Philip's supporters.

Even more significant in this period were Indian attacks on towns along the Connecticut River. Indians attacked beleaguered English settlements with rapid strikes, torching buildings and crops and slaughtering livestock while residents huddled and prayed in fortified buildings in the town center. Those who failed to gain refuge in time found themselves prisoners of the raiding forces. September and October proved especially disheartening for the colonists and their Indian allies: Philip and his supporters could celebrate the entrance of many, if not most, of the Indians in the Connecticut River Valley into the war on their side. For a generation, the Indians along the Connecticut River in Massachusetts had had close ties with the English, underpinned by a fur trade and peace with the Mohawks. That peace and that trade deteriorated in the 1660s, but Springfield magnate John Pynchon still had relationships with neighboring Indians that he believed transcended ethnic ties. He felt confident that residents of Deerfield, Hatfield, Hadley, Northampton, and Springfield could rest assured that nearby Indians would remain neutral and perhaps even support the English.

But colonial officials in Boston were suspicious of Connecticut River Indians, and they sent forces in pursuit of them under Captains Thomas Lathrop and Richard Beers. The chase led to the war's first loss of life in western Massachusetts on August 24 and 25 when fleeing Norwottocks ambushed the English troops, killing nine south of Deerfield. At the same time, Nipmucks conducted minor raids on Springfield. When that town's English residents placed suspicion for the raids on the local—and until then neutral—Agawams by seizing their weapons and taking some of their children as hostages, those Indians, too, joined Philip's rebellion.

They learned, as Philip had through the Sassamon trial, that their ties to the English did not guarantee their protection.

Throughout September, numerous Connecticut River Valley towns suffered from Indian raids. Indians subjected Deerfield, Hadley, and Northfield to large-scale attacks, preventing the inhabitants from harvesting the crops necessary to get them through the winter. When troops under Captains Lathrop and Samuel Moseley patrolled a region south of Deerfield called Muddy Brook, they stumbled into a punishing ambush on September 18. The English lost seventy-one soldiers, and Muddy Brook has been known ever since by colonists and their descendants as Bloody Brook. Finally, Springfield, the preeminent English town along the river, suffered its most devastating attack on October 5, when a combined force of Agawams and Nipmucks burned thirty of its houses. The main bright spot for the English in the region came on October 19, when an English garrison staved off attack at Hatfield. Despite this minor success, the English settlements in the Connecticut River Valley lay in shambles with winter approaching. Small remnants of the English population persisted; they had been garrisoned in town centers such as Hadley and Hatfield while Indians had foraged through their orchards and fields. The changing seasons, however, brought the English along the river respite from attack as the Indians retreated to consolidate their food supplies and take stock of their gains during the cold New England winter.

The attacks against the English towns along the Connecticut River demonstrate that the region's diverse groups of Indians had managed to implement a coherent and effective military strategy. The Indians kept most of the towns of the region distracted with small, surprise raids. Meanwhile, they focused most of their energy and resources in large attacks on single towns. Between August 1 and November 10, 1675, Indians did not leave a single one of Massachusetts's eight towns on the Connecticut River unscathed. Five of the eight towns sustained major attacks, and three of them, Brookfield, Northfield, and Deerfield, were abandoned and did not see resettlement by the English for more than a decade. Brookfield suffered the first rout, which severed an important communication link between eastern Massachusetts and the Connecticut River. Then came the northernmost river towns, Northfield and Deerfield. Following these attacks, Massachusetts authorities managed to get reinforcements to the next three towns downriver from Deerfield—Hatfield, Hadley, and Northampton. In response, the Indians wisely chose to attack well below these settlements and hit Springfield hard on October 5, 1675, destroying thirty houses, twenty-five barns, and a mill. Only after destroying Springfield did rebels return north to strike at Hatfield in earnest. Through this campaign in the fall of 1675, the Indians had reduced the English presence in the region, using what in retrospect appears as an efficient and intelligent military strategy.[16]

What made events in the Connecticut River Valley so disturbing to the English and pivotal in the course of the war was that the colonists had viewed the Indians in the region as loyal. John Pynchon, the Springfield trader and frequent intercultural mediator who had worked so hard to keep "his"—as he viewed them—Indians from joining Philip was exasperated and disillusioned when towns along the Connecticut River, including his own Springfield on October 4 and 5, were attacked and burned.[17] Learning that these Indians had cast their lot with the enemy intensified the English fear of ostensibly neutral Indians. Not knowing what else to do as rebels repeatedly appeared out of nowhere to attack and then vanish into the woods, many colonists drew on their prejudices and stereotypes of the savage to lash out at the most tangible symbol of their enemy—Christian Indians professedly loyal to the colonies. From the first pursuit of Philip after the attacks at Swansea, a significant number of Indians had steadily supported the prosecution of the war. In many instances, Indians did a disproportional share of the fighting for the colonial forces. Yet throughout the war this support failed to receive the recognition it deserved. Aside from a few vocal advocates of loyal Indians, such as Daniel Gookin and John Eliot, as well as well-meaning officials trying to preserve civil order, the colonists in general, of different stripes, had piled abuse on allied Indians since the beginning of the conflict. A renegade captain from Massachusetts, Samuel Moseley, was censured by the government in August 1675 for arresting without warrant a group of praying Indians at Marlborough, whom townspeople had nearly lynched on the spot.

In this instance and others during the first few months of the war, high-level public officials stood up for the rights of loyal Indians. Following the October attacks on Springfield, however, the tide had turned to such an extent that officials at the highest level sponsored the internment of Massachusetts's praying Indians on Deer Island in Boston Harbor. In many ways analogous to the internment of Japanese Americans during World War II, Massachusetts's praying Indians suffered severe hardship solely because of their ethnicity. On Deer Island food and shelter were in short supply, and the Indians found themselves suffering at the hands of the government to which they had sworn loyalty. For those not put on the island, English prejudice was only one of their worries; rebel Indians, likely Nipmucks, attacked Christian Indian villages at Magunkaquog, Chabanakongkomun, and Hassanemesit in early November.

The rapid and highly successful spread of Indian insurrection fueled the worst fears in the minds of the English men and women. To be sure, a sizable number of Indians in Connecticut and Rhode Island and most of the praying Indians had either fought on behalf of the English or stayed neutral. As for the remainder, by October 1675 many of the English began to suspect all of New England's Indians, despite past cordial relations and diplomatic efforts to ensure their neutrality. The expansion of Philip's effort compounded cross-cultural ignorance and misunderstanding. For decades Indians had purposely used false accusations and misinformation to gain political advantage for themselves, individually or as a group. Such strategies often worked because the English struggled with Indian languages. Now they had to deal with the foreignness of Indian war. The contrasting military cultures of the Indians and the English heightened fear and paranoia among members of both cultures. Fear and paranoia made neutrality difficult, and the need to choose a side, prepare for war, or even make a preemptive strike seemed urgent.

For the English, anxiety arose because of the Indians' "skulking" way of war. In 1675 the Indians did not confront their enemies in a way that conformed to English military protocol, choosing instead to combine elements of the English military culture with means and methods they had utilized in the past. In fighting the English and their Indian allies, many war parties used the element of surprise to maximum advantage. Avoiding conflict unless the circumstances were favorable to success, Philip and his allies preferred ambushes and raids on unsuspecting towns to the open confrontations of pitched armies more common in European-style warfare. Attacks against English forces and towns were not the low-casualty warfare common in so many precontact indigenous American cultures; rather, the assaults sought the wholesale destruction of combat units and towns. To pursue these aims, the rebels used English flintlock muskets in addition to the traditional tomahawks and bows and arrows. The most effective weapon they had, however, was one that they had been familiar with well before contact with Europeans but in the past had restrained themselves from using because it was so destructive: fire. The torching of the Pequot fort at Mystic in 1637 by the English had lessened the Indians' restraint and pushed them toward a high-casualty form of total warfare.[18]

The English fear of the "skulking" way of war often manifested itself in English efforts to influence or weaken those Indians whose loyalty was unknown. Colonial leadership would receive letters from town inhabitants "certain that our woods are possessed with Indians" and begging assistance because of their "weak capacity to defend ourselves" against "skulking" or "lurking" Indians. In reaction, many colonies eventually tried to force the issue of loyalty among Indian groups, sometimes only making matters worse. Massachusetts forces, much to the chagrin of many in Connecticut, tried to disarm Indians professedly friendly to the colonies in the upper Connecticut River Valley. James Fitch of Norwich advised the governor of Connecticut that the attacks on upper Connecticut River Valley towns such as Hadley had been precipitated by English efforts to disarm Indians. Connecticut secretary John Allyn also wrote Winthrop that these new conflicts had been brought forth "by the imprudent demands of Captain Lathrop made upon the Norwottock Indians, for their arms, which else might possibly have been prevented for the present." Samuel Willys commented in a letter to Winthrop, "[T]he forwardness of many . . . English make the Indians their enemies." Efforts to disarm the Indians undoubtedly helped to undermine any perception these Indians might have had of mutual obligation or reciprocity with the English. Disarmament efforts combined with bonds of kinship to Nipmucks loyal to Philip and efforts by Philip to sway them to his side ultimately resulted in attacks by the Connecticut River tribes on the Massachusetts towns along that waterway.[19]

Following attacks against Connecticut River Valley towns by Indians who had previously professed their loyalty to the English, Connecticut's war council warned Massachusetts of the impending spread of hostilities: "[T]he overbearing of the Springfield Indians, to break their solemn engagement of friendship to the English, as upon pain of death . . . doth so deify them in their own eyes & deter other Indians (yet our professed & pretended friends) that its high time . . . to stir up all their strength, to make war their work and trade." The English had to strike against the

Springfield Indians quickly: "nor must their be any delay herein . . . to prevent these proud natives from tyranizing over them all; and to be worse neighbors than the English have been to them hitherto."[20]

The fear and paranoia generated in the summer and fall would affect the question of how to deal with the Narragansetts in Rhode Island, a group with enough members and power to swing the course of the war. Since some Indians whom the English thought were loyal had recently joined Philip, how should the Narragansetts be treated? In the debate over this question, lingering schisms among the colonies resurfaced, even after the war had spread throughout Massachusetts and Plymouth. Samuel Gorton of Warwick, Rhode Island, criticized the growing tendency of the English to view Indians as enemies. He wrote Winthrop on September 11, 1675:

> People are apt in these dayes to give credit to every flying and false report; and not only so, but they will report it again, as it is said of old, report and we will report; and by that meanes they become deceivers and tormenters one of another, by feares and jealousies. There is a rumour as though all the Indians were in combination and confederacie to exterpate and root out the English, which many feare (for my own part I feare no such thing), as though God brought his people hither to destroy them by delivering them into the hands of such Barbarians.[21]

Those Indians who supported Philip were traitors. But those Indians "which do not yet so appeare [hostile to the English], it may seeme to be good to take the actings of such in the best sence." Gorton reminded Winthrop that they had "voluntarily subjected themselves to his Majesties royall father and his successours for ever." Should these loyal Indians have to arm themselves in defense against the English, it would only compound rebel efforts. It would symbolize to others that their political strategies had failed, and "stirre up many natives to beare a part with them."[22]

MOST OF THE English were, at least for a short time, content to cast a suspicious eye on the Narragansetts rather than risk military confrontation. In the meantime, Gorton's analysis of indigenous perceptions raises the question of what motivated indigenous New England. The Indians differed from the English, who were, despite doctrinal differences, relatively similar because they were members and descendants of a broad Puritan migration to the Americas. The natives had deep historical, social, and ideological rifts among themselves. It is not surprising that they were far more divided in their loyalties than the English and that most of them pursued local interests. Yet the most consistent and pernicious idea conveyed by three hundred years of writing on the war is the characterization of it as a conflict in which the sides drew up rigidly along lines of ethnicity—a war *between* the Indians and the English. This notion hinders the recognition of the large number of Indians that joined the colonists and stems from the absence of histories of the conflict written by Indians. The lack of Indian-produced histories contrasts starkly with the tidal wave of material by English authors. English contemporaries of the war produced nineteen different tales of it at printing presses in London, Boston, and Cambridge. At least fifteen thousand books on the war were produced for the tiny Anglo-American book market in just seven years.[23] The authors of these books usually referred to the conflict simply as "the Indian war." Not only is the ethnocentricity of "the Indian war" readily apparent, since undoubtedly most of the Indians in the conflict did not refer to it as such, but it also masks the complex texture of the alliances that sprang out of the war. The label sowed the seeds of a bias that has persisted until the present, for today the most commonly used name for the conflict—"King Philip's War"—gives proprietary rights to the war to an Indian. The war was a bad thing; the Puritans and subsequent Americans writing on the war attributed the war to Indians.

Despite appellations such as "Indian war," "King Philip's War," and "Metacom's War," Indians played a large role in putting down Philip's rebellion. Within many regions they even contributed more than the English did. When war broke out, for example, Connecticut had an English population somewhere between 12,600 and 17,250. Estimates for the number of Pequots and Mohegans living within the colony who had submitted to the English range from 1,500 to 5,000. When called on to help suppress the rebellion, the colony provided a force of 300 Englishmen and 150 Mohegans. With an English-Indian ratio of two to one in the army and, conservatively, twelve to five in the population at large, it is clear that the Indians of Connecticut made a greater commitment to putting down Philip's rebellion than did the English inhabitants.[24]

The point here is not to give precise estimates of the per capita commitment of the Indians and the English to the two sides of the war and derive some sort of value judgment from them; that would be nearly impossible. The sources are lacking to define the boundaries of each Indian group, their population, which side they supported, and how many combatants they put in the field. Even for the English, the treasury accounts with lists of soldiers survive for only one colony, Massachusetts. And these documents do not include the Indians that joined English forces, since Indians usually kept wartime plunder as their pay instead of receiving specie from the colonial governments. The goal here is merely to unsettle the long-held belief that the conflict was exclusively an Indian-English one.

Impressionistic samples rather than comprehensive quantitative data confirm that Indians, Christian and non-Christian, played a large role from beginning to end in suppressing the rebellion. According to William Hubbard, Capt. Daniel Denison led a force from Connecticut of 66 volunteers and 112 Pequots. In a letter written July 31, 1675, to the governor of Massachusetts, Daniel Henchman noted that he had 68 English and 17 Indians in his company. In Plymouth during the latter parts of the war, most of the successful military leaders had in their companies large numbers of Indians. Major Bradford of that colony had under him 150 English and 50 Indians. The English military leader perhaps most famous for his use of Indians, Benjamin Church, led a force of 200 English and 100 Indians in spring 1676.[25] Aside from these prominent companies, nearly every smaller force in the field had, if not a sizable number of Indians working as soldiers, at least one or two Indians guiding English soldiers through unfamiliar terrain to find those Indians associated with the uprising.

What led so many Indians to ally with the English while others rebelled in large numbers? Something that Indians shared was a memory of the Pequot War. By 1675 all Indians in New England had undoubtedly heard of its carnage. That memory taught the Indians that the English conduct of war differed dramatically from their own. Indians in 1675 knew, as they had not in 1637, that to be in a war against the English meant risking what seemed to them astronomical casualties and suffering, and therefore many considered it essential to take immediate action. Capt. John Underhill reported the Narragansett belief that the English style of warfare displayed in the Pequot War was "too furious and slay[ed] too many men." The Narragansetts knew they could not continue their ordinary day-to-day lives, as had the Pequots at Mystic, for fear of facing massacre at the hands of the English. Like many of the English, large numbers of New England Indians had a fear and paranoia rooted in their experience of past decades; being caught off guard by an English attack was not something they could afford.[26] This fear created an urgent "beat them or join them" mentality. When the earth's shadow eclipsed the moon on June 26, 1675, memories of the Pequot War reinforced the Indian belief that this was an omen of fantastic bloodshed. Thus, native groups, like their English counterparts, worked quickly to solidify and secure a position on the war that reconciled their security concerns with a level of commitment corresponding to their unique identity within the political system.

Yet countervailing pulls could be just as strong. Although fear and paranoia of English tactics made the need to pick a side seem urgent, facets of southern New England Algonquian mythological tradition led Indians to take an accommodating, conciliatory approach toward the actions of others. Indian oral tradition suggests that all Indians of southern New England shared the legend of Maushop, which tempered their urge to jump into the war. Maushop was a giant who had, before the arrival of Europeans, given New England most of its topographical features, protected its inhabitants from predatory birds, and generally assisted the population. Maushop constituted, according to anthropologist William Simmons, "a local manifestation of a broader northeastern culture-hero pattern of giants that included Gluskap of the Algonquian-speaking tribes of Maine and eastern Canada. Examining the Gluskap legend, Kenneth M. Morrison argues that it encouraged Algonquians of the Northeast to seek peaceful, constructive alternatives to violence. The myth of Gluskap showed the "possibility of cooperation" in the face of "threatening otherness"—the same cooperation that allowed for the evolution of a covalent society in the first place. Thus, the legend of Maushop led Indians to seek conciliation, while the memory of the Pequot War combined with a daunting eclipse made it urgent to prepare militarily. William Hubbard recognized the vacillation those contradictory impulses produced among the Indians. He wrote that after the initial skirmishes at Mount Hope, "many of the Indians were in a kind of Maze, not knowing well what to do; sometimes ready to stand for the English, as formerly they were wont to do, sometimes inclining to strike in with Philip.[27]

For many Indians the compass suggesting a way out of their maze was heavily influenced by forces beyond their control. Historian Neal Salisbury has made some shrewd generalizations concerning the pattern by which a generation of economic interdependence among the Indians and the English in New England broke down. He has correctly noted that this deterioration cannot be explained without looking beyond New England to broader economic and demographic trends. More specifically, he pointed to a wampum glut, the expansion of English settlement, and a decrease in the supply of furs as determinants of growing Indian-English hostilities. These three factors help to explain why the majority of Philip's support, with, of course, a number of exceptions, came from a swath of territory stretching from "both sides of Narragansett Bay northwestward through 'Nipmuck country' to the Connecticut River Valley."[28]

Until the 1660s, the lack of specie in New England allowed natives, especially the Narragansetts—whose population survived some of the earliest epidemics and was not decimated in the Pequot War—a central role in an integrated New England economy. The Narragansetts lived on the south-central coast of New England, where the wampum shells were, and provided the skilled labor that turned these shells into a highly valued commodity in the Northeast. Indians throughout the region highly valued wampum, largely for spiritual reasons, and English settlers rapidly adapted to its use as a currency to trade with Indians in exchange for fur and land. So long as wampum remained a highly valued commodity among European settlers and Indians, the natives in the wampum-producing regions—along the southern coast of New England from the Narragansett Bay to the Connecticut River—retained a powerful, interdependent role within the New England economy.

In 1662, however, wampum lost its status as the official currency of New England following an influx of English specie that came about because of a resurgence of English overseas trade. A wampum glut resulted, which also reduced demand for the beads in Iroquoia and New Netherland. The wampum-producing Indians of southern New England lost much of their usefulness within the integrated Indian-English economy. And colonists and their polities lost one of their main incentives both to respect these Indians' rights to their land and to fulfill their various agreements of mutual protection. Increasing settler encroachment on Indian land and a weakening commitment on the part of English polities to do anything about it undoubtedly altered many Indians' beliefs that the colonial system offered a useful avenue to protect their political autonomy.

The deterioration of the wampum-producing Indians' role in the New England economy corresponded with a dramatic jump in the demand for land among the English inhabitants of New England. This increase had its most dramatic effect on the Indians of central Massachusetts, between the Boston area and the Connecticut River. The Indians of this region—broadly referred to as the Nipmucks—had been relatively insulated from the land pressures of the English, because most of the English migrants to New England between 1630 and 1640 came in families headed by parents between their late twenties and early forties. The children in these families tended to be young, and they did not seek land independently of their parents in great numbers until the 1660s. Once they did seek land, however, the Nipmucks had to face a relatively sudden encroachment that provided them little time to adapt. Herein lay some of the roots for most of these Indians' deciding to join Philip's forces.

The Indians of the upper Connecticut River Valley, the final segment in the swath of Indians mostly supportive of Philip, which stretched northwesterly from Narragansett Bay, were also affected by broad forces largely beyond their control. For over thirty years, these Indians and the English along the middle Connecticut River Valley had engaged in a fur trade that both found important enough to make them put aside their differences. Connecticut River Indians had acted as middlemen in the fur trade between the English and natives farther to the north and west. Many Indians in this part of New England had offered their land as collateral to borrow either wampum or sometimes currency to trade for furs. From the English they received items such as wampum, cloth, metal tools, and firearms. Such items not only had utilitarian benefits but also reinforced native social and political networks. Exchange for these Indian peoples symbolized the establishment of reciprocal alliances. Indians along the Connecticut River had also eagerly sought the protection that the English might provide them against the attacks of Mohawks to the east. As this peace began to deteriorate in the 1660s, so, too, did the fur trade.

The English in the region viewed the fur trade as more of a pure profit-seeking enterprise than did the Indians. This became apparent as furs became harder to procure beginning in the 1660s, because of a combination of Iroquois wars in fur-hunting regions, a decrease in the number of fur-bearing animals, and a devaluation in wampum. When the Indians in the upper Connecticut River Valley could not provide furs to pay their debts to the English merchant-gentry of the region, they sold them their land. In the short run, trading away land satisfied the English creditors and the Indians' desire for goods, yet the strategy was not a sustainable one. The Indians' land loss benefited English yeomen tremendously as they moved into the region and focused increasingly on the production of wheat instead of the trade of furs. Indians worked more frequently as laborers in Englishmen's fields or makers of their baskets and brooms rather than as their equal trading partners. Changes in native culture instigated by the fur trade accelerated with land loss. Many Connecticut River Indians began to see less advantage in the colonial system. In this time of rapid and dramatic cultural change and deteriorating economic relations with the English, the Indians in the Connecticut Valley faced the dilemmas of Philip's War. Under these circumstances, most, especially among the younger males, opted to lash out at their old trading partners and potential allies against the Mohawks.[29]

All of these groups had experienced alterations in material conditions that adversely affected their relationships with neighboring English groups. But vast impersonal forces such as economic and demographic shifts were not determinative, nor were the memories of English warfare or the cultural impulses to seek peace. Rather, a constellation of variables—culture, age, kinship, perceptions of the degree of reciprocity in the colonial system, preexisting political rivalries, and the course of the war—intermeshed dialectically with changing material conditions to shape the decision-making process. It is impossible to know how these variables played out and became prioritized in each community. Nevertheless, it is safe to say that these were the parameters within which various groups operated.

IN JUNE 1675, with colonists from Massachusetts and Plymouth bearing down on them and Connecticut's soon to follow suit, groups of Wampanoags in the southeastern part of Salisbury's swath had to act fast, and other Indians would eventually have to do so as well. Among the Wampanoags, the Saconet band of western Plymouth provides one well-documented example of the extent to which an Indian group's allegiances could be torn. And, just as important, the Saconets demonstrate the centrality of both Indian-Indian and Indian-English tensions in shaping wartime alliances. In the early 1670s, the sachem Awashunkes had managed to reaffirm her authority among the Saconets, despite challenges from Christian Indians, through her land dealings with and political submission to the colony of Plymouth.[30] When war was imminent between Plymouth and Philip's Pokanoket band of Wampanoags, both Philip's forces and the English vigorously lobbied for Awashunkes' assistance. In June

1675 Philip sent six of his men to meet with Awashunkes and try to persuade her to join his side. She in turn summoned Benjamin Church and an interpreter as representatives of Plymouth to counter the arguments of Philip's emissaries.

At the meeting, Awashunkes explained to Church that Philip planned to gain her loyalty by making the English hostile to her. He would do this by having some of his men "privately" attack nearby English settlements, leading the English to assume that Saconets were responsible and to retaliate against her band. Church railed against Philip's representatives and pleaded with Awashunkes to remain loyal to the English. She then asked Church to go to the governor and see if she could "shelter herself and people under his protection." Church promised to do so and bade her farewell. Awashunkes had, at least temporarily, succeeded in playing the Pokanokets and Plymouth off each other.[31] Being a Wampanoag was not as important to her as being English was to a colonist.

Awashunkes' divided loyalties and liminal status appear equally striking in her wartime actions. Her name does not appear in written records for quite some time after the early rendezvous with Philip. Yet the deeds of her followers sent a chill through the spines of English colonists. Church failed to sway Awashunkes to the side of Plymouth, and her followers undoubtedly had a role in some of the raids that devastated many Plymouth towns in June and July 1675. After disappearing from the written record behind the veil of Philip's rebellion, she reappears a year later in July 1676. Despite having spent the majority of the war fighting for Philip's cause, Awashunkes managed, with some aid from Church, to switch sides without having to face the punishments accorded most rebels who surrendered to English control.[32] This switch highlights the fact that Awashunkes was ambivalent in her commitment to the "Indian side" and that the Englishman Church recognized it. Awashunkes, with her shifting dedication, seemed to be pursuing a strategy of self-preservation. When she initially sided with one alliance and then switched to the other, the tide of the war turned.[33]

Another Wampanoag group, the Pocassets led by Wetamoo, wavered right from the beginning as to which side they would join. Plymouth governor Josiah Winslow wrote to Wetamoo trying to persuade her to join the United Colonies and their Indian allies. He warned her that Philip "endeavoured to engage you and your people with him, by intimations of notorious falsehoods as if we were secretly designing mischief to him and you." Trying to get Wetamoo to support the English, he told her, "[Y]ou shall assuredly reap the fruit of it to your comfort, when he [Philip] by his pride and treachery hath wrought his own ruin." By the end of June, the loyalty of the Pocassets was still uncertain. And on July 6, 1675, Winslow wrote Massachusetts governor John Leverett that Wetamoo had witnessed many of her men joining Philip against her wishes.[34] After much wavering, however, the Pocassets eventually divided: many joined each side.

In this life-or-death decision, when consensus could not be reached, the group could divide, even though strands of kinship had bound it together. Wetamoo and her "husband" Peter Nunnuit (Petonowowett) ended up on opposite sides. Petonowowett told Benjamin Church on the eve of the conflict that there would be a war "for Philip had held a dance of several weeks' continuance and had entertained the young men from all parts of the country." Daniel Gookin subsequently wrote that both Wetamoo and Petonowowett opposed joining the war effort, but the younger band members were adamant in wanting to fight the English. In the end, Wetamoo accommodated the young and "married" Quinnapin, a Narragansett hostile to Plymouth who, according to Church, had another "wife" married to Philip. Petonowowett, for his part, offered allegiance to the Indians allied with the colony. Wetamoo, we know, fought against the English until her death, whereas some of her followers managed to switch sides under Awashunkes' leadership before the bitter end. One Pocasset who had been under Wetamoo even fired the shot that later downed Philip on August 12, 1676.[35]

How did the fractures among the Pocassets take shape? Age clearly divided many Indian communities, and it is reasonable to assume that it was a factor in this case. Usually the fault line was between the more aggressive young who wanted to join the insurrection and the older members of the community who desired either to aid the colonists or to remain neutral. English observers noted these divisions. William Hubbard reported that a messenger returned from a meeting with some Narragansett sachems having found that "the young were very Surly and Insolent, the elder ones shewing some Inclination to maintain the wonted Peace." These schisms often revealed themselves when older Indian leaders, in meetings with English representatives of colonial governments, professed loyalty to the English but made no promises about their ability to maintain a consensus within their community. Roger Williams warned

John Winthrop that Canonicus (a Narragansett sachem) had told a messenger "that his Heart affected and Sorrowed for the English, that he could not Rule the Youth and Common people." The divisions within Canonicus's community were sharp enough that he "advised the English at Nahiggonsik to stand upon their Guard, to keepe strict watch, and if they could, to fortifie one or more howses strongly wch if they could not doe, then to flie."[36]

These divisions along the lines of age were apparent even within Wampanoag rebel forces up to the closing stages of the war. Upon capture, one of the leading Pokanoket sachems under Philip, Annawon, surprised Benjamin Church by blaming the war not on Philip or the English, but on the praying Indians. Younger Indians, however, carried a much stronger anti-English sentiment and blamed the war on the English to the end.[37] Thus, even when the younger and elder Indians could agree on which side to fight on, they often had disparate motives. The schisms along the fault lines of age are attributable to the fluid sociopolitical nature of these groups. Because the sachem's power rested on achieved status, especially the ability to perform well in rivalries with the English and other Indians, there was tremendous competition for leadership roles. One perceived avenue toward increasing status lay in successful warfare. The younger male Indians were often much more inclined to fight than their elders: by fighting they hoped to move further up the tribal hierarchy. Because Indian political culture necessitated that decisions be broadly consensual, these schisms between young and old often fractured unity and fragmented groups.

But kinship, both biological and metaphorical, could also often have a tremendous cementing influence on the alliances of individuals or groups, English or Indian. This influence can be seen rising as the war spread to central Massachusetts and the upper Connecticut River Valley, the middle and northern parts of Salisbury's swath. Kathleen Bragdon has suggested that on the eve of contact, at least, a different social dynamic was at work in "riverine" and "upland interior" communities than in those located near the coasts. She sees less centralization, more village autonomy, and possibly a stronger clan system in Connecticut River and upland settlements. The Indians of 1675 who lived in these areas seem to have inherited the legacy of these distinctions. Kinship, as far as it can be gathered, played a stronger role in their decisions than in those of the Wampanoags.[38]

The Indians near the Massachusetts towns along the Connecticut River, in particular, had long professed their fidelity to the English. The leading colonist in the region, John Pynchon, continually referred to them as "our Indians," assuming they were allies. When the Connecticut River Valley Indians turned against the English from August to October 1675, it reflected not so much an ethnic alliance between those natives and the Wampanoags as it did the breakdown of commercial ties and the resurfacing of old rivalries with the Mohegans to the south. Connecticut had committed large numbers of Mohegans to the field under the leader Uncas, who, in the words of Pynchon, "hath of old a grudge against the Upriver Indians."[39] Although this served the interest of Connecticut and Uncas, Pynchon was left in the lurch. The entrance of Uncas into the war had the unintended consequence of putting the Indians along the Connecticut River to the north in an awkward position: either they ally with the English, the side of their rival Uncas, or they break their long-standing ties with the English residents of the valley and throw their lot with Philip.

When the Nipmucks of central Massachusetts began attacking English towns in August 1675, the Indians of the upper Connecticut River were in an unenviable position. Although many of them had benefited from their association with the English, they saw many of the Nipmucks who were hostile to the English as their kin. Their predicament became more severe when they were out on patrol with some Englishmen. Increase Mather related a comment of the minister John Russell of Hadley: "'When they [river Indians] were out with our Army, they shewed much unwillingness to fight, alledging they must not fight against their Mothers and Brothers and Cousins (for Quabaog [Nipmuck] Indians are related unto them).'" Eventually, the ties of kinship outweighed any allegiance to the English and the River Indians began to attack English towns, much to the surprise of John Pynchon and others. The attack proved pivotal in the expansion of the war. Daniel Gookin expressed the shift in English sentiment toward Indians after these attacks when he wrote that "their [the Connecticut River Indians'] defection at this time had a tendency to exasperate the English against all Indians, that they would admit no distinction between one Indian and another." William Hubbard singled out the River Indians' attacks as especially evil, because he believed these Indians had reneged on their word and their long friendship with the English. Some commentators could not even comprehend that the Springfield Indians had instigated these attacks and initially placed the blame on others.[40]

Another reason that many Indians in central and western Massachusetts decided to fight against other Indians and the English was that they had been directly persuaded to do so by Philip or his emissaries. He tried to establish metaphorical or "fictive" (to use the terminology of anthropologists) kinship through gift exchange to encourage alliances. Evidence for this appears in the historical record a number of times. After successful raids in Plymouth, Philip and many of his followers fled northwest through the Nipmuck territory on the way to New York, trying to garner supporters as they traveled. In the fall of 1675 Philip traveled to the Mohawks in eastern New York to offer large amounts of wampum in exchange for assistance.[41] Further south, the Narragansett sachem Ninigret reported that Philip had sent wampum and coats to the Mohegan leader Uncas in order to gain him to his side.[42] It is unclear whether Philip actually did this or whether Ninigret fabricated the story to raise the ire of the English against Uncas, a man with whom he had had a lasting rivalry. Whether true or not, Ninigret's story suggests the importance of gift-giving in New England diplomacy. Gift-giving was so important that colonial governments had to conform to this Indian tradition if they hoped to gain Indian allies. Responding to his enemy's military successes, the deputy governor of Connecticut argued for a concerted effort to lobby the Mohawks living within New York to intervene in the war on the colony's side. He wondered if the colony could "by purchase or pay . . . make it in their [the Mohawks'] reall interest" to fight it.[43]

As IMPORTANT as variables of kinship and age were, they alone did not determine one's alliance. This was especially true outside the swath of territory extending from Narragansett Bay to the upper Connecticut River. On either side, and whether it be Christian or non-Christian Indians, past and continuing successes in the colonial system were central to many Indians' decision to help suppress Philip's insurrection. The praying Indians, who made up most of the Indians who supported the English in eastern Massachusetts, saw greater benefit in bolstering the United Colonies than in rebelling against them. Many of these Indians, as previously documented, had carved out a measure of autonomy by subjecting themselves to the English political system. Many praying Indians had promi-

nent Englishmen such as Daniel Gookin and John Eliot successfully advo-
cating their cause in English courts. Literacy and a willingness to at least
hear the Gospel facilitated their success relative to others in holding on to
land. Natick and Nemasket helped make it clear to Philip that the praying
Indians' strategy had worked better than his own. Once war broke out, it
is not surprising that those praying Indians who had the most experience
protecting their autonomy within the English colonial system either
stayed out of the fray or immediately helped Plymouth and Massachusetts. As the war progressed, however, the praying Indians learned that
although they may have had advocates among the English such as John
Eliot and Daniel Gookin, they did not have the wholehearted support of
the colonies. To the contrary, those who championed Christian Indians
became outcasts to the point of receiving death threats, and Christian
Indians were subjected to some of the war's gravest injustices.[44] Not surprisingly, this caused some Indians to throw in their lot with rebel forces.
Others, such as the Pennacooks under Wanalancet, tried to temporarily
weather the storm in woods to the north.[45] But enough praying Indians
served alongside English forces to overcome the momentum of Philip's
rebellion.

The praying Indians might have contributed even more to suppressing
Philip had the English trusted them. English skepticism of Christian Indian loyalty increased as the colonies groped to understand why the
conflict was growing out of control. Some had feared that the initial
skirmishes at Swansea signaled the beginning of a widespread Indian uprising. The spread of violence only heightened these fears. Nipmuck attacks against the central Massachusetts towns of Mendon, Brookfield, and
Lancaster in July and August 1675 made colonial officials suspect that
some of the praying Indians had allied with rebel Indians. Accordingly,
the Massachusetts Council ordered Christian Indians confined to praying
towns. The same day this order was issued, Massachusetts captain Samuel
Moseley arrested fifteen Hassanemesit Indians (praying Indians) whom
he found near Marlborough and dragged them to Boston to be tried for
the assault on Lancaster. The episode proved embarrassing for colonial
officials and revealed that their authority over their own English subjects
was tenuous. Moseley was a problem for officials trying to restrain the
colonial conduct toward Indians, because he had a reputation for unwar-
ranted violence. His grounds for arresting the fifteen Indians was the con-

fession of one, gathered by way of torture. Once in Boston, the captured Indians narrowly escaped vigilante attempts on their lives and were imprisoned. On their day in court, thirteen were declared innocent, but popular opinion, in the words of Daniel Gookin, "would have had these Indians put to death by martial law, and not tried by a jury, though they were subjects under the English protection."[46]

Feeble attempts to carry out justice in Boston did little to suppress the violence elsewhere. Most damaging to the cause of praying Indians seeking the trust of the colonies was the torching of settlements along the upper Connecticut River, especially Springfield on October 5. If these Indians—who had earlier professed loyalty and had close ties to the Pynchon family—could turn against English towns, was there anything preventing Christian Indians from doing the same? Colonists' fears that praying Indians might turn against them seemed confirmed when a barn was set aflame at Dedham, which bordered on the praying town of Natick. Facing a war raging beyond their control and a crisis in their own authority, colonial officials took drastic measures. Massachusetts ordered first Indians living at Natick and then those in other praying towns to be herded up and put on Deer Island in Boston Harbor. The General Court claimed to have ordered the Indians to the island "for their and our security."[47]

To be sure, some Christian Indians had requested protection as early as July 19, 1675, and even Gookin saw some good in "their preservation from the fury of the people."[48] But conditions on Deer Island were far from healthy, and leaving the island, unless with permission of the colony, subjected one to "payne of death."[49] Gookin and Eliot traveled to the island and found "they lived chiefly upon clams and shell-fish, . . . the Island was bleak and cold, their wigwams poor and mean, their clothes few and thin." To make matters worse, popular opinion toward Christian Indians did not improve. Mary Pray tried to raise doubts about the loyalties of the praying Indians when she wrote Captain Oliver of Massachusetts, saying that "those Indians that are called praying Indians never shoot at the other Indians but up into the tops of the trees or into the ground and when they make show of going first into the swamp [in pursuit of the enemy] they commonly give the Indians notice how to escape the English." Pray did not stop there but went on to accuse the praying Indians of selling powder obtained from the English to the enemy. She also alleged that they had advised the Narragansetts to attack the English, "telling them that they are sure that if they do not the English will fall upon them."⁵⁰

Facing confinement during the harsh New England winter on a windswept island in Boston Harbor with insufficient food, it is not surprising that many praying Indians saw flight, and maybe even fighting with Philip, as better options. Many faced a window of opportunity to rise against the English in early November when rebel Nipmucks attacked the praying towns of Chabanakongkomun, Hassanemesit, and Magunkaquog. Even the Indian James Printer, a literate Hassanemesit Indian who set type for John Eliot's Bible at Cambridge Press, ended up among the Nipmucks following these attacks. It is unknown whether he was captured or voluntarily fled to the Nipmucks. Perhaps his actions fell somewhere between these two extremes. Having seen the threat of English vigilante justice and confinement on Deer Island, Printer's will to resist capture would certainly have been diminished.⁵¹

That Printer and others may have been relatively indifferent to whether they continued their relationship with the English or forged new ties with rebel Indians became apparent as the war drew to a close. They had sufficient initial motivation to join the rebellion but lacked a sustaining drive. They had causes for fighting but were without a cause. Although some Christian Indians who ended up among rebel forces faced capture by colonial troops and trial for treason, others managed to forestall this fate and take advantage of later English offers of amnesty. On June 19, 1676, Massachusetts offered Indians who surrendered, except major leaders in the rebellion, the opportunity to escape the death penalty due traitors. Many of those who accepted the offer, including James Printer, were required to assist English forces against enemy Indians. By the time of Philip's death on August 12, 1676, Massachusetts and Plymouth had an unprecedented number of Indians serving alongside their troops, many of whom did so to escape confinement on Deer Island.

THE PRAYING Indians were not the only natives who had garnered the support of prominent English colonists. The non-Christian Cowesits were a group that hoped to fulfill sincere promises as well as to profit by suppressing the insurrection. During the war a Cowesit sachem submitted a petition to the Plymouth Court complaining that several English colonists had settled on his land. The leader pointed to a twenty-six-year-old agreement made between his father and Englishman James Brown according to which some English people had been allowed to let their cattle graze on his land in exchange for a mutual alliance of protection: "Mr. Brown promised my father if occasion should be he would really and effectually joyn with him for his preservation; And assist him for the preserving of a happie and well grounded peace."[52] Under the provisions of the agreement, no English were to settle on Cowesit land. Most Cowesits fought alongside colonial forces in the war, and, as the petition demonstrates, still saw advantage in establishing and using ties of mutual obligation with the English.

Many individual Indians who worked for Englishmen also found these ties adequate to keep them from joining Philip while others around them did. In October 1675, the well-to-do Englishman John Paine petitioned the commissioners of the United Colonies for the release of an Indian named Jack and his family who had been captured by rebel Indian forces near his house but were now in United Colonies' custody. Since the early 1660s these Indians had had Paine as their "landlord" on Prudence Island in Narragansett Bay, and once the war broke out the relationship became a nearly feudal one. Paine petitioned that "upon Jack's faithfulness to us and engagement to abide by me, peace or war, life or death, I promised to secure him so far as I could." On a night following this promise, some United Colonies forces had surprised and captured these Indians. In the subsequent petition Paine fretted that "the Indians conceive that I betrayed and sold them . . . whereby I may also suffer wrongfully by their private malice if not public." Paine concluded by asking for these Indians' release, so "that the innocent may not suffer with or for the unjust murders lest God avenge the wrong."[53] Paine took his obligations toward these Indians seriously, and so, too, did the Indians, as evidenced by Paine's fear of retaliation for broken promises.

To the west of the swath of territory from which most of Philip's supporters came, many Indians and English people still considered valid their ties of reciprocity to one another. Unlike Philip, who through his individual experience had come to believe that he was betrayed by the colonial system and that he could no longer utilize it to his advantage, many sachems had arrived at the opposite conviction and maintained their ties of mutual obligation to the English. Ninigret, a sachem of the Eastern Niantics (located in western Rhode Island and closely related to the Narragansetts), tried to protect his band members and advance their cause in their competition with the longtime rival Mohegans and Pequots by remaining loyal to the English. This was tricky given that the English and the Mohegans fought on the same side. Shortly after the war began, some English colonists were suspicious of his willingness to help them and suggested that he surrender his band's arms to demonstrate fidelity. Ninigret proclaimed his fidelity to the United Colonies, arguing that he could not "forget the kindness that he received from King Charles." Nevertheless, he said he could not surrender his arms because his band had to protect itself from Uncas and the Mohegans who had killed some of his men. Ninigret's motives in responding this way were twofold. First, he hoped to protect his band from both the English and the Mohegans. Second, he aimed to make the English suspicious of the Mohegans.[54]

For Ninigret and others in southwestern New England, fighting against Wampanoag rebels and their allies constituted as much an opportunity to enhance one's position in a complicated shell game among the English, the Mohegans, the Niantics, and the Pequots as a war against Philip. The various Indian groups guardedly made sure that the English did not play favorites. Sometimes Indians would feed false accusations to the English, attributing the killing of some English people to rival Indians who never would have done so. Such was the case in August 1675 when John Mason wrote letters to Fitz-John Winthrop questioning Uncas's loyalty because some Pequots had accused some Mohegans of attacks that had previously been attributed to rebel Nipmucks. To sort through this, Mason urged that Uncas and the Pequot leader Robin Cassassinnamon be brought together before some leaders of Connecticut. Again in the spring of 1676 the rivalry among Indians threatened the unity of the delicate English-Indian alliance in Connecticut. Englishman Edward Palmes argued for a uniform policy when dealing with the Pequots, the Mohegans, and the Niantics, noting that "the great Difficulty . . . is how to keepe freindship with all three." Ninigret had complained that Uncas had stolen wampum from his family, and the Pequot leader Robin Cassassinnamon had asserted that Ninigret owed him money. The Connecticut Council, not knowing what else to do, pleaded that these Indians put aside their difference at least until the end of the war.[55]

Of the Indians involved in this triangular rivalry, the Mohegan leader Uncas best used the colonial system to his advantage. Despite efforts of Philip to sway him to his side, Uncas supported the English throughout the conflict. With a long history stretching back to the Pequot War of nurturing a relationship with the English for personal gain, Uncas jumped on the opportunity to assist the English attempt to subdue Philip.[56] About a month after the first Wampanoag attacks on Swansea, armed Mohegans marched into Boston to offer their assistance to the United Colonies.[57] They also accused the Narragansetts of harboring the women and children of Philip's band, beginning the English suspicion of that group.[58] The Mohegans undoubtedly knew that if they solidified their relationship with the English at the outset of the war, their rivals the Narragansetts would be in an awkward position. In the past, Uncas could and did court English assistance whenever trouble arose between the Mohegans and the Narragansetts. In 1643 he used the United Colonies to help him kill Miantonomo, the Narragansett sachem who had begun calling for an Indian rejection of English ways.[59] After many years of benefiting from his ties with the English, Uncas was not about to let the problems of Philip and his rebellion interfere with his ongoing success.

It is also clear that Uncas limited his war involvement to suit his own personal needs. John Mason said in September 1675 that the Mohegans "seem not to be willing to fight with the upland Indians unless they understand the ground of the English warring with them."[60] As late as July 1676 the English noted that Mohegans would not pursue the Wampanoags out of Rhode Island and into Plymouth, suggesting that their real grievance was with the Narragansetts rather than those closest to Philip. On July 2, 1676, with Philip's rebellion crumbling, a force of Mohegans, Pequots, and Connecticut colonists celebrated a stunning victory against a Narragansett encampment in which they killed three hundred and captured "not much above sixty."[61] "Lest by a Denial they might disoblige their Indian Friends, of whom they lately mad so much use," the English officers on the scene acquiesced to Indian demands that one of the prisoners be put in their hands.[62] What unfolded provides a chilling reminder of how violent the seventeenth century could be:

> They first cut one of his Fingers round in the Joynt, at the Trunck of his Hand, with a sharp Knife, and then brake it off, as Men used to do with a slaughtered Beast, before they uncase him; then they cut off another and another, till they had dismembered one Hand of all its Digits, the Blood sometimes spirting out in Streams a Yard from his Hand . . . his Executioners . . . dealt with the Toes of his Feet, as they had done with the Fingers

of his Hands; . . . At last they brake the Bones of his Legs, after which he was forced to sit down, which 'tis said he silently did, till they had knocked out his Brains.[63]

Having tortured the Narragansett to death, the Mohegans and Pequots demanded that the mixed force return to Connecticut rather than continue pursuing Philip through Rhode Island and into Plymouth. The English, in the words of William Hubbard, "were necessitated . . . to return Homewards to gratify the Mohegin and Pequod Indians."[64] Aside from demonstrating the brutality of seventeenth-century warfare, this vignette is telling evidence that the Indians who allied with the English were not necessarily fighting the colonists' war or pursuing English war aims. King Philip's War was far from being just an Indian-English war. All Indian groups and individuals had unique motives in the conflict.

Uncas did not think of King Philip's War as Philip's. It was his own. Indian decisions as to which side to join were grounded in past experiences in New England society and the social and material relationships that had been forged during the past generation of interdependency. Perceptions of these relationships varied according to ethnicity, religion, age, kinship, geographical position, and political success within the colonial system. Even the various English colonists, who developed relative unity, fought with diverging, even competing aims—if they fought at all. Once a group made the decision to fight, the next issues it confronted were how and for how long.

5

"BARBAROUS INHUMANE OUTRAGES"

UNLIKE UNCAS and the Mohegans, the Narragansetts, the last major group to become embroiled in the conflict, struggled to keep Philip's war from becoming their own. Not surprisingly, efforts to sway Narragansett loyalty brought out the worst in intercolonial conflict. Nearly all in the region recognized the Narragansetts as the potential crown jewel in their confederation; at the same time they feared defeat should the Narragansetts join their opponent. With estimates for the number of Narragansett fighting men ranging between one thousand and two thousand, their loyalty constituted a highly coveted prize.[1] When war broke out in June, Roger Williams worked actively to secure guarantees of their support. He initially found what he wanted. But five months later he believed "that it is not possible at present to keepe peace with these barbarous men of Bloud who are as justly to be repelld and subdued as Wolves that assault the sheepe." A contingent of Indian and English forces acted accordingly the day after Williams wrote these words, staging a punitive surprise raid against the Narragansetts in what has since become the most famous battle, or massacre, of the war—the Great Swamp Fight of December 19, 1675.[2]

The Narragansetts had compelling reasons to stay out of the conflict as soon as their rivals—the Mohegans—quickly offered assistance to the English in July 1675. Fighting against Philip would essentially mean assisting their arch rival Uncas. The Narragansetts expressed their general hostility toward Uncas when, in meeting with Williams, they brought up the role he had had in killing their leader Miantonomo. They also fueled English suspicions toward Uncas, telling Williams of his "many fowle practices and how he treacherously sent an head (or heads) of the Qunnihticut Indians to the Mauguawogs, and would send Your Heads allso, as presents if he Could Come at them."[3] Equally important in dissuading the Narragansetts from fighting were the potential size and power of the forces that quickly arrayed against Philip and the memory of the Pequot War. The legacy of the Pequot War undoubtedly made them fearful of being caught off guard. Surrounded by the relatively large population of English colonists on three sides and having witnessed with horror the casualty rates of English warfare in 1637, they hoped to demonstrate their position of neutrality to the English to prevent becoming victims of English attack.

For many historians, the Pequot War of 1637 exemplifies the ruthlessness and lack of respect for their opponents that the Puritans would again reveal in King Philip's War. Descriptions of the carnage resulting from the burning of a Pequot settlement at Fort Mystic, such as this from William Bradford, leave little wonder why groups such as the Narragansetts feared entanglement in King Philip's War in 1675: "It was a fearful sight to see them [Pequots] thus frying in the fire and the streams of blood quenching the same, and horrible was the stink and scent thereof; but the victory seemed a sweet sacrifice, and they gave the praise thereof to God, who had wrought so wonderfully for them, thus to enclose their enemies in their hands and give them so speedy a victory over so proud and insulting an enemy." Violating the sensibilities of twentieth-century American historians, such incidents from the seventeenth century have prompted comparisons with various acts of genocide and atrocity committed in the present era. Such responses echo those of the Narragansetts who witnessed the scene, Puritan allies who recoiled in shock and horror at the slaughter.[4]

Yet "atrocity" and "slaughter," despite their implications of extremism, are relative terms, and widening the angle of vision allows us to see King Philip's War with greater resolution, distinguishing it from other contests. As Barbara Donagan, a historian of the English Civil War, has demonstrated, seventeenth-century English men and women viewed European wartime behavior in comparative terms; that attitude also prevailed in the North American colonies. Civil wars, conflicts between sovereign nations, and religious wars each involved a distinct set of behavioral norms, although differentiating among the types of clashes was often a subtle and challenging task. Formal political identities, cultural affinities, utilitarian motives, interpretations of the rules of war, and the actions of one's opponent all influenced the course of conduct. The Pequot War, in other words, was not King Philip's. No one war was like another, but rules were constantly brought to bear to regulate behavior. Therefore, no matter what values we might ultimately want to attach to King Philip's War, we cannot understand it in its proper historical context unless we view it against the background of contemporaneous conflicts, both in America and abroad, involving English Puritans. Doing so shows conduct peculiar to a civil war. This is not to say that the colonists fought as if they were pitched against their brothers, because they saw themselves occupying a higher rung on a natural hierarchy. Keeping within the metaphor of kinship, they fought more as if it were a conflict between father and child. For Indians on both sides of the conflict, of course, King Philip's War often was a war among brothers, in a literal and a figurative sense.[5]

PHILIP VINCENT, an Englishman who recounted the events at Fort Mystic for a London audience the year after they occurred, considered them rather benign in light of the atrocities Christians had committed against one another in the Thirty Years War (1618–48). In 1638, the same year his account of the fight at Fort Mystic appeared, Vincent published *Lamentations of Germany*. So far "beyond all precedent of former ages" had Germany regressed in prosecuting its war that Vincent felt compelled to devote his entire work to its horrors—complete with graphic illustrations of torture, rape, and famine—so that civilized peoples might fully understand the consequences of violating the rules of war. In Vincent's view, those rules had been admirably observed in the Pequot conflict. Unlike the combatants in Germany, who killed all of their captives, Christian or not, the Puritans allowed most of their prisoners to live. Vincent also justified the offensive by highlighting its utilitarian benefits. New England colonists were "assured of their peace by killing the Barbarians. . . . For having once terrified them, by severe execution of just revenge, they shall never heare of more harme from them." Not only had the war proven effective against the Pequots, but it had also sent a message to the Mohawks, a group Vincent considered "cruell bloodie Caniballs."[6]

Although Vincent's pejorative descriptions of Indians would today brand him a racist, he was actually quite cognizant of their humanity as of "the same constitution, & the sons of Adam, and that we had the same Maker, the same matter, the same mould. Only Art and Grace have given us that perfection, which yet they want, but may perhaps be as capable thereof as we."[7] It was precisely because they could be viewed as equals, in a sense—equals simply in need of correction and "civilization"—that the Indians could be held to the rules of war.

Under conventions of international law well known and understood by Englishmen, especially professional soldiers such as military leader John Mason, the colonists felt fully justified in their actions against the Pequots, for a town or a fort refusing to surrender merited little, if any, protection. In the words of historian Maurice Keen, "In a city taken by storm almost any license was condoned by the law. Only churches and churchmen were technically secure, but even they were not often spared. Women could be raped, and men killed out of hand."[8] Thus, setting fire to a village and granting quarter to many of the captives, as the colonists did, was well within the bounds of law and supported by English conceptions of religion and morality, even had the opponents been Christian.

Instead of dismissing the Indians as racially or culturally inferior, colonists debated the extent to which the "laws of nations" applied to them. Forty years after the Pequot conflict, William Hubbard wrote in his history of King Philip's War that the 1637 attack on the Pequots was justified because they had acted "contrary to the Laws of Nature and Nations." Such language differs from that used during King Philip's War, which refers to the hostilities as a rebellion or an insurrection. In 1637 the colonists considered the Pequots outside of their polity. No texts survive documenting Pequot submission to a colony. Then governor of Massachusetts John Winthrop, Sr., referred, in his journal, to a trade agreement between Massachusetts and the Pequots. But he also noted that the magistrates refused to promise to "defend them." Historian Francis Jennings has gone so far as to interpret Winthrop's comments to mean that, "emphatically, the Pequots had not permitted Massachusetts to assume a protectorate over them."[9] Before the conflict, English patents and charters never granted settlers formal title to Pequot land; not until they understood themselves as having conquered a sovereign nation in a just war, did the colonists believe they had earned that right.

King Philip's War differed from the Pequot War in that by 1675 the English no longer understood the Indians within New England to be sovereign nations. Since declared representatives of most, if not all, of the

Indian groups had by that time sworn loyalty—at least formally—to a colony, the colonists saw groups of Indians not as foreign nations but as inhabitants and subjects of colonial polities. They also paternalistically saw Indians as subordinates to them like children or younger brothers. The widely recognized rules of war governing conduct between sovereign nations no longer applied; rather, now considered traitors or rebellious children, the Indians could be subjected to civil laws. According to regulations applicable in such cases, Indians who killed colonial soldiers or civilians were guilty of treason or murder, or both; they now lacked the criminal immunity enjoyed by a soldier in a foreign war. The penalty for both treason and murder was death—in the case of treason, death by quartering and beheading. Massachusetts law prescribed that "If any man CONSPIRE and ATTEMPT any INVASION, INSURRECTION or publick REBELLION against our Commonwealth; or shall endeavour to suprize any Town or Towns, Fort or Forts therein; or shall Treacherously and perfideously attempt the Alteration and Subversion of our frame Polity or Government fundamentally, he shall be put to death."[10] Indians would be subject to an equally severe punishment if viewed as rebelling against the "civilizing" influence of their English rulers. In November 1646 the Massachusetts General Court had decreed that "If a man have a stubborne or rebellious sonne of sufficyent yeeres of understanding, viz., 16, wch will not obey the voyce of his father or the voyce of his mother, & that when they have chastned him will not harken unto them, then shall his father & mother, being his naturall parents, lay hold on him, & bring him to the majestrates assembled in Courte, & testify to them by sufficyent evidence that this their sonne is stubborne & rebellious, & will not obey their voyce & chasticement, but lives in sundry notorious crimes, such a sonne shall be put to death."[11] Whether they saw enemy Indians as full-fledged traitors or just rebellious children, colonists believed they had the legal right to execute them.

Yet the colonists did not uniformly seek the most severe punishment for all rebel Indians. As Barbara Donagan has demonstrated, even in the English Civil War of the 1640s, combatants on both sides refrained from holding their opponents liable for civil offenses and usually afforded them the treatment reserved for prisoners of war under the jurisdiction of military rule. It was only in the later years of the English Civil War, once the eventual outcome could be reasonably predicted, that the dominant force began to exert a kind of victor's justice on its enemy by holding some of the most prominent combatants liable for treason. The conduct of the colonists during King Philip's War followed a similar pattern. The English forces and their Indian allies tended to exact stricter punishments as time progressed and the confidence of victory grew stronger.[12]

BECAUSE THEY believed they could execute traitors, colonists saw themselves as treating the Indians leniently when they did not do so. But English perceptions of self-restraint often failed to prevent atrocity. This becomes apparent in examining the relations of the English with the Narragansetts. By December 1675 the United Colonies came to see the Narragansetts as having a town or fort that was harboring the enemy, as having committed treason, and as occupying some of the best land in New England. The English also saw in the Narragansetts a large population, and they remembered the pivotal role played by the Narragansetts in the conquest of the Pequots. Realizing that they had the largest number of fighting men of any group in the region, John Mason wrote to Connecticut's Captain Wait Winthrop, son of Governor John Winthrop, Jr., in July 1675 advising extreme caution in any war effort against the Narragansetts. In addition to raw size, the foreignness of Indian culture made the English uncertain and fearful of their ability to discern Narragansett motives. This fear was substantiated by reports that some of Philip's forces had indeed tried to lobby the Narragansetts to join their side. Thomas Stanton and Thomas Minor had reported to the Connecticut leadership that some natives had sent the Narragansett sachem Pessicus the heads of Englishmen to sway his loyalty. Wait Winthrop wrote his brother Fitz-John stating the common belief "that if we do not speedily engage the Narragansetts to the English they will be tempted to fall in with Philip."[13]

Geographic location played a large role in shaping English attitudes toward the Narragansetts. Both Rhode Island and Connecticut, having poorly protected towns in or bordering on the Narragansett territory, understandably worked hard to maintain Narragansett neutrality. Fear of Narragansett reprisal and the machinations of other English colonies spurred inhabitants of these colonies to advocate restraint. Thomas Stanton, of Stonington, Connecticut, on the border of the Narragansett territory, believed that unless the Narragansetts were on his colony's side, "we shall in these parts be in greater danger than ever." Richard Smith, living at Wickford, Rhode Island, also advocated caution: "It will be good to be moderated as respecting the Narragansetts at present I humbly conceive, for that a great body of people of them are here gathered together, may do such mischief, and it if not brought into better decorum, here will be no living for English." Similarly, a Connecticut official residing in Hartford emphasized the need to maintain peace with the Narragansetts because they could not afford to fight a war on two fronts—one against the Narragansetts and the other against New York. Connecticut secretary John Allyn wrote a letter to Wait Winthrop stating that the stirring of New York governor Edmund Andros made maintaining peace with the Narragansetts that much more of a priority.[14] Representatives of these two colonies were far more accommodating of Narragansett requests than was Massachusetts or Plymouth.

Although some English colonies urged a conciliatory approach toward the Narragansetts, heavy suspicion existed. This was especially the case in Massachusetts because of its inhabitants' perceived superiority to Indians as a whole and their paranoid mindset created by decades of jeremiads and the flow of the war. Accordingly, colonial leaders pressed the Narragansetts to collateralize their fidelity to the English with hostages. The Narragansetts resisted supplying hostages to demonstrate their loyalty to the English; at a meeting between some sachems and English military leaders, the sachems said that their long history of friendship with the English was proof enough of their fidelity to their cause. According to Roger Williams, who had a long relationship with the Narragansetts and was probably more sensitive to their worldview than any other Englishman, the Narragansetts preferred to demonstrate their loyalty by providing the heads of dead rebel Indians.[15]

Mindful of appeals from those who bordered on the Narragansett territory urging them not to irritate the Narragansetts with demands for hostages, the United Colonies eventually established a treaty with these Indians that included a provision that the Indians would provide hostages to the English. Diplomacy was delicate; Connecticut governor John Winthrop urged the colonies not to press the hostage issue too hard, the Narragansetts "being a people not so acquainted with such ways." Nevertheless, on July 15 and on October 18, 1675, the United Colonies persuaded the Narragansetts to provide hostages and also guarantee that they would hand over any rebels who tried to flee into their territory.[16]

Although provisional agreements had been reached, language problems and cultural misunderstandings over the meaning of *hostage* led to tension over how to fulfill their terms. The difficulty that John Eliot and his Indian assistants had in translating the term in their Algonquian Bible suggests that the Narragansetts were unfamiliar with the English conception of hostages. The term *hostage* appears in two places in the English Bible, yet Eliot's translation uses two completely different words in these locations. That the English and the Narragansetts could have had competing conceptions of the meaning of *hostage* seems even more likely in light of subsequent disagreements. The Narragansetts apparently thought that their hostages could be freed once they had handed over to the colonies the heads of some their enemies.[17]

The Narragansetts also treated the Indians who had fled to them differently than the English expected them to. Rather than providing for them and keeping them under close watch until they had an opportunity to hand them over to the English, the Narragansetts allowed these Indians to provide for themselves. As a result, many of them were out hunting when the English tried to summon them from the Narragansetts. As Richard Smith explained to John Winthrop, when asked why the Narragansetts had not handed over all the enemy Wampanoags, "they [the Narragansetts] are forward and willing to do it, but say it is not feasible for them to do at present, many of them [Wampanoags] being out a hunting."[18] This episode heightened English suspicion of the Narragansetts, because they were not fulfilling their treaty obligations exactly as the English had envisioned.

Additional misunderstandings between the English and the Narragansetts occurred because the Narragansetts underwent, in the words of anthropologist Paul Robinson, a "struggle within." Like other Indian and English groups, internal divisions made uniform action difficult. Richard Smith noted that "Canonicus of himself and some others incline to peace rather than war, but have many unruly men which care not what becomes of them." Roger Williams learned from Canonicus that "he could not Rule the Youth and Common People." Williams also found that one sachem, "the old Queens," had even rewarded some of Philip's forces who sent her the heads severed from English bodies.[19] The English forces had trouble understanding Narragansett intentions not only because they differed culturally but also because the Narragansetts were divided and sent mixed signals.

They also had competitors for the Narragansetts' loyalty. Right from the beginning, some of Philip's forces actively sought Narragansett services. To the horror of the English, Philip's forces sent the heads of dead English people to prominent Narragansett leaders in an effort to sway them to their cause. Such efforts coincided with a fear among many of the English that if they did not form an alliance with the Narragansetts soon, Philip would.[20] Within this competition, confusion arose because of Rhode Island's neutrality. That colony's position led many Indians to see it as a refuge from hostilities. Richard Smith, writing from Rhode Island, observed that "many Indians lately come hither, and some of the enemy amongst them." In one case, Wetamoo, the Pocasset sachem, wanted to surrender there because she thought she might receive more lenient treatment than in any other English colony.[21] The influx of non-Narragansett Indians into Rhode Island proved detrimental to the Narragansetts' attempt to distance themselves from hostile Indian groups.

Indian rebel attacks against Springfield in October worsened matters. They not only led to the internment of Christian Indians, but they also triggered a chain reaction that eventually resulted in the United Colonies' invasion of the Narragansett territory. Because the Indians who had assaulted Springfield had for so long expressed their fidelity to the English, their actions left the English bewildered and even more distrustful of Indians professing neutrality, including the Narragansetts. The resulting hysteria among the colonists led to abuses of Christian Indians, which no doubt only aided rebel efforts to get the support of the Narragansetts. Groups that were loyal to Philip pointed to atrocities committed by the English against praying Indians to argue that loyalty to the English did not guarantee escaping their wrath. Richard Smith, writing to John Winthrop, related that the Narragansett sachem Canonicus had told him that he had heard from some other Indians that "their [the English's] friends all the praying Indians were seazed first and then killed by Boston men, only they escaped, and that you intended a war with the Narragansetts suddenly."[22]

It was in this scenario that the United Colonies had to decide how to deal with the Narragansetts. The splits within the United Colonies' alliance narrowed as fear of Indian motives increased, and gradually the more aggressive colonies gained greater influence in policymaking. The United Colonies adopted policies at meetings attended by six representatives—two each from Massachusetts, Plymouth, and Connecticut. For a decision to be binding, five of the six representatives had to agree to it, meaning that each colony had to have at least one representative in favor of the proposed action. Plymouth and Massachusetts—the colonies that expressed the greatest anti-Indian sentiment—could not act without at least the partial support of Connecticut.

Gaining the support of Connecticut was no easy task. At the time of the United Colonies' meeting in Boston scheduled for November 2, 1675, one of Connecticut's representatives, James Richards, sat in Hartford unable to travel because of the war and the weather. The other, Gov. John Winthrop—long an advocate of conciliation and moderation in dealing with the Narragansetts—insisted that the United Colonies could not act in Richards's absence. Tensions built as the representatives of Plymouth and Massachusetts accused Connecticut's Winthrop of stalling. On November 5, representatives pleaded with him to allow the proceedings to go forward, but Winthrop resolutely stood his ground. Exasperated, the four representatives of Plymouth and Massachusetts castigated Connecticut, calling that colony's action "an absolute violation of the main ends of the Articles of Confederation."[23]

Nevertheless, the colonies reached a compromise within several days; Connecticut allowed Wait Winthrop, who was already in Boston, to sit in Richards's place at the meeting. The commissioners arrived at a consensus quickly. Following the surprise attacks in the Connecticut River Valley, the question raised by the commissioners was no longer whether they could risk irking the Narragansetts into joining the rebellion, but whether the colonies and their Indian allies could afford not to conduct a preemptive strike against them. By now, even John Winthrop conceded that action had to be taken against the Narragansetts. On November 12, 1675, the commissioners of the United Colonies unanimously agreed to enforce the terms agreed upon with the Narragansetts on October 18. To this end, the United Colonies raised a one-thousand-man army under the command of Josiah Winslow to march into the Narragansett country and demand that they hand over all Indians who had sought their shelter.[24]

Why, after urging the United Colonies to pursue a policy of moderation and even trying to stall its militaristic efforts, did the Connecticut delegation accede to the desires of Plymouth and Massachusetts? The records do not offer any explicit answers to this question, but it does seem that ethnicity played a large role. For both the English and the Indians, kinship, at times metaphorical, bound communities together. The English metaphorical bond of kinship embodied in nationhood made the commissioners feel a sense of duty to act with a consensus concerning the

Narragansetts. A latent cultural infrastructure—a pan-English identity—rose to the fore in this time of crisis. As noted earlier, most of the English colonists, marginalized from "orthodox" Massachusetts or not, felt bound together by virtue of their nationality. Sentiments such as those of Massachusetts minister William Hubbard, who pleaded that "[t]o be short we are all but one political Body, which ought to be sensible of the Sorrows that befell any particular Members thereof," and Samuel Gorton of Rhode Island, who referred to "the body Pollitique of English in these parts," crystallized and led to the United Colonies' consensus.[25] Whereas pan-English identity had not been prioritized over issues such as local security and ties of obligation during the early stages of the war, the experience of the conflict, especially the generalized fear of Indians among the English that was heightened by the Connecticut River Valley raids, made what was previously latent more manifest.

The decision to punish the Narragansetts for treaty noncompliance culminated in the most famous confrontation of the entire war. To ensure that the attack against the Narragansetts was decisive, the United Colonies put together a force recruited from the colonial militias, under the command of Plymouth governor Josiah Winslow. Massachusetts provided 517 men, Plymouth 158, and Connecticut 465. Connecticut's contribution warrants special attention because a sizable number of the men it provided, 150 to be exact, were Mohegans or Pequots. On December 19, 1675, the army comprised of Indians and English colonists staged a punitive raid against a Narragansett stronghold and palisaded village surrounded by swampland near what is today West Kingston, Rhode Island.

When the forces arrived at the fort, guided by captured Narragansetts, it was still under construction and thus provided some possible weaknesses the United Colonies' forces could strike at first. The gap in the fort apparently was not big enough for the first wave to infiltrate; the Narragansetts repelled the troops and inflicted heavy losses. The second wave ordered in did not do much better. After suffering heavy casualties, the United Colonies set fire to the fort. In a scene reminiscent of events at Fort Mystic in 1637—and in one of the most brutal and lopsided military encounters in all of New England's history—huge numbers of Narragansett men, women, and children perished. When the fires died out and the bullets stopped flying, the United Colonies had lost 70 men and had 150 wounded. The Narragansetts had lost at least 97 warriors and between 300 and 1,000 women and children. The casualties were the highest of any battle in the war and were unusually lopsided.[26] Needless to say, any thoughts the Narragansetts had of remaining neutral vanished after what came to be known as the Great Swamp Fight. They learned the hard way that ties binding them to Rhode Island and the king of England were not enough to stave off members of the United Colonies. The survivors fled to join Philip.

With the Great Swamp Fight, nearly, if not all, groups living within New England became embroiled in the war or at least were forced to choose a side. The battle represented the climax of a six-month period after the outbreak of war at Swansea during which various groups tested and jockeyed for position. The English, although they inflicted tremendous casualties, found little joy in the event. Their dismay did not stem from their conduct and its bloody results; rather they viewed themselves as having acted with restraint, since they believed they were dealing with traitors. What disappointed them was that the campaign failed to produce the immediate results they desired. Winslow's army waged an unsuccessful pursuit of the fleeing Narragansetts. Because of the exceptionally harsh winter, the shortage of supplies, and their unfamiliarity with the terrain, his soldiers acquired nothing but hunger, exhaustion, hypothermia, and low spirits. In what became known as the "Hungry March," Winslow's troops headed home, supposedly having to kill and eat some of their horses along the way.[27] On February 5, 1676, Winslow disbanded the army, feeling that it had done little to advance the overall position of the United Colonies. Bickering between the supposedly allied colonies of Connecticut and Massachusetts also intensified as it became apparent that their soldiers had looted one another's dead in the aftermath of battle.[28] At this point the shared threat of an Indian rebellion was not enough to unify these factious people, with their localized webs of relations—they did not even respect the dead from other English colonies.

THE ENGLISH believed that, facing a rebellion of "savage" subjects, they could subject their enemy to the ultimate penalty. But they usually refrained from doing so. English restraint was always fragile, but when it gave way, the results were not always as catastrophic as those of the Great Swamp Fight. All of the colonies in King Philip's War decided the fates of enemy Indians by trying to measure their degree of guilt and then doling out a punishment according to the dictates of law and morality. To a large extent the norms governing conduct in war had developed from English perceptions of the laws of nature, religious doctrine, internationally recognized professional conventions for soldiers, and army regulations. When English men—a significant number of whom had had experience in English military establishments or had served in the English Civil War, or both—and women transplanted to New England, they brought those conventions with them.[29]

Of course, laws and morality are rarely, if ever, immutable principles, and prevailing conditions are seldom disregarded. The English obviously had practical motives that influenced their interpretation of events and the character of their justice. Because morality and utility differed across time and space in the conduct of King Philip's War, the degree to which the colonists and their Indian allies followed formally prescribed codes varied from case to case. Yet patterns can be seen in this variation. Utilitarian concerns emerged again and again, whether explicitly or implicitly, as a rationale regulating behavior. Fear among the English and their Indian allies that the war would expand and that they might lose created a strong impetus for restraint.

During the first half of the war, the colonial forces suffered repeated setbacks. Because they feared defeat or future capture, colonists and their Indian allies treated their captives in such a manner as to discourage reprisals and encourage leniency should they themselves fall into the hands of their enemy. Checks on abuse also created conditions favorable for surrender, which in turn helped prevent the war's prolongation or escalation. Capt. Benjamin Church of Plymouth articulated the principle when he reflected upon the sale of 160 rebel Indians in the fall of 1675. They had surrendered with the promise of life and liberty, Church complained, and "had their [the captors'] promises to the Indians been kept, and the Indians fairly treated, 'tis probable that most, if not all the Indians in those parts, had soon followed the example of those that had now surrendered themselves, which would have been a good step towards finishing the war."[30] A more pragmatic approach was to grant Indian rebels the status of legitimate prisoners of war.

Curtailing violence would also help limit the geographical scope of the war, the colonists believed. Several contemporary accounts attributed the spread of the conflict to the improper deeds of English settlers. The most vocal critic of such actions was the Ipswich minister William Hubbard, who explained in his *Narrative of the Troubles with the Indians* (1677) that Indians near Chelmsford on the Merrimack River became hostile because they "had been provoked by the rash, unadvised, cruel Act of some of the English." Later in the same work, he noted that the wife of Squando, an enemy Indian leader, "was abused by a rude and indiscreet Act of some English Seamen," which resulted in her child's drowning. The incident spurred Squando to "ever since set himself to do all the Mischief he can to the English in those Parts."[31] Such outbreaks of excessive, random violence were thankfully rare, Hubbard acknowledged; elsewhere, especially in the more southerly parts of New England, the colonial forces generally proceeded according to legitimate rules of war.

The colonists did not need to look far in the winter and spring of 1676 for a reason to limit their conduct; they were losing the war, and fear of reprisal for their actions ran high. Despite the overwhelming force used by the English and their Indian allies at the Great Swamp Fight, Algonquian attacks against English settlements had the colonies reeling at the beginning of the year. Eager to maintain momentum, Philip's supporters traveled to Schaghticoke on New York's Hudson River in January. There they hoped to enlist the support of the Mohawks, a group of Iroquois whom many southern New England Algonquians feared, comparing their ferocity to that of wolves. The move was a risky one, and not surprisingly, it backfired. Philip competed for Mohawk loyalty with the English governor of New York, Edmund Andros. Though Andros did not see eye to eye with the New England colonies on many issues, he was not about to let rebellious Wampanoags seek refuge in his colony and enlist the support of its native peoples. Moreover, he quite possibly saw it to his advantage to crush the Wampanoags in New York. Doing so might aid him in his boundary disputes with Connecticut and Massachusetts. Connecticut's colonial government had long been reluctant to ask for New York's assistance in the war out of fear that it might provide an opportunity for that colony to seize some of their land.

Whether Andros had any significant influence over the Mohawks in early 1676 is unknown. The Mohawks, after all, had been fighting New England Algonquians since at least the early 1660s. What seems almost certain, however, is that the Mohawks, either for their own reasons or partly at the urging of Andros, lashed out at Philip. Hundreds of miles from their home, which had become a war zone, in the middle of winter, Philip's forces suffered a devastating defeat. In subsequent months, fear of Mohawks would drive many rebel Indians to surrender to the English, but not before they had pushed the colonists to their greatest depths of despair.[32]

In February 1676 the English and their Indian allies were unaware of Philip's failings in New York, and the remaining rebels went on the offensive. In rapid succession Lancaster, Medfield, Groton, Marlborough, Sudbury, and Providence were torched; other towns experienced smaller raids.[33] The first town to fall, Lancaster, succumbed within a week after the disbanding of the United Colonies' Army, which followed the unsuccessful pursuit of Narragansett refugees from the Great Swamp and the Hungry March. The rebel Indians offered one of their greatest displays of force when four hundred Nipmucks, Narragansetts, and Wampanoags attacked Lancaster in central Massachusetts. When they left, they ushered away twenty-two English captives, including Mary Rowlandson, and left fifty dead.

The daughter of Lancaster's largest landowner and the wife of the town's prominent minister, Rowlandson spent three months living with rebel Nipmucks, Narragansetts, and Wampanoags before she was finally ransomed and released when the war turned in favor of the colonies. Her captivity narrative published six years after the war, *The Sovereignty and Goodness of God*, provides us with the only written eyewitness account of life among Philip's forces. She tells us how "by their noise and hooping they signified how many they had destroyed." Along with its descriptions of life among the "savages," Rowlandson's work offers the most personal account of the war and its suffering. She relates how she witnessed the death of her daughter "with a very heavy heart" and how she herself was saved not only from death but from degeneration into savagery by the providence of God. Because it was unique as a firsthand report, her account came to be regarded as a symbol of the despair into which the war had lowered the colonists and the intensity with which God had tested them.[34]

The despair and the tests the colonists and their Indian allies faced beginning in February were the stuff not only of literary symbolism, but also of decisive military defeat. Following the Lancaster attack, Indians struck a well-defended Medfield, just twenty miles from Boston, on February 21. Two days later, Indian raids came within ten miles of the town. The Massachusetts government encouraged inhabitants of smaller towns to abandon them and flee to larger ones. Many Boston residents took the proximity of attacks to the most concentrated areas of English settlement as a sign that not even their town was safe. At this point, rebel confidence was high, and one of the Indian assailants on Medfield left the following note attached to a bridge as he fled: "Know by this paper, that the Indians that thou has provoked to wrath and anger, will war this twenty one years if you will; there are many Indians yet, we come three hundred at this time. You must consider the Indians lost nothing but their life; you must lose your fair houses and cattle."[35] March and April's warmer temperatures did little to alleviate the colonists' military woes. During that month Indians attacked Groton, Northampton, Marlborough, and Sudbury, Massachusetts, successfully. In Plymouth Colony they hit Clark's Garrison and Rehoboth. And even in ostensibly neutral Rhode Island they managed to destroy the largest town, Providence, forcing the flight of Roger Williams, elder statesman to the Indians. To make matters worse, epidemics struck the colonists and killed many, including Gov. John Winthrop, who died on April 5 while in Boston attending to the affairs of the United Colonies.

The reactions of the troubled colonists reflected their desperation and sense of futility at the peak of the rebellion. The government of Massachusetts put forth the idea of abandoning huge parts of the colony and retreating behind a line of fortifications, natural barriers in the form of ponds and rivers and an eight-foot palisade. To the chagrin of the diehard defenders of towns such as Lancaster, Concord, Sudbury, Chelmsford, and Marlborough, they would be on the wrong side of the line. It was residents of such towns who shouted down the proposal, citing its high cost and lack of guaranteed success. The colonists had had little success fortifying isolated towns, much less a vast section of eastern Massachusetts.[36]

It is also remarkable, given their Calvinist beliefs, that they tried to influence their relationship with God throughout the war and especially during this time of desperation. Many, if not most, of the English did not perceive the root cause of the war to be legitimate grievances among Indians but a failure on their part to keep their covenant with God. Reflecting this perception, the colonies waged war not only against the rebel Indians but also against the sins of English men and women. Almost immediately after the war began, colonies proclaimed occasional fast days, days of prayer, and days of public humiliation. These became more frequent once it became clear that the war would not consist solely of brief, localized skirmishes, but instead threatened the very existence of the New England colonies.[37]

Yet the most telling evidence of how desperate the English had become during the winter was the revival of discussion concerning the use of Indian troops. Although Connecticut steadfastly relied on Mohegan and Pequot allies, Plymouth and Massachusetts had ceased using Christian Indians in the second phase of the war, when it first spread beyond Plymouth and eventually into the Connecticut River Valley, leaving many colonists unsure which Indians they could trust. Starting in February 1676, however, several military commanders in Massachusetts urged the reconsideration of Christian Indians as soldiers. The council of the colony agreed on April 21 to begin supplementing its forces with more Indian troops. A month later Indians were released from Deer Island, with many of the men "in the service of the country" as soldiers or guides.[38] Far more complicated than a "race war" or a conquest, King Philip's War also forced colonists to draw on Indian subjects to put down perceived traitors. This reliance proved instrumental in turning the tide of the war.

The effectiveness of the insurrection in the first ten months of the war suggests that, contrary to what many historians have asserted, the differences in military strategy and technology between the Indians and the English favored the former. All rebels were Indians; the majority of the forces they confronted, despite the sizable contribution of Indians, came from English ranks. These demographics meant that, in the initial stages of the war, the differences in military culture between the Indians and the English largely translated into the differences between the two sides. The lifestyle and subsistence strategies of Indians made them more mobile than the English. Wigwams, unlike English houses, could be torn down and reconstructed relatively easily. And Indians were accustomed to moving their residences and settlements to take advantage of diverse, seasonal food sources; they hunted, fished, grew crops, and gathered wild plant foods. Their mobility proved advantageous during the war, as reflected in the frustrated comments of English military leaders who complained that they could not even find their enemy. Responding to letters from Maj. Simon Willard, for example, the Massachusetts Council wrote, "we understand that our forces cannot meet with the enemy, the lord humble us under his afflictive hand." Similarly, Increase Mather somberly noted the Indian advantage of "knowing where to find us, but we know not where to find them."[39]

Even when the army could locate the enemy Indians, it was often too late, because by then they had escaped. For the English, war with the Indians felt like "fighting with a wild Beast in his own Den," as William Hubbard put it.[40] Frustrated colonists on several occasions recounted how Indians had fled to safety across rivers, either using lightweight canoes or crossing bridges that they destroyed immediately afterward. The captured Englishwoman Mary Rowlandson noted how the Indians used rivers to protect themselves from English pursuit. William Hubbard repeatedly portrayed Indians as foiling English attempts to capture them by fleeing across rivers to safety. And Daniel Gookin recounted an incident in which Indians raided the English settlement of Dedham, Massachusetts, until they "saw cause to withdraw on a bridge towards Sherburne, and, firing the bridge impeded the pursuit of English soldiers." Once across, these Indians "drew up in a body on the other side of the river, and, being secure, vapored and talked high."[41] The frequency of such incidents suggests that rebel strategists were able to take advantage of natural features such as rivers to flee decisively when the terms of engagement did not favor them.

The Indians' skilled use of weaponry accentuated the advantages of their mobility. The Indian men and boys of New England were generally better marksmen than their English counterparts. Accuracy with firearms offered little benefit in English military culture. Militia training encouraged the use of mass volleys rather than aiming at individual targets. Hunting had not given the English much practice shooting their muskets accurately, either. Domesticated livestock and seafood were the main sources of meat in the English diet; the principal source of meat in the typical Indian diet was wild game. When the English colonists needed some hunting done, for instance, when they wanted to kill wolves that preyed on their livestock, they often hired Indian men to take care of it, because they were better sharpshooters.[42]

At the time of contact with Europeans, the Indians hunted game with bows and arrows; at a young age Indian boys began working on the sharpshooting accuracy required to kill an animal with this weapon. Indians generally found that they could strike with greater precision with their arrows than with the highly inaccurate matchlock muskets carried by the English in the first half of the seventeenth century. Indian accuracy with arrows so exceeded that with matchlocks that they found little value in them. It was only with the advent and growing popularity of the much more accurate flintlock musket in the second half of the seventeenth century that Indians integrated English weaponry into their arsenals in large numbers. Indian sharpshooting skills with arrows facilitated the adoption of the flintlock musket into their culture, once it had been developed and introduced to the Indians as a trade item. They quickly learned to use it with great prowess. By the time of King Philip's War, New England's male indigenous population had become so adroit in the use of the flintlock that the military historian Patrick Malone has written: "The colonist had brought the firearm to the New World; in King Philip's War, the Indian would demonstrate how to use this machine."[43]

The Indians also knew how to repair this machine and manufacture its ammunition. Indian blacksmiths learned their craft under the tutelage of Englishmen before the war began. As early as 1640, William Bradford expressed trepidation that some Indians might use artisanal skills that they learned from the English to support a military effort against the English. He observed that Indians had "moulds to make shot of all sorts, as musket bullets, pistol bullets, swan and goose shot, and of smaller sorts" and that they could "mend and new stock their pieces . . . as well in most things as an Englishman."[44]

Despite the close relationship that these Indian blacksmiths must have had with English colonists, at least some of them opted to join Philip's cause once the war began. Some of the major military confrontations resulted in the confiscation of rebel forges and tools or the killing of their blacksmiths. Nathaniel Saltonstall reported that at the Great Swamp Fight in Rhode Island on December 19, 1675, the English and their Indian allies killed "an Indian blacksmith" and "demolished his forge and carried away his tools." Five months later a company patrolling western Massachusetts "demolished two forges they [the Indians] had to mend their arms; took away all their materials and tool . . . and threw two great pigs of lead of theirs (intended for making bullets) into the said river." In addition to these seventeenth-century discoveries, archaeologists in more recent years have unearthed evidence suggesting that Indian blacksmiths lived in regions other than the Narragansett country and western Massachusetts. Excavations of a seventeenth-century Wampanoag burial ground near Philip's territory have uncovered shot molds. Archaeologists have also found shot molds in seventeenth-century Indian villages in Connecticut.[45]

Such geographically widespread evidence demonstrates that Indians were not dependent upon the English to repair their arms. Indians did, however, depend on Europeans—French or English, directly or indirectly—for gunpowder. Yet there is no evidence suggesting that they ever lacked it during the war. Stockpiles, plunder, and trade evidently satisfied Indian demands. Unfortunately no sources document the inter-Indian trade that likely existed between New England's Indians and those to the north and west who had access to French gunpowder. But colonial courts often accused individuals of illegally selling powder to hostile Indians, suggesting, at the very least, that powder leaked from the English to their enemies during the war. Regardless of where they got their powder, and even if they wished they had more, no rebels who surrendered ever cited lack of powder as a motive for their capitulation.[46]

Although the issue of Indian firearms and the ability to maintain them relative to the English is important, it should not overshadow the extreme simplicity, abundance, and effectiveness of the weapon most frequently used by the rebels: fire. Because of fire, Indians might have been able to wage an effective war even without gunpowder. The idea of waging "total" war and trying to burn villages to the ground probably occurred to New England Indians in the Pequot War of 1637 when the English, supported by Narragansett allies, torched the entire Pequot village at Fort Mystic. Indians, both Narragansett and Pequot, were shocked at the time by the high casualties that resulted from this technique. Thirty-eight years later, however, Indians were the ones relying most heavily on the torch. The sedentary lifestyle of English colonists made their habitations highly susceptible to fire damage, and a burned-down English house took much longer to rebuild than a torched wigwam. These advantages meant that of all the forms of technology available to the rebels, fire—simple and abundant—suited their purpose best and allowed them to fight most effectively.[47]

THE TECHNOLOGY and tactics of rebel Indians were effective enough that the colonial leadership felt it could not afford to expand the war and advocated limitations on its prosecution. In particular, they urged moderation in the matter of punishing captured rebel Indians. Often, however, those admonitions fell on deaf ears. Although military leaders with formal training and government officials tended to show restraint in their punishment of Indians and to attempt to differentiate among them according to degrees of guilt, colonists of the "lower sort"—volunteers, civilians, and those English combatants without formal military training—tended to execute Indians simply because they were Indians. They despised all Indians, rebel or not, and spent little time trying to differentiate among them. Magistrates and military officials disapproved of such unreflective behavior, but civilians anxious for revenge applauded it.

Two English military leaders with different backgrounds, Daniel Gookin and Samuel Moseley, illustrate these opposing attitudes. Gookin, who had a military background in England and, after coming to Massachusetts, was voted captain of the Cambridge military company in 1648, immediately championed the use of Christian Indians in colonial forces. Horrified at the way some of the English had treated New England's Christian Indians during the war, Gookin issued "An Historical Account of the Doings and Sufferings of the Christian Indians in New England" [1677]. He portrayed the praying Indians as loyal subjects and victims of English prejudice. After Indians burned Lancaster in February 1676, Gookin castigated those who rushed to implicate some praying Indians in the attack: "Some men were so violent that they would have had these Indians put to death by martial law, and not tried by a jury, though they were subjects under the English protection, and not in hostility with us." He declared that he could not "join with the multitude, that would cast them [praying Indians] all into the same lump with the profane and brutish heathen, who are as great enemies to our Christian Indians as they are to the English." By "multitude," Gookin referred not to colonial magistrates, who "generally were very slow to distrust those poor Christians," but to the "common people," the "disorderly rout in Boston," and "women."[48]

In addition to the "common people," Gookin held one particular military leader in contempt for cruelty toward Indians: Samuel Moseley. Unique among English military leaders, Moseley, in the words of George Madison Bodge, "held no military office, and not even his success and popularity, and close family relation to Gov. Leverett, could prevail to break the strict rule of official succession in the colonial militia." That the militia was a closed society may have had less to do with Moseley's inability to gain a formal position, however, than his predilection to act beyond his orders. A Jamaican privateer, Moseley led a company of volunteers who, for the most part, had not been enrolled in town militias because they were former pirates, servants, and apprentices. The Massachusetts General Court, and even Moseley himself, recognized that his volunteers often disregarded rules of proper conduct and were responsible for some of the war's most notable atrocities.[49] On August 30, 1675, Moseley's forces

marched toward a village of Indians who were ostensibly friendly to the
English near what is now Concord, New Hampshire. Finding it abandoned, they burned the village, even though they had been instructed not
to. A week later, Massachusetts officials ordered Lt. Thomas Henchman
to send a contingent of loyal Indians to offer reparations to those who
had had their village burned.[50] In the next month, Moseley found himself
apologizing to Governor Leverett for encouraging other questionable executions in the field. He wrote:

> I confes, that I have written some things to that purpose as Concerning the
> hangeing of those Indians of Malbery, I desire to be Excuse of my tongue or
> pen has out run my witt being in a passion and seeing what mischief had
> beene done by the Indians which I have beene eye witness to, would make
> a wiser person than I am, willing to have revenge of aney of them, but
> notwithstanding what I have written there as to that purpose it is fare from
> my heart to Doe, for I am willing to undertake any commands Imposed
> upon me to serve the country.[51]

Moseley's atrocities not only infuriated friends of the praying Indians,
such as Gookin; they also created problems for the colonial officials who
had to make amends for his actions.

The correspondence of John Pynchon also speaks to the common hysteria for revenge that could frustrate a pragmatic approach to avoiding
skirmishes with Indians. Pynchon, like Gookin, emphasized the need to
court potential Indian allies. Yet in the town of Springfield, where he was
the most powerful citizen, large numbers of the English distrusted the
very Indians Pynchon most valued. Championing the rights of a Northampton Indian accused on weak evidence of joining the rebellion, Pynchon wrote Connecticut governor John Winthrop of his dismay that his
point of view was so widely disdained. "Sir, people cry out that he is not
dispatched; I wonder at such a spirit in people for our most faithful Indians tell me they cannot think but that he was coming in from his hunting
wigwam to the English out of dislike of the enemy, he having a father,
mother, wife, and children at Northampton . . . I am said to be overfavor-
able." Apparently many of Springfield's English inhabitants were prepared
to disregard the protections afforded a prisoner of war and even the due
process reserved for a civilian traitor. The discrepancy between their
point of view and Pynchon's demonstrates the sharp schisms between
various colonists that sometimes hindered customary restraints on violence that most leaders advocated.[52]

In a war out of control and with the colonies forced to rely partially on volunteers and impressed soldiers, restraint was sometimes lacking and atrocities were committed. Moreover, the colonists and their Indian allies only became more ruthless as the course of the war shifted in their favor and they sensed impending victory. In spring 1676 it appeared to many colonists that their prayers had been answered. Depending upon location, the tide of the war began to shift sometime between March and April. From then until the war's end in August, English soldiers and their Indian allies mopped up a suddenly listless enemy in southern New England. Not fearing retaliation as they would have earlier, some colonists and Indian allies often wreaked vengeance on the enemy—man, woman, or child. They continued to justify such ruthlessness in part by the rationalization that the rebels had committed treason, a civil crime rather than an act of war, punishable by death.

The colonists first gained momentum in western Rhode Island, territory long controlled by the Narragansetts. In late March 1676, Connecticut captains James Avery and George Denison put together a force of forty Englishmen and eighty Mohegans and Niantics to wage an offensive against rebel Narragansetts led by Canonchet. After the Great Swamp Fight, which conclusively drew most Narragansetts into the conflict opposite the English and their Indian allies, Canonchet's preeminence as a military leader had risen. By April, in the aftermath of Philip's disastrous winter in New York, Canonchet arguably had the most power of any rebel Indian.

Yet Captains Avery and Denison also commanded a sizable number of Indians. And these Indians in large measure drove the Connecticut forces to success. Indian scouts located Canonchet's group near the Pawtucket River. Alerted to the presence of the colonial force by his watch, Canonchet practiced the tried and true. He led his soldiers in flight away from the force with the expectation that they could eventually lure their pursuers into an ambush. This strategy had worked in the past when colonial commanders followed the tenets of European military culture. Yet the tactics of Avery and Denison's force reflected its Indian majority. Fast-moving Indians pursued Canonchet. As his group fled, they suddenly discovered they had already been outflanked by a contingent of Mohegans and Niantics. A Mohegan captured Canonchet, and forty-three more Narragansetts were in Avery and Denison's hands by the end of the day.

Though Indian tactics led to Canonchet's capture, his treatment as a prisoner initially followed English norms. Having captured the preeminent Narragansett leader, Avery and Denison made an offer that they might have made to a European general. They would grant Canonchet and his men their lives in exchange for the surrender of all Narragansett rebels. Canonchet refused the offer, hoping the rebellion would continue without him. His intransigence prompted the Connecticut force to slay the forty-three captives on the spot. They spared Canonchet's life only long enough to transport him to the nearest Connecticut town, Stonington, for trial.

On April 2 Connecticut officials sentenced him to death, and at this point Indian cultural codes of conduct came to the fore. Canonchet requested that Oneco, son of the Mohegan who had slain his father years ago, carry out the execution. Connecticut officials jumped at the opportunity to test Mohegan loyalty. Thus on April 2 Oneco beheaded Canonchet. Canonchet's hopes that other Narragansetts would continue in the struggle were unfounded; his death proved to be only the first episode in a period of decline and loss of will among the Indian rebels.[53] Sensing events turning in their favor, the colonies and their Indian allies treated rebel holdouts vengefully.

Indians in the Connecticut River Valley experienced the next crushing blow. For the colonists, steeped in the European military tradition, a complacent camp of Indians at Peskeompscut offered a prime opportunity to wage a war in which the goal was unconditional surrender or annihilation. On May 18, 1676, Capt. William Turner, the garrison commander at Hatfield, inspired by intelligence reports, led an early-morning surprise attack against the encampment. Turner and Massachusetts magistrates had not always seen eye to eye. He had spent a lot of time in prison in 1668 and 1670 for his Baptist views. And, according to one historian, Turner was denied a military commission when the war began. As conflict spread and more English towns burned, Massachusetts's leadership could no longer afford religious intolerance and commissioned him.[54]

Well-trained soldiers were hard to come by, and Turner could scrounge up only 150 volunteers and impressed men: "single men, boys, and servants." If the earlier actions of Samuel Moseley's forces were any indicator, the composition of Turner's party bode ill for the Indians going about their seasonal subsistence routine. Turner had hoped for, but failed to get, reinforcements from the more formally trained and disciplined Connecticut militia. Without these men, he would have to make do with a handful of garrison soldiers and a large pool of local inhabitants. Some historians have since called the subsequent actions of Turner's forces "innovative," whereas others have labeled them "amateurish," depending upon which side they sympathized with.[55]

What is clear, however, is that Turner and his men had grown frustrated with the seemingly rigid strategic approach of the colony's high command. Turner's followers were local residents weary of the siege-like state they had been in for the previous seven or eight months. Their demonization of Indians had escalated during this period. Presented with the opportunity to lash out at Indians, and perhaps acquire loot in the aftermath of a battle, Turner's poorly trained men abandoned all restraint advocated by the colony's leadership. As they saw it, the traditional rules of war did not apply to their attack on the Indian encampment. Not allowing such cultural restraints to limit their actions, Turner's group successfully surprised the camp, killed as many inhabitants as possible, and destroyed their supplies. Estimates of the number of Indians killed that morning range from one hundred to several hundred, including many women and children. Turner's men took no prisoners. The natives also lost part of their machinery of war when the attackers destroyed two forges used for repairing muskets and a large quantity of lead that could have been molded into shot.

In the initial attack at Peskeompscut, Turner's men suffered only one death and a handful of wounds. Undoubtedly they were jubilant as they left the scene. Their joy proved short-lived, however, because on their retreat they fell into an ambush and lost thirty-nine men, including Turner. Even though more than one-fourth of the party was lost, the exchange at Peskeompscut on May 18 proved extremely beneficial to the colonies from a military perspective. Many colonists, especially high commanders, undoubtedly frowned upon Turner's method and apparent lack of restraint, but his success made atrocity easier to overlook. We know today, as the colonial leadership probably knew at the time, that Turner committed one of the war's greatest atrocities by slaughtering a camp that offered no resistance. But his death made dwelling on his failure to follow culturally prescribed codes of conduct fairly pointless since he could not be court-martialed.[56]

Peskeompscut demonstrated, at least from a twentieth-century perspective, the fragile nature of the colonists' restraint in King Philip's War.

But the colonists themselves would have nonetheless viewed the conflict as having been, on the whole, conducted well within the bounds of law. They also believed that the rebel Indians had tried to limit their own atrocities, and so the opponents had a sense of sharing mutually reinforcing codes of conduct. Atrocities, or at least alleged atrocities, in the Irish Rebellion of 1641 and in the Thirty Years War provided a background against which the Indian actions appeared relatively benign. Like any group engaged in war, the English constructed a demonized enemy "other." Yet this "other" did not exist simply as a binary opposite of the self; the English recognized degrees of otherness. And enemy Indian conduct came much closer to the colonists' norms than did that of the Irish rebels in 1641.

Thirty-four years before King Philip's War, English presses had spewed forth graphic descriptions of atrocities that Irish Catholics had allegedly committed against English Protestants. Acting much like the Germans in Philip Vincent's *Lamentations of Germany,* the Irish had supposedly subjected combatants and noncombatants alike to horrifying tortures, the most despicable of which, according to the pamphleteers, was the raping of women. Undoubtedly, the English press exaggerated, even fabricated, a large number of the atrocities it reported; even so, the English perception that the Irish routinely raped Protestant women—that they were thus routinely committing war crimes—was very real. Many of the English responded by calling for sharp reprisals.[57] In 1644 Parliament passed an ordinance condemning to death Irish rebels who had been captured in England.[58] Thereafter it no longer differentiated shades of guilt among the Irish, all of whom were now considered savage or inhumane. Throughout King Philip's War, the English never reached that point with the Indians.

Even though English writers frequently described enemy Indians as "barbarous" or "savage," many also acknowledged that the Indians generally accorded respect to their captives. As William Hubbard noted in 1677, "The Indians how barbarous soever in their own Nature, yet civilly intreated their Prisoners." After the raid on Lancaster, Massachusetts, for example, Hubbard asserted that the Indians did not "offer any uncivil Carriage to any of the Females, nor ever attempted the Chastity of any of them."[59] Witnessing such behavior forced colonists to reexamine their stereotypes of savage, lustful Indians to determine more precise motives for those atrocities their enemies did commit.

Indian behaviors that may strike modern students of King Philip's War as horrific were often mutually practiced or are otherwise understandable within context. Bodies of dead colonists, their Indian allies, and livestock were sometimes stripped, "mutilated," and their heads placed on poles.[60] Mounting heads in such a fashion was not unique among the Indians; indeed, it was a familiar sight in seventeenth-century European conflicts, including the English Civil War, and both sides followed the practice in King Philip's War.[61] Mutilation, of course, was an obvious result of toma-hawk warfare, and stripping bodies was common on seventeenth-century battlefields as well. By 1675 English clothing had long been the Indians' most sought-after trade good. Before the war, coats and cloth were the goods most frequently extended in ceremonies recognizing the establish-ment of political alliances, and during the war the English paid their In-dian compatriots with coats and cloth. English women held captive by the Indians spent a good deal of their time knitting clothing at their captors' insistence, and clothing was also the ransom often demanded for a hos-tage's release. Given the English view that taking plunder was a victor's right in combat, stripping bodies for their clothing must have been con-sidered a legitimate activity, however distasteful it must have been to the colonists.[62]

Familiarity, intimate ties, and kinship formed another set of motives for behavioral restraint in King Philip's War. Whereas the counterforce in the Irish Rebellion was a standing expeditionary force from a relatively distant mother country, New Englanders had to fight enemies they knew, sometimes well. Rebel leaders calling out to English captains across the battlefield would refer to them as "old neighbors," and combatants could often could list the names of those they had killed. The Indians allied with the colonists, of course, were most likely to be familiar with their opponents. The Reverend John Russell related how some of the loyal Indi-ans in the Connecticut River Valley, "[w]hen they were out with our Army . . . shewed much unwillingness to fight, alledging they must not fight against their Mothers and Brothers and Cousins." Familiarity also affected the treatment of captives. In one case, some Indians who had surrendered to the English were placed among the Narragansetts, whom they claimed as their kin. Petitioning the Massachusetts Court in June 1676 for leniency for their kin, whom they had captured, a group of pray-ing Indians who had fought alongside the English advanced the utilitarian argument that such treatment might induce other Indians to surrender.

Kinship ties among Indians also raised English suspicions. To assess the
loyalty of their Indian allies, the English often forced them to be the pun-
ishers. Benjamin Church had one of his Indian soldiers kill a captured
kinsman with a hatchet blow to the head.[63] That Indians were often willing to carry out the sentence and withhold restraint attested to their loyalty and the sincerity of their ties to the English.

ALTHOUGH THE level of violence in King Philip's War was not out of balance with what the English had experienced in European wars, the frequency with which captives were enslaved was unusual. That practice
intensified throughout the course of the war, which was quickly empty-
ing New England coffers. Selling surrendered Indians as slaves, a practice
the English felt they could justify through Scripture and international law,
provided much-needed revenue. Just as a contemporary perspective allows us to evaluate the violence within its cultural context, instances of
slavery must also be viewed within their particular place and time. In the
unique historical situation of 1675 and 1676, many of the English and their
Indian allies saw the enslavement of enemy Indians as an opportunity
both to dispense mercy and to reap a profit.

Given their belief that Philip's supporters were rebels and traitors, the
colonists maintained their right to execute prisoners. Yet many Indians
whom the colonists might have so treated under this law did not face the
executioner. The majority of those surrendered or captured Indians not
considered ringleaders were "spared" in part because, although they were
taken to be subjects of the colonies, the English felt that they occupied a
rung lower than themselves in a natural hierarchy.[64] Thus, the English
often approached Indians paternalistically.

The official symbol of the Massachusetts colony depicted an Indian
entreating the English, "Come over and help us." John Eliot, who took
that plaintive request seriously, responded joyfully in a prefatory letter to
Daniel Gookin's favorable "Historical Account of the Doings and Sufferings of the Christian Indians in New England": "As Natural fathers, so
foster fathers, are well pleased to hear well of their children."[65] Eliot, who
thought of the New England Indians as the "foster children" of the Society for the Propagation of the Gospel in New England, exemplified the
beneficent aspect of a paternalism that also had its darker side.

Nothing makes the colonists' perception of Indians' inferiority more
apparent than the mass selling of enemy Indians into slavery. Although it

was considered acceptable for Christian victors to enslave Christian captives, in practice it was primarily non-Christians who suffered this fate over the long term, for when both victor and vanquished were Christians, the offer of an exchange of prisoners for ransom was generally accepted as an obligation.[66]

Perhaps the English would not have resorted to enslaving enemy Indians had another commonly administered form of punishment, banishment, been logistically possible. New England Puritans had a history of banishing those individuals that they perceived as threats to their communities, for example, Roger Williams and Anne Hutchinson. But even in

Seal of the Massachusetts Bay Colony, 1672. Courtesy, American Antiquarian Society.

these cases, some wondered how much of a punishment banishment really was. Referring to Williams, John Cotton pondered whether it be "punishment at all in such a Countrey as this is, where the Jurisdiction (whence a man is banished) is but small, and the Countrey round about it, large, and fruitfull: where a man make his choice of variety of more pleasant, and profitable seats, than he leaveth behinde him. In which respect, Banishment in this Countrey, is not counted so much a confinement, as an enlargement, where a man doth not so much loose civill comforts as change them." Like Williams and Hutchinson, Indians posed a threat, but because so many of them already lived within the colonies but outside the bounds of English villages, they quite simply could not be banished within New England.[67] Slavery, a more rigidly enforced type of banishment, therefore more closely approximated the punitive action taken against errant English men and women in the region.

Forcing Indians into slavery or servitude also helped satisfy the dilemma of what to "do" with them. The war produced hundreds of Indian refugees, who lived as vagabonds within or on the edges of New England towns. Historian Stephen Innes, echoing Max Weber and others, has described the Puritans of New England as having a "culture of discipline." This translated into a "war on idleness" that mandated that everyone fulfill their calling through labor.[68] Servitude or slavery, depending upon the level of implication in the rebellion, satisfied the English desire to eliminate idleness forthwith. Accordingly, the treatment of Indians reflects as much the English disgust with idleness as their loathing of rebellious Indians.

Slavery and servitude had the additional advantages of helping to ameliorate a labor shortage in the New England colonies and helping to pay for the war. English soldiers and their Indians allies kept captives as payment for their services. Plymouth colony allowed Benjamin Church's English forces to have "half the prisoners and arms" that they took; his Indian force was granted only "the loose plunder." Connecticut treated its Indian troops more generously: The Indian leader Ninigret received two rebel Indian children for turning over enemy Indians to the colony, and Uncas kept a number of his captives, including some of Philip's relatives.[69] Struggling to pay for the war, the colonies found enemy Indian captives a human gold mine.[70] Financial incentives, combined with the formal rules of war, the subordinate status of Indians in New England society, the difficulties inherent in banishing Indians, the culture of discipline, and the shortage of labor, justified, in the English mind, the sale of rebel Indians into servitude or slavery. Slavery, in this particular historical context, seemed to many of the English an especially benevolent and rewarding alternative to execution.

Contextualizing the colonists' actions in King Philip's War against the background of contemporaneous conflicts involving Englishmen reveals that their conduct in many respects paralleled that to be expected in a civil war more than in a conflict between sovereign powers or even a war between a civilized society and a savage other. Both sides felt the brutality and viciousness of its battles. But atrocity is relative. When William Hubbard referred to the conflict as "Troubles," characterized by "barbarous inhumane outrages," he wrote from the perspective that the conflict was an internal rebellion. In absolute terms, the English had perceived far greater "outrages" in past wars. King Philip's, however, did not "deserve the Name of a War," since it was technically treason. The English viewed the traitorous murder of a fellow subject to be more reprehensible than a soldier killing a foreign enemy during wartime. It was because Hubbard could judge the conduct of King Philip's War through the lens of civil law, rather than the rules of international war, that it seemed so "barbarous."[71]

The conflict was not, however, a civil war "among brothers," because the colonists considered themselves more advanced in the natural hierarchy than their Indian opponents. Instead, they fought the war more as if it were a conflict between father and child. For Indians on both sides of the conflict, though, it often was a war among brothers. For the colonists, paternalism carried responsibilities of the very gravest sort. When Philip and others challenged colonial rule in 1675, the English faced wayward children and traitors. Although they never intended to exact the ultimate punishment for disobedience on all rebellious Indians, in effect the restraint of the English and their Indian allies, limited and fragile at best, did little to prevent the collapse of New England's Indian population. In the end, the cultural gestalt of the colonists allowed them to carry out effectively genocidal policies while steadfastly believing to the end that they stood upon the moral high ground.

6

VICTORY AND DEFEAT

ONE OF the most remarkable aspects of King Philip's War is that all of its destruction, all of its twists and turns, happened in such a compressed time period. Philip's was no Thirty Years War. It took only six months for nearly all of New England's groups to become involved in the conflict. After eight months, in February 1676, the English and their Indian allies were at the depths of despair. Just three months later they were confidently meting out a brand of victor's justice to opponents who refused to submit to their authority. And in August 1676, King Philip's War, one of the most violent in North American history, drew to a close, just fourteen months after it began. How was it that after such a short period the United Colonies and Indians loyal to them were able to defeat Philip's rebellion? History shows that having superior numbers, technology, and access to supplies does not make victory inevitable. The American Revolution and the Vietnam War demonstrate that powerful militaries with superior weaponry can defeat their opponents in the vast majority of battles and still lose the war.

Although military strength and technology were important in King Philip's War, they provide limited explanatory power for the war's outcome. Instead, we must look at each side's relative will to continue fighting to understand the outcome. By the time the rebellion had reached its zenith, the English had developed a more widespread, coherent, and ideologically based motive to fight than their Indian enemies had. At the same time they began to rely more heavily on their Indian allies for military guidance and support. This change in tactics helped swing the pendulum in favor of the colonists and their Indian supporters and resulted in

Philip's demise. Seeing Indians fighting alongside Englishmen made surrender seem more palatable to rebels. It weakened their will to resist,
ultimately leading to their defeat.

To be sure, the will to fight is closely related to military success in the
field. Yet many warriors had at best an ambivalent commitment to Philip's cause from the outset. Lack of commitment led to divisions and a
splintering of Indian forces, despite their military achievements. The English, too, had a multitude of internal schisms, but these were less significant than those of their enemy. Moreover, the English overcame many of
their internal divisions during the course of the war, in spite of a wide
array of military setbacks. As time passed, they developed a wider and
deeper will to fight than did their Indian enemies. For this reason they
won the war.

FROM A PURELY military standpoint, the war could have continued much
longer than it did. An examination of the internal group dynamics and
motives of the two sides and how they changed over time reveals why it
did not. The English, who made up the majority of those fighting against
Philip's forces, were relatively committed and ideologically coherent.
They outlasted an Indian enemy force containing many individuals and
groups with often only a partial commitment. Moreover, the English and
the Indians differed in their conceptions of victory. Because the English
viewed themselves as superior to the Indians, they would accept nothing
less than a "total" victory. Their sustained motive to fight exceeded that
of their Indian opponents; the will to fight fizzled among most of the
rebels before it had a chance to among the English.[1]

Although Indians contributed relatively heavily to suppressing Philip's
uprising, much of the work was done by colonists, and no groups of the
English actively fought on Philip's side. For this reason the colonists' ideological motives to fight bore heavily on the rebellion's defeat. The colonists' commitment to fight was not only deeper but also more widespread
than that of their enemies. This is not to imply that there were not strong
divisions among the English. Indeed, those divisions had contributed to
a sense among Philip's supporters that their resistance had a strong
chance of succeeding in the first place. The Indians of New England knew
all too well of the colonists' divisions, having succeeded in playing the
English colonies off one another for more than a generation. Colonies
such as Connecticut and Rhode Island legitimated their political existence

before the Crown and other English colonies by reference to their close relationships with local Indians. It is no wonder, then, that the Indians expressed surprise at the willingness of Massachusetts and Rhode Island to support Plymouth soon after the skirmishes at Swansea, demanding of Roger Williams "why the Massachusetts and Rode Iland rose, and joynd with Plymmouth agnst Phillip and left not Phillip and Plymmouth to fight it out."[2]

The Indians who made this observation understood that the English colonists living among them had tended to identify first and foremost with local polities. During the war, these local allegiances occasionally rose to the fore, leading to tension among the English. Lack of trust among the English colonial governments and among soldiers from different colonies was most apparent in the aftermath of the Great Swamp Fight. James Richards, a Connecticut magistrate and delegate to the United Colonies, wrote Gov. John Winthrop, Jr., relaying news of the bad blood between Connecticut and Massachusetts troops. Accusations that the English of Massachusetts were ransacking the dead bodies of Englishmen from Connecticut in search of plunder disturbed the magistrate. Connecticut soldiers no longer wanted to fight with those of Massachusetts because the latter had "dreadfully pillaged of their clothes, guns, horses, provisions." It seemed that "sundry of the soldiers were more ready to secure plunder than help and relieve in bringing off dead and wounded men whereby many of our dead, and wounded men's arms are lost which we cannot spare." Connecticut secretary John Allyn seconded these concerns when he reported to the governor that the colony had not only suffered a disproportionate number of casualties, but also had lost "about one hundred arms." These arms "were stolen from them at Narragansett, it is grievous to us that we should so lose our arms amongst our friends, & have not wherewithal to arm our men."[3]

Beyond such disputes that threatened the unity of the colonies, tensions strained relations within units as soldiers challenged the chain of command. One militia committee complained of the "averseness of the generality of the [town's] inhabitants to obey military orders." They hoped that the governor and council would "direct some special order to such in this town as may bring the inhabitants to the obedience of the military laws."[4] Several months earlier, the Massachusetts General Court had had to deal with impressed foot soldiers' failure to show up for duty or, when they did appear, their "refractoriness, reflection or contempt upon authority." The court arrived at the solution that "such persons shall be punished with death or some other grievous punishment." Two days later the same court had to address a related problem when Capt. George Corwin allegedly displayed a "very evil example in his demeanor & carriage" toward Capt. Daniel Henchman that "tended to disturbe & mutinize the souldiers under his command." Corwin, although a captain, was second in command to Henchman. The court realized that this alleged insubordination by a person of high rank could not go uninvestigated, "for the prevention of the like disorders, and to stop any clamors against the government . . . that poorer men are punished for lesser offences, when richer men escape with greater."[5] Appearances of injustice and inequality within the ranks, like disputes between colonies, threatened to unravel their military coalition. Minimizing these differences relative to those among their enemy proved crucial in their march toward victory.

The English colonists, although they tended to identify first and foremost with local polities, nevertheless had a more intense feeling of ethnic identity than did the Indians of the region. This sense of unity enabled them to maintain their will to fight longer than most of their opponents did. It stemmed largely from their shared history, language, and religion. In responding to Indian confusion as to why Massachusetts and Rhode Island had sided relatively quickly with Plymouth in its conflict with Philip, Roger Williams told some Narragansett sachems that "all the Colonies were Subject to one K. Charls [King Charles] and it was his pleasure and our Dutie and Engagement for one English man to stand to the Death by Each other in all parts of the World."[6] That such a strong statement came from a man who had been banished by Massachusetts and who has earned a reputation as the Puritan most sympathetic to Indian culture and interests highlights the intensity of the fairly dormant English ethnic identity, which many Indians had failed to appreciate.

This latent cultural infrastructure in which the English differentiated themselves from the Indians intensified as the war progressed. Colonists found inspiration in the construct positing them on a higher level of cultural evolution than the Indians. As English tutors to Indian pupils, the colonists were unwilling to make concessions to an Indian rebellion. They were fighting an inferior, even though their opponent was succeeding militarily. Sometimes this belief translated into anti-Indian sentiment that failed to differentiate among Indians or recognize the significant contributions that many of them had made to putting down the rebellion. Some

English people demonized all Indians as their enemy, especially after the rebellion swelled with the ranks of supposedly loyal Indians in fall 1675. Metaphors came into use portraying Indians as savage "wolves" preying on English "sheep."[7] Those colonists perceived to be sympathetic to Indians, such as John Eliot, Daniel Gookin, and Thomas Danforth, came under sharp attack. Gookin and Danforth, in particular, received threats on their lives for their efforts to protect praying Indians. A conspiracy against them developed with the circulation of handwritten leaflets by an anonymous author: "Reader thou art desired not to suppress this paper, but to promote its design which is to certify (those traytors to their king and Country) Guggins [Gookin] and Danforth, that some generous spiritts have vowed their destruction as Christian we warne them to prepare for death, for though they will deservedly dye, yet we wish the health of their souls."[8] Gookin, although he had succeeded in bolstering the strength of Massachusetts forces through the addition of praying Indians, became especially unpopular among many of the English. One night a drunk Richard Scott "broke out into many hideous wailing expressions about the worthy Captain Daniel Gookin, calling him an Irish Dog that was never faithful to his country, the son of a whore, a bitch, a rogue, God confound him and God rot his soul." Scott then threatened to kill Gookin. Many colonial leaders tried to restrain anti-Indian sentiment and protect the loyal Indians in their jurisdictions from those English who felt the war should be pursued against all Indians; yet they were not always successful.[9]

No doubt some of the difficulty the leaders had in restraining hostility toward loyal Indians resulted from their simultaneous efforts to reinforce a communal sense of identity among the English. The English worked hard and made sacrifices to broaden and intensify their notion of a collective self. Puritan notions of a communal self expanded in response to an Indian threat. As historian Perry Miller has noted, a dramatic change in Puritan attitudes toward church membership occurred between the 1660s and the end of the seventeenth century. A Puritan debate over whether or not to baptize the children of non–church members caused controversy yet was eventually resolved in the Half-Way Covenant of 1662 that did allow the baptism of these children. Opponents of the Half-Way Covenant remained vocal for years after the decision. But even the compromise of the Half-Way Covenant became eclipsed by pragmatic efforts to keep church membership high when the children of the nonprofessed church members who were baptized under the doctrine of the Half-Way Covenant failed to become communicants themselves. That led to a further liberalization of church membership policies. As Perry Miller has put it, "In the 1660's a cautious, logically supported proposal to extend a partial membership to the grandchildren of the founders excited ferocious opposition; by 1700 the New England Way was little bothered with ancient scruples, and was pressing visible membership, including the precious rite of baptism, upon all who would own the external covenant." King Philip's War marked a pivotal moment in this shift, causing a flurry of covenant renewal ceremonies. Widespread communal, external covenant renewal was foreshadowed before 1675, but the shared hardship of King Philip's War crystallized it.[10]

Not only did the English inhabitants of New England renew covenants among themselves; they also justified the conflict by arguing that the enemy Indians had broken their covenants with the English. In a broadside addressed to "our Brethren and Friends the inhabitants of the colony of Massachusetts" and published on December 7, 1675, the Massachusetts Council appealed for support. Their argument hinged upon the plausibility that Indians had been subject to English laws and had broken their promises of loyalty to the colony. The council believed that such an argument would resonate with the general populace and that most English colonists would have sincerely seen Indians as having been previously engaged in covenants with the colonial government. The combination of covenant renewal among the English and the justification of the war based on Indian violations of covenants served to redefine and reinforce communal identities within New England. The English ostracized the enemy Indians while minimizing ideological differences within their own ethnic group.

As difficult to overcome as ideological differences were disputes over material resources, including land. The colonies bickered and accused one another of failing to contribute their fair share to the war effort. Long-standing boundary disputes complicated these arguments; colonies accused one another of impressing inhabitants outside of their jurisdictions to satisfy the United Colonies' conscription requirements. Massachusetts secretary Edward Rawson sent a note to Connecticut on April 7, 1676, asking that colony not to "[i]mpress any of our inhabitants that are following thiere occasions in your parts." Within colonies, too, towns as well as individuals appealed for leniency in the enforcement of conscription laws. The Massachusetts General Court received numerous requests for clemency based on hardship. James Bate of Hingham complained that he had suffered unnecessarily from the impressment of both of his sons while others in the town had sons who had not been conscripted. Thomas Eams petitioned successfully to have his horses freed from impressment because his livelihood depended upon them. Similarly, the entire militia of Woburn pleaded that the colony draft no more of that town's inhabitants into a United Colonies army for fear that the town would no longer be able to protect itself from "skulking" Indians.[11] These petitions for relief within Massachusetts undoubtedly translated into that colony's pushing other colonies to contribute more to the military effort, heightening disputes between Massachusetts and its neighbors.

Yet disputes over the material contributions and ideological differences among the various polities did not overcome the elements that bound those same groups together. The perception among them that they shared a common enemy led them to try to put their differences aside. Massachusetts's Edward Rawson referred to this sentiment in his December 7, 1675, letter to the Connecticut Council: "That wee avoyd all occasion of offense & Trouble each to other & that we strengthen each others hands in these times of Comon Dainger & Distresse is Doubtless our great duty."[12]

Best symbolizing the perception among the English that they faced a common enemy and must put aside differences among themselves to combat it is Massachusetts's abrogation of Roger Williams's banishment. On March 29, 1676, Indians attacked and burned numerous houses in Providence, Rhode Island, including that of Roger Williams. The long-smoldering political and religious rivalries between Rhode Island and Massachusetts shaped the reactions of many of the English toward news of this attack. Many saw the attack as poetic justice for Williams's transgressions. Despite such smugness, the English of Massachusetts identified with Williams's plight and felt sympathy for him. The poet Benjamin Thompson expressed in verse the common view that for all of the acrimonious disputes between Massachusetts and Rhode Island, and despite the latter's efforts to escape the rule of the former, they could not avoid their divinely ordained fate. Rhode Islanders might have been "Out of the reach of Lawes but not of God, / Since they have felt the smart of common rod." For Massachusetts, the belief that they suffered at the hands of a common enemy with Rhode Island made religious principles less of a priority, and the colony rescinded Roger Williams's thirty-nine-year banishment so that he could seek refuge in the Bay Colony. They did so "out of compassion to him" and because he "hath served the English interest" in his past dealings with Indians.[13]

The perception among diverse groups of English colonists that they shared a common identity and faced a common threat from a culturally inferior opponent sustained their motivation to the point where surrender seemed incomprehensible. Unlike many Indians who debated which side to join when the conflict first began, no group of English colonists remotely considered actively joining the rebellion. Neutrality, pacifism, and vocal opposition to the scope and scale of the war were as close as any came to supporting it. As the war progressed in its first half and began to favor Philip, still no group of English colonists considered surrendering, fleeing their colonies, or subjugating themselves to rebel Indians. English colonists living under Indian rule was beyond their conception of the possible. Believing that they were God's chosen people and superior to Indians, the colonists assumed that the divine hand of providence would eventually deliver them from their troubles. The cultural gap in their minds between Indian savagery and English civilization, as well as a shared history, religion, and language, bonded the English together and boosted their faith that they would eventually prevail. Their will to fight hardly faltered; it weathered intraethnic factionalism.

RELATIVE TO the English, the rebels had weak motivation; it is best understood through an analysis of Indian political and military culture. Aside from a few isolated English individuals who had abandoned their brethren to join Indian communities before the outbreak of the war, all rebels were of Indian descent. Yet shared ethnicity did not bond these Indians as strongly as it did their English counterparts. The diversity among southern New England's Indians made it difficult to cultivate a common identity. They spoke a variety of languages and could not have even had a common conception of themselves as "Indians" before their relatively recent encounter with Europeans. Unlike the overwhelming majority of the English, who believed that if they had to fight it must be against Philip, many Indians could imagine joining either side. Many had initially joined the fray only because they did not see neutrality as a valid option, and relatively little sustained them in their drive to fight.

Daniel Gookin, who had interacted heavily with praying Indians during the war, captured this ambivalence when he tried to justify why some of these Indians had joined the rebellion. In choosing sides, they were "inclined . . . of two evils to choose the least." In relaying this observation, Gookin aimed a sharp attack at the general anti-Indian sentiment that spread through Massachusetts as the war progressed. He believed that without the transgressions of justice committed against loyal Indians, no praying Indians would have joined the enemy. Gookin underlined the sensibility of those praying Indians who joined Philip's cause when he argued that "perhaps if Englishmen, and good Christians too, had been in their case and under like temptations, possibly they might have done as they did." As it turned out, the rebels were able to capitalize on the mistreatment of Christian Indians during the war to persuade many of them to join their cause nominally, even if they would not have been inclined to do so previously.[14]

Months of wartime hardship weakened what little resolve many Indians had to support Philip. Late in the war, a Christian Indian sent among the enemy as a spy, James Quannuponkit, testified before the Massachusetts Council about the ambivalent commitment felt by many of Philip's troops. Quannuponkit identified two in particular, Wuttusacomponum and his eldest son Nehemiah, who had been taken from the praying town of Hassanemesit. Although these individuals were captured praying Indians, they also disliked the idea of staying with the English for fear of confinement with the other praying Indians on Deer Island in Boston Harbor. Having spent some time "among those wicked Indians," Wuttusacomponum and Nehemiah "greatly desired to be among the praying Indians and English again." Nehemiah told Quannuponkit that he "never had or would fight against the English."[15] These Indians had unwillingly found themselves caught in the cross fire and either joined or allowed themselves to be taken by Philip's supporters without forcible resistance. Realizing they felt little loyalty to the rebellion, they sought to return to their fellow Christian Indians and the English.

Christian Indians were not the only rebels who felt an uncertain commitment to Philip's cause. Mary Rowlandson's captivity narrative offers historians another look at the internal workings of the insurrection during the period of its greatest military success in winter 1676. During Rowlandson's captivity, when her captors' confidence seemingly should have been reinforced by accomplishments in the field, some Indians wavered and looked for a way out of the conflict. Rowlandson spent time with some of the most ardent rebels, including Philip himself, yet she could report, "In my travels an Indian came to me and told me if I were willing, he and his squaw would run away and go home along with me."[16] This Indian, even though he associated with impassioned rebels, did not see the war as worth fighting and was willing to surrender at a time when the course of the war favored his side.

Others who witnessed deliberation within the insurrection were representatives sent to negotiate for the emancipation of captives. In early April 1676, the praying Indian Tom Dublot, alias Nepponit, met with Philip and others to negotiate the release of Mary Rowlandson. Upon returning to the English, Nepponit reported that the issue of how to treat prisoners had caused deep divisions among the rebellion's leadership. Daniel Gookin relayed Nepponit's findings of a disagreement between two groups of enemy forces. On the one hand, Philip and "some others of the enemy's chief men . . . were utterly against treating with the English or surrendering the captives." On the other, "some other of their principal sachems" favored "a reconciliation with the English, [and] thought that their compliance with the English about surrendering the captives (especially being well paid for their redemption) would mollify the Englishmen's minds in order to a peace."[17] The issue of captives drove a wedge between ardent rebels and those hoping to reconcile their differences with the colonies.

Gookin realized that this internal dispute "had no small influence into the abatement of the enemy's violence and our troubles." In part, he argued, "[t]his contest about the treaty [concerning captives], caused them to fall out and divide."[18] Gookin astutely observed that Philip's cause faltered because many in its ranks lost their will to fight and not because of English military superiority and success. He also reminded his readers that until this time rebel attacks had been "frequent and violent" and "they made daily incursions upon us."[19] The enemy had the power and the means to wage effective war against the English and their Indian allies, but they began to lose their commitment to do so.

Some Indians had no desire to fight the English, but the war and the more hostile members in their group prevented them from communicating their intentions. Two praying Indians, Anthony and James, reported to the Massachusetts Council that some Nipmucks in central Massachusetts had loyal intentions toward the English, but other Nipmucks prevented them from reaching any colonists. Similarly, the praying Indian

Peter Ephraim, acting as the English emissary to some Narragansetts in the spring of 1676, learned that several of that group's older and more prominent sachems "desired peace." When asked about their involvement in the war, these Narragansett elders blamed it on the younger leadership. They portrayed themselves as consistently unwilling accomplices to those with rebellious inclinations.[20] These Narragansetts and Nipmucks had no desire to fight the English, despite their association with rebels.

SOME INDIANS chose to surrender to the English only because it appeared a more attractive alternative than captivity with the Mohawks. Many Indians of southern New England had a long history of warfare with Mohawks who waged "mourning wars" in search of captives. Before the war, many southern New England Indians had viewed subjecting themselves politically to the English as a way to shelter themselves from the Mohawks. Surrendering to the English during King Philip's War continued this tradition under harsher circumstances.

A major goal in warfare for the Iroquois, including the Mohawks, was to gain live captives, whom they either tortured to death, adopted, or eventually ransomed. Historian Daniel K. Richter has superbly contextualized the Iroquois practice of fighting to acquire captives, rendering it comprehensible at least through the eyes of the Iroquois. But that context would have offered little consolation to the southern New England Algonquians who were prospective victims; the English treatment of captives probably appeared more humane than that of the Mohawks. Increase Mather heard from an Englishman formerly held captive that they "would not suffer any fires to be made in the night, for fear lest the Mohawgs should thereby discern where they were." Mather logically interpreted this fear of the Mohawks as "a great reason why many of them have, of late been desirous to submit themselves to the English."[21] Surrendering to the English during wartime, like submitting to them politically during times of peace, provided New England's Indians a means of sheltering themselves from the Iroquois mourning wars. Facing a two-front war, Philip's forces had to reassess their desire to continue the struggle. For many, the risks of fighting outweighed the rewards, and they either surrendered to the English or fled the region.

Unfortunately, more is known about Mohawk motives to fight than those of the southern New England Algonquians, especially when it comes to the goals of the Indian rebels in the latter parts of the war. The encampment at Peskeompscut that fell victim to Capt. William Turner's men in May 1676 provides a tantalizing clue about their aims and conceptions of victory and defeat. In the Connecticut Valley, Indian attacks against English settlements had virtually ceased after mid-March 1676; the area saw relative peace for two months excepting a few minor cattle raids. English intelligence reports had suggested that the encampment was vulnerable to attack and that the Indians there lacked the heightened alert expected among Englishmen during time of war. They were focused not on war but on catching and drying fish and planting crops.

Why, at the peak of their success, did these Indians at Peskeompscut seem to lose interest in waging war? Their inaction can be explained largely by the ways in which their conception of warfare contrasted with that of their European opponents. Unlike their opponents, these fighters did not see warfare as a continual struggle to complete victory evidenced by the unconditional surrender of their opponent. Their tactics had changed since the low-casualty affairs that typified Indian warfare in earlier centuries, but their conception of victory and defeat had not. A military history of quick raids with limited goals colored their motives in 1676. These Indians between Deerfield and Hatfield, although still capable of fighting, lacked the will. For them, the state of affairs that spring did not warrant more fighting.[22] For the English and their Indian supporters, however, this simply presented an opportunity for an annihilating victory against cultural subordinates, and on May 18, 1676, Turner's force wreaked vengeance against the camp, killing hundreds.

Peskeompscut, combined with the Avery and Denison campaigns in the Narragansett territory, proved pivotal in turning the tide of the war. They lifted spirits among the English in the Connecticut River Valley by virtue of their decisive blows against rebel Indians, and they also signified an overall shift in English tactics. They undoubtedly pleased Plymouth's Benjamin Church. Church had championed the English utilization and reliance on Indian allies since the war's first skirmishes. The story of Church and his followers from June until August 1676 exemplifies the war's final phase, and we know far more about the particulars of Church's campaigns than any others, because he was the quintessential self-promoter. With the help of his son Thomas, Church provided one of the war's most famous accounts: *The Entertaining History of King Philip's War* [1716]. Although much in his text has to be taken with a grain of salt, some of its main themes are in keeping with patterns in other parts of New England. Church, having returned to the war after a six-month sabbatical, led his forces in mopping up an enemy that for the most part had lost its will to fight. Indians surrendered to Church's forces in droves in June, July, and August. Many of those who submitted soon found themselves fighting on the side of the English. Church's lenient acceptance of Indian captives had the backing of the colonial leadership, because on June 19 the Massachusetts general court had declared that rebel Indians could surrender to English mercy.[23] For many Indians, seeing their one-time allies fighting with Church's forces—and knowing that those who did not surrender might face the same fate as those at Peskeompscut—made surrender appear as a palatable alternative, furthering the decline in their will to fight.

Early in the summer of 1676, the English circulated written notices asking Indians to accept the mercy of English justice. Shortly thereafter, the Indian James Printer—a servant who had been instrumental in helping John Eliot publish his Indian-language Bible yet fled to the enemy once the war began—turned himself in, having read the announcement. Through the literate James Printer, many Indians learned of the English offer of "mercy." It is important to note the technical difference that the English recognized between the offer of surrendering to "mercy" and surrendering to "quarter." The English, in offering "mercy" to those who came in, by no means intended a general amnesty; they reserved the right to judge each case individually. Following their traditional rules of war, the English also felt that, having offered mercy, they could prosecute the war more vigorously against those who did not surrender. It seems entirely possible, if not probable, that James Printer was unaware of the technical meaning of "mercy" under English rules of war. Printer's possible misunderstanding of the announcement would have heightened the belief among many that surrendering was an attractive alternative to fighting.[24]

Sure enough, "[n]ot long after [the offer of mercy] many of them came and offered themselves, to the Number of near two hundred." Officials quickly sorted out the new captives by degree of complicity in the rebellion. They forced some of the Nipmucks to prove their loyalty by executing their leader Matoonas. Others faced Caribbean slavery or indentured servitude within New England. Some Indians sought out Church's force before surrendering to it. Several of these Indians, in particular William

Wannukhow, Joseph Wannuckhow, and John Appamatahquoon, petitioned the Massachusetts Court of Assistants to keep the promise that they believed the colony had made of "life and liberty unto such of your enemies as did come in and submit themselves to your mercy." They conceded that they were among the enemy but claimed to have had only a passive role in the rebellion: "If it should be said that we are known to be notorious in doing mischief to the English, we answer none can so say in truth & prove any such thing against us." Even if they had been active accomplices in rebel attacks, these Indians believed that should have no bearing on their treatment, because "depredations and slaughter in war are not chargable upon particular persons, especially such as have submitted themselves to your honors upon promises of live as we have done." Whether the Indians produced this document themselves or had someone help them, it reflects an effort to play upon the English distinction between military and civilian jurisdictions. The writers hoped that the Indians would be viewed as soldiers under the rules of war rather than as murderers under the rules of the state.[25]

Those who did not learn of the English announcement of "mercy" often found themselves fighting former allies, which was in itself a powerful indication that surrendering was a viable option. Comprised of 60 English and 140 Indians, Benjamin Church's force included a large number of non-Christian Wampanoags, suggesting that neither faith nor tribe necessarily determined the treatment of Indians.[26] In his diary, Church says that he followed his government's orders to grant "quarter"—the technical term for allowing prisoners to live—to all that peaceably surrendered to him except for prominent leaders and "some particular and noted murderers."[27]

Church's heavy reliance on Indians produced results, and his unit enjoyed remarkable success. The Puritan minister Thomas Walley praised his achievements in a letter to John Cotton: "I am glad of the success Benjamin Church that it is the good fruit of the coming in of Indians to us, those that come in are conquered and help to conquer others. To observe throughout the land where Indians are employed there hath been the greatest success if not the only success which is a humbling providence of God that we have so much need of them and cannot do our work with out them." Church's unit was only the most prominent of many with English leadership that utilized the techniques and combatants proven effective in the first half of the war. The pervasive change in tactics prompted John Eliot to write in the aftermath of the war to Robert Boyle that "God pleased to show us the vanity of our military skill, in managing our arms, after the European mode. Now we are glad to learn the skulking way of war."[28]

Church's return to combat after a six-month hiatus began with one of the war's most colorful recorded encounters. Traveling around Cape Cod on a mission to recruit his fighting force, Church stumbled upon several Saconets, a band led by Awashunkes and hostile to the English. In the past Church and Awashunkes had been friends, and on the eve of war he had lobbied unsuccessfully for her help in suppressing rebel Indians. Sensing an opportunity to sway the once intransigent Awashunkes to his side, Church arranged to meet her on her terms. Alone, he journeyed into her camp, surrounded by Saconet soldiers. After sharing some rum with Church, Awashunkes offered to abandon Philip's cause and help Plymouth to suppress it. One of her leading military men promised "Philip's head before Indian corn be ripe." Church, of course, had no problem with this, but he needed the Plymouth leadership to grant her amnesty. She sent her son, Peter, to petition the Plymouth court for an alliance. Although these Saconets had admitted fleeing from the English and acknowledged that they may have burned some English houses at the outbreak of the war, they also claimed that they "had not bin active in fighting with the English." With the Plymouth court demanding evidence of their loyalty, the men in the band offered to fight alongside United Colonies forces as long as the English allowed the women and children to live securely on their lands at Saconet. Benjamin Church, who had a long history of contact with Awashunkes, vouched that the Saconets were not resolute in their attachment to Philip's rebellion, and it is likely that his intercession tempered the actions of the Plymouth Court.[29] Despite the misgivings of some, Church soon had Awashunkes' warriors under his leadership with colonial approval.

Meanwhile, as Church made his preparations for war, forces to the north and west of Plymouth softened the enemy he would soon face, driving them in his direction. Maj. John Talcott led a mixed force of Connecticut volunteers and Indians on far-flung campaigns from western Massachusetts to the Narragansett country. Traveling in the area around Hadley throughout June, Talcott's men found only minor skirmishes. It seems that following a string of defeats, Indians were fleeing the region. Many of these Indians headed in the direction of homes they had earlier abandoned. This sent Narragansetts into Rhode Island and Philip and other Wampanoags into Plymouth.

Under orders from the Connecticut leadership, Talcott led his forces into northern Rhode Island. The large number of Mohegans in the expedition undoubtedly sought to advance their cause against their Narragansett rivals. Connecticut, too, had ulterior motives beyond simply ending the war, having long disputed its boundary with Rhode Island. The Narragansetts, with their submission to Rhode Island and the king of England in 1644, provided their home colony with leverage in its dispute with Connecticut. In conquering the Narragansetts, Connecticut stood to pull the rug out from under Rhode Island's claim to some of the most fertile real estate in New England. The Narragansetts were so integral to the internal workings of New England that their defeat or decimation would effectively destroy the scaffolding upon which the region's political institutions had been built.

With such high stakes, Talcott struck the Narragansetts as hard as the collective conscience of his mixed force allowed. On July 2, 1676, they surprised a large encampment of Narragansetts near a swamp. Comprising mostly nonsoldiers, the encampment resisted only mildly. Such weakness did not prevent Talcott's men from wreaking vengeance. They knew that on June 19 the Massachusetts General Court had offered "mercy" to those who surrendered. Given that these Indians were in Rhode Island rather than before officials in Boston, they could technically be interpreted as still in a state of flight. After three hours 126 Narragansetts were dead, including 34 men and 137 women and children. Mohegans loyal to Talcott seem to have had a role in convincing him to grant the lives of 45 Indian women and children. The attack made future Narragansett participation in the war negligible. Events of that day also set the framework for a bitter dispute between Connecticut and Rhode Island, because the campaign took place in violation of a Rhode Island decree that no United Colonies forces were allowed within the territory. Rhode Islanders knew that a Narragansett defeat would threaten their own political existence.[30]

Wampanoag resistance to the English and their Indian allies also faced its final moments in July and August. Two forces, under the leadership of William Bradford and Benjamin Church, respectively, pursued the remains of the rebel Indian forces who had returned to their corner of New England after months of flight and hardship. Although these Indians had returned to their homeland and had apparently given up prosecuting the war in other parts of the region, they also displayed a reluctance to surrender; indeed, they put tremendous effort into avoiding detection by the English and Indians hostile to them, leading to a game of cat and mouse. Nevertheless, Bradford's forces succeeded in inflicting high casualties on Indians who presented little threat to western Plymouth. Intelligence reports allowed them to repulse an attack at Taunton on July 11. That same week they managed to kill dozens of Indians hiding in swamps. All of these moves had been made with the hope of encountering the elusive Philip and bringing the war to at least a symbolic end. At times Bradford's men seemed to be right on Philip's tail only to lose him.

It was Church's forces that eventually found the most sought-after Indian rebel. In July Church led his company of English and Indian volunteers, many of whom had visions of booty and profits from the sale of captives into slavery, through central and western Plymouth in search of Indian rebels. They had tremendous success, suffering almost no casualties and killing or capturing hundreds of their enemy. Church, following orders, sent most of the captives to Plymouth for trial, but he hoped they would find benevolent treatment there. Upon hearing that his leaders had sold many of them into slavery, he reportedly felt tremendous anguish.[31]

For Philip, however, Church had little sympathy. Though mercy could be accorded lackluster rebels, most committed leaders were fully prosecuted. During a chase, an Indian fighting with Benjamin Church shot and killed Philip near his home on Mount Hope Peninsula on August 12. "Thus did Divine Vengeance retaliate upon this notorious Traitor, that had against his League and Covenant risen up against the Government of Plimouth, to raise up against him one of his own People, or one that was in League with him, as he was with the English," Hubbard editorialized. Not content that Philip was simply dead, Church exacted the full measure of English law when he had the traitorous corpse beheaded and quartered. In a final act of vengeance that went beyond law, Church ordered that "forasmuch as he had caused many an Englishman's body to lie unburied and rot above ground, that not one of his bones should be buried."[32]

Philip's prominent supporter Annawon was also among those captured by Church's forces. With specific orders in his commission restricting his treatment of captives, Church relayed to them verbatim that he could "treaty and composition to receive to mercy, if [he] see reason (provided they be not Murderous Rogues, or such as have been principal Actors in those Villanies)." He was generous with his mercy insofar as he was able. He informed the captives that "their lives should all be spared, excepting Captain Annawon's and it was not in his power to promise him his life, but he must carry him to his masters at Plymouth, and he would entreat them for his life."[33] The leaders at Plymouth were not moved; Annawon was beheaded.

Shortly thereafter Church's forces captured Tuspaquin, the sachem whose land in Plymouth had ended up in John Sassamon's hands just a few years earlier. The sachem had supported Philip to the bitter end. His powers during the war were legendary among rebel Indians, who believed that "no bullet could enter him."[34] Those powers could not, however, prevent the colonists from beheading him. The armed contest for control of southern New England had come to an end in the same colony where it had begun. The rebel heads were taken to the town of Plymouth, where they remained mounted on posts as a public reminder of the fate reserved for traitors.

MUCH OF the rebels' motivation waned because surrendering or seeking refuge with other Indians outside of New England seemed like more palatable alternatives than risking one's life in combat. This was especially the case as the war progressed and it became clearer that the English would accept nothing less than complete victory. When some of Philip's forces surrendered, the effects snowballed. Those who capitulated to the English left the remaining forces weakened, and those who continued fighting found military success harder to achieve. Under such circumstances, the appeal of surrendering or fleeing New England altogether increased, leading more, in turn, to give up fighting.

Critical in facilitating surrenders in the first place was the perception that the English and their Indian allies restrained themselves in fighting the war, even though in reality they often exacted ruthless retribution. In the early stages of the war, Indians could not have conceived of surrendering to the English if they had thought they would be summarily executed. Yet many believed they could reconcile their differences with the colonies and put down their arms. Philip's supporters eventually found themselves fighting against former allies whom the English not only allowed to live but trusted to serve. In allowing at least some Indians to live and serve under them, the English bolstered their strength and simultane-

ously communicated the possibility of reconciliation to those still in rebellion.

Just how close the rebels' perceptions of English treatment of captives
came to the reality will never be known. From a twentieth-century van-
tage point, the number of Indians executed or sold into slavery by the
English is striking. It is apparent, though, that the English struggled to
dispense justice, taking into account the crimes they felt had been committed as well as pragmatic concerns. They tried to be just in the treatment of their former enemies—even restrained—when they saw utilitarian benefits. Indians fighting against the colonies fell into several
categories: (1) leaders, or "Grand Contrivers," such as prominent sachems,
whom the Puritans executed; (2) more ordinary insurrectionaries, who
killed colonists or their Indian allies in an "unsoldierly fashion"—they
faced trial for murder and, if convicted, execution; (3) those who surrendered or were captured—they were either sold into slavery or held as indentured servants; and (4) a small number of only nominal rebels, who,
having demonstrated a lack of conviction toward their cause and volun-
teering to assist colonists militarily, received immunity on their lands not
previously confiscated. In practice the categories were not rigid, but they
do help us to understand English efforts to differentiate among Philip's
supporters and to assess their degree of guilt. Examples will illustrate
the point.

On March 12, 1676, a party of Indians attacked the garrison of William
Clark, several miles south of Plymouth, and killed eleven people. The
English considered the attack an act of senseless cruelty toward defense-
less noncombatants. Four months later, colonial forces presented to the
Plymouth General Court a group of surrendered Indians, among whom
were three men accused of instigating the attack on Clark's garrison and
committing the "bloody murder of Mistris Sarah Clarke." Their confes-
sions and the accusation of an "Indian squa" prompted the Court to con-
demn the three to death, the rationale being that, "forasmuch as the
councell had before this engaged to severall Indians, desirous to come in
and tender themselves to mercye, that they should find favor in soe doe-
ing, it was fully made knowne to such Indians as were then psent that the
said engagement was to be understood with exception against such as by
murder as abovesaid had soe acted, and not against such as killed his en-
imie in the feild in a souldier like way."[35] These Indians, not operating
within the bounds of military conduct as traditionally defined, were thus

held accountable in a civil court for having committed a crime against humanity. Having demonstrated no restraint and no mercy, they deserved none. The immunities reserved for prisoners of war did not apply to these three, who were scrupulously distinguished from the others who had surrendered.

The magistrates of Massachusetts held that colony's captives to even harsher standards. When called to decide the fate of some captured Indians in September 1676, the court decided that "such of them as shall appeare to have imbrued their hands in English blood should suffer death here, and not be transported into forreigne parts."[36] Such a judgment followed the dictates of a civil rather than a military jurisdiction, as captives increasingly faced charges of murder and treason rather than receiving the immunities accorded a soldier who killed during wartime. The record is silent about Massachusetts's shift in policy, but we can theorize that the colonies and their Indian allies had a sense of certain victory in September, Philip now dead, that they had lacked in July. With the death of Philip, whose symbolic importance was perhaps as significant as his strategic skills, the English settlers undoubtedly felt they had less to fear if they treated captives harshly. A kind of vengeance that was not permissible in a military setting could find its place in a civil one.

Looking at how Massachusetts treated its own English colonists reinforces the notion that the waning of hostilities facilitated strict justice against Indians. In September 1676 two Englishmen, Stephen and Daniel Goble, hanged for their involvement in the brutal murder of six innocent Christian Indians. Earlier in the conflict, other English people who had killed Indians received only minor penalties. An angry, endangered populace threatened and sometimes succeeded in ousting those magistrates who tried to implement the letter of the law in cases involving English violence on Indians. But when danger had subsided, colonists felt more bound by their conscience to punish murderers such as the Gobles. The return to order meant a reassertion of Massachusetts civil law and authority. Just as Massachusetts magistrates could hang Englishmen for civil crimes—even if committed against Indians—so, too, could they hold Indians liable for treason rather than accord them prisoner-of-war status.[37]

Rhode Island, which had remained neutral in the war, was inundated with Indian refugees who had fled the United Colonies in search of leniency. As in the other colonies, the Rhode Island Court attempted to determine an Indian's degree of guilt before deciding his fate. In general, the court forced refugee Indians into a period of indentured servitude, limited by a vote of August 7, 1676, to a term not to exceed nine years, except for those "notorious persons duly detected or guilty, this act shall not excuse such." Indians found guilty of joining Philip's cause were ultimately disappointed in their expectations of laxer treatment, however, for they faced punishments similar to those their fellows suffered in other colonies. At Newport a court convicted and executed four Indians on August 23, 1676.[38]

The records of the town of Providence reveal much more information about Rhode Island's efforts to differentiate among Indians. Upon apprehending the Indian Chuff in August 1676, the English of Providence "cried out for Justice against him threatning themselves to kill him if the Authorities did not." Then "the Councell of War gave sentence & he was shot to Death, to the great satisfaction of the Towne universally." Officially, the council passed the sentence of death because, as the town records note, Chuff had supposedly "bene a Ring leader all the War to most of th[e] Mischiefs to our Howses & Cattell, & what English he could."[39] Such an episode smacks of vigilante justice, and there may be a kernel of truth in that characterization; yet other events of the very same week tend to complicate the analysis.

Four days after Providence inhabitants called for Chuff's death, a town committee "[v]oted that all the Indians above 12 years of age now in Towne or that shall come in shall not be suffured in but sent out of the Towne untill the Towne take further order." The next day the same committee decided that "Kewashinit & his wife & 3 children & the old man Mamanawant Titus his Fath[ ] in Law & the old Crooked Woman & the old Woman Peter the Smiths mother shall stay in the Towne about Sheapards well."[40] The obscurities of the records are significant: they offer only fleeting glimpses of the Indians who placed themselves at the mercy of the English at the close of the war, even fewer of the relationship between the Indians and the English before or during the war, and no clear explanation of what the English thought the individual Indians did during the war. Despite all of these shortcomings, the English impulse to reserve particular fates for different shades of guilt rather than holding all Indians liable for murder or treason is striking. Clearly, the English felt a sense of moral obligation to avoid wholesale slaughter or enslavement of the Indian peoples.

Connecticut and its Indian allies, the Pequots and Mohegans, had fewer rebel and refugee Indians to deal with than did the other colonies, yet their actions reveal similar patterns of categorization. "Respecting the Indians which have or shall before January next surrender themselves to mercy of this Government," the Connecticut General Court ordered on October 23, 1676:

1. That such of them as cannot be proved murtherers shall have theire lives and shall not be sould out of the Country for slaves.
2. They shall be well used in service with the English where the Councill shall dispose of them.
3. After tenn yeares service, all growne persons (viz. when sixteen yeares old) shall, upon certificate from their masters of their good service in their tenn yeares service, after service have their liberty to become so-journers or to dwell in our respective townes to worke for themselves, they observing the English fashion and lawes, which shall be as well observed to them as from them.[41]

Of the Indians who surrendered to English officials in Connecticut, the colony distributed many to those Indians who had helped put down the rebellion, most often Uncas and the Mohegans. Those captured or sur-rendered Indians who had, from the colonists' perspective, fought directly against them faced execution at the hands of the English or their Indian allies.[42] Not all Indians who had chosen to ally themselves with the rebels faced the death penalty, however, for many less actively hostile Indians surrendered under offers of amnesty and received it in the form of inden-tured servitude.

Throughout the colonies there were instances of negotiation of the fates of specific individuals. When Indians perceived that Englishmen had broken their promises concerning the treatment of those who had capitu-lated, they often appealed, which suggests that they had not completely lost hope that they could use the English legal system to their advantage. Sometimes, colonists protested on behalf of Indians. James Barker and Joseph Clarke represented the interests of two Indians, Peter and John, in a letter to the Plymouth Council. Peter and John "freely yielded them-selves" to three Englishmen in Plymouth sometime in 1676. Following this surrender, they informed the English that there were "several Indians out" that they could bring in exchange for their freedom. The English assented, but when the Indians fulfilled their part of the bargain, the En-glish "forgot their promises . . . and sold them, their wives and children with the rest." Barker and Clarke pleaded that the court "give satisfaction and justice unto those poor Indians, who take it very hard and grievous that the English should be so false as to break their words and promises."[43]

Often, Indians who were allowed to surrender would lobby for amnesty for their former colleagues. During the war colonists had recognized that allowing enemy Indians to surrender to loyal Indians might constitute an "expedient towards peace." Such a practice would usually pose little risk since many of these potential surrenders would come from those who were "unwillingly involved" with the rebellion in the first place.[44] To determine the risk of granting amnesty to some former enemies, colonial governments would listen to the lobbying efforts of their Indian allies who requested that specific surrendered individuals be put under their control. In February 1676 Ninigret was permitted to take charge of some surrenders who were in English hands on the grounds that they were his kin. Two praying Indians, Samuel and Jeremy Hide, used their good service among English forces as an inducement to gain the "release unto them [of] a prisoner now at Boston . . . these men being uncles to this young woman." This petition, as well as that of Ninigret earlier, may even have paved the way for more Indians to surrender to English forces. The acts these Indians took opened up another avenue of possible reconciliation between members of the two sides. For many rebels, the chance that they might be able to reunite with relatives, rather than being held by the English indefinitely or even sold into slavery, made surrender more appealing.[45]

It was a hot August day in 1676 when the English military leader Benjamin Church ordered Philip's corpse dragged out of a bog and carried out the punishment for treason posthumously. As an Indian executioner came forward with his hatchet and beheaded and quartered the body, the English and their Indian allies must have heard the sounds of the blade hacking at joints and ligaments as a celebratory drumbeat. Philip's head was taken to Plymouth, where it remained mounted on a pole as a stark reminder of a traitor's fate.[46] Warfare among Indians and colonists did not cease entirely in August 1676, but King Philip's War had come to an end. After fourteen months of terror, southern New England had quieted. Although conflicts to the north, in what is now New Hampshire and Maine, continued for decades, this fighting was very different from that of King Philip's War. English contemporaries usually viewed it as distinct from the Indian rebellion in southern New England. They saw the fighting to the north not as a civil insurrection but more as a frontier war. For the twentieth-century student of New England, the conflict in what is now Maine and New Hampshire serves as a useful foil that demonstrates the extent to which King Philip's was a civil war.

Northern New England's Indians were less sedentary and more fragmented than those to the south, and thus they had different relations with colonists in both peace and war. Parallels exist between New England and other parts of the Americas. In the sixteenth century, the Spanish had far different relations with the Nahuas in central Mexico than with the nomadic Chichimecs to the north. The United States had similarly contrasting relations with the relatively sedentary Cherokees in the southeast and the nonsedentary Apaches in the southwest. In both cases the more sedentary Indians pursued paths of relative accommodation that made them easier to dominate, and the more nomadic Indians fought bitterly and were far more difficult to conquer.

The Indians and the English to the north lacked the covalent relationships found in southern New England. The northern Indians had not submitted to any colonies. Colonists of southern New England even tended to scorn their English brethren in this region as "uncivilized." Moreover, the English colonists throughout New England found few parallels between their political culture and that of Indians in the north, making it difficult, if not impossible, for the two to intermesh their polities. Thus, when fighting erupted in the parts of Massachusetts that are now Maine and New Hampshire, it was punctuated by more atrocities and dragged on intermittently for many years. Northern Indians had a much stronger will to fight. Not surprisingly, contemporaries tended to view fighting to the north as distinct from King Philip's War.

Despite its temporal and geographic proximity, modern historians have struggled unsuccessfully to link subsequent fighting in Maine to King Philip's War.[47] English contemporaries were not nearly so persistent in their efforts. A quick look at the content and structure of some of their earliest histories of King Philip's War reveals much about their worldviews. Richard Hutchinson entitled his account of Philip's death *The Warr in New-England Visibly Ended*. Increase Mather neglected the fighting in Maine almost entirely in his *Brief History of the War with the Indians in New England* (1676). Conflict in the north, as a nineteenth-century editor of the text noted, "is singularly slighted by our author." Benjamin Church's account of the conflict totally ignores the fighting in Maine. The only major author to document the fighting to the north, William Hubbard, did so in a way that distanced it from events to the south. Rather than weaving the events there into the main narrative of the text, Hubbard devoted a separate section to them, noting that "[b]efore the War with Philip was well ended to the Southward, there was a fresh Alarm" to the north. The war was even distinct enough to warrant a separate book by Hubbard.[48]

It was more than convenience that caused Hubbard to treat King Philip's War separately from the subsequent fighting. The central narrative thread that he found woven through the events of King Philip's War was absent in events to the north. Conflict there was not a rebellion against established authority: it was chaos. Not only had Indians in the region failed to swear loyalty to English authority as most within southern New England had, but even English colonists there lived in a state of virtual anarchy: "[I]t hath been observed of many of these scattering plantations in our borders that many were contented to live without, yea desirous to shake off all yoake of government, both sacred and civil, and so transforming themselves as much as well they could into the manners of the Indians they lived amongst." Indians in the region were at best "a strange kinde of moralized savages . . . not without some shew of a kind of religion, which no doubt but they have learned from the Prince of Darkness, (by the help of some Papist in those Parts)."[49] English living in anarchy, Indians under the influence of Catholicism. This was not a mix to which Hubbard felt a strong attachment, and to him the fighting in that area was not King Philip's War. Hubbard and others viewed the north as an uncivilized backwater. Its conflict constituted a frontier war, not a civil one.

The first treaty between colonists and the Eastern Abenakis of northern New England was drawn up in 1676, a product of wartime relations rather than peaceful society building. In the past there had been looser "agreements" between Indians and the English in the east, but, in the words of William Hubbard, "Matters of Government in those Parts being since collapsed, no Authority more than what was meerly Voluntary and Perswasive being owned, Things are brought to that miserable State." Treaties made during the "miserable state" of war proved no more effectual at maintaining peace or subduing Indians. When the Eastern Abenaki leader Mugg entered into a treaty with Massachusetts in November 1676, the document differed from those agreed to by praying Indians,

Wampanoags, Narragansetts, and other Indians in southern New England. There is no mention of submission in exchange for protection. Instead, this treaty and subsequent ones appeared to be a desperate effort on the part of the English to end fighting in the region. Arrangements were made for release of prisoners and for Indians to pay for damages to English settlements. Even more telling is that, aside from the release of some English prisoners, the Indians largely ignored the agreements. Little supports the idea that these were sincere treaties of submission, like the ones southern New England Indians had agreed to in earlier decades. A second treaty was agreed to in 1678—war had already been going on twice as long as King Philip's War in the south did—leaving the Indians victorious. They gave up nothing, whereas the English colonists were forced to abandon most of their coastal settlements in Maine.[50]

Far from submitting to the English in Massachusetts, the Eastern and Western Abenakis maintained trading ties with the French, a sure sign to the English that the region had not been completely subjected to their rule and was essentially uncivilized. Hubbard blamed the French for keeping the Abenakis well armed. But, even worse, English traders violated the prohibitions against trading with Indians in the region. Not only the Indians had avoided colonial rule, but so too had some of the region's English inhabitants.[51]

Without a structured, civilized society, as Hubbard saw it, wartime atrocities were far more common to the north than in King Philip's War. War began in the region when the infant child of an Indian leader on the Saco River, Squando, was thrown into the water and drowned by some English seamen.[52] Atrocities continued to occur. Hubbard noted that many Englishmen in the region "would kill any Indian they met." Perceptions of Indian restraint were no better: "such was their Salvage Cruelty exercised in this Place, as is not usually heard of." In a particularly gruesome example, Indians "dashed out the Brains of a poor Woman that gave suck, they nayled the young Child to the dead Body of its Mother, which was found sucking in that rueful Manner, when the People came to the Place."[53]

Given the intensity of violence in the north, it is not surprising that the region's Indians were unwilling to surrender and that the colonies had trouble getting soldiers to fight there. The Abenakis fought the English in King William's War (1688–99), Queen Anne's War (1702–13), Dummer's War (1721–25), King George's War (1745–48), and the French and Indian

War (1755–59). It is not surprising that fighting that began during King Philip's War lasted until 1678 with little benefit for the colonies. Nor is it surprising that most colonists were reluctant to participate in what seemed at the time like a far-flung frontier war.

Massachusetts used the other colonies' membership in the United Colonies as a lever in trying to obtain their assistance. In a letter to the Connecticut Council, Massachusetts complained about that colony's resistance to sending troops to what is now Maine, claiming that Connecticut, unlike many other English colonies in North America, was bound by covenant to do so. Responding to a similar request from Massachusetts, made almost a year after the death of Philip for military support in what is now Maine, the Plymouth General Court grudgingly complied. At first Plymouth hesitated, it "being questionable whether those places be within limits of confederation." Moreover, Plymouth's court believed that "those Indians have been greatly abused and provoked [by the English of Massachusetts] to take arms." In the end, however, a shared sense of community among the English as well as Plymouth's gratitude for the past assistance of Massachusetts prevailed; Plymouth reluctantly opted to participate in "the defense of the common English Interest against so barbarous an enemy."[54] Even then, many of the soldiers who fought in this and future wars to the north were Indians, who, severely weakened by King Philip's War, were "mercenaries in all but name."[55] Colonial leaders did not display the hesitation about arming Indians in these wars that they did in King Philip's War, partly because of the distant, frontier nature of these conflicts. When New Englanders faced civil war in their own neighborhood, the leaders were far more willing to commit troops, and they wanted soldiers they trusted. Contemporaries viewed the wars to the north as separate from King Philip's War. Recognizing the civil component of Philip's rebellion renders the distinction comprehensible to us in the twentieth century.

The defeat of Philip's supporters did not reflect the inexorable progress of a more technologically "advanced" culture at the expense of a "primitive" one. Rather, it stemmed from the differing motives and desires of the two sides. War did not continue longer than it did because Indians who had joined Philip's rebellion saw themselves as having more attractive options than fighting. Many of them hoped to reconcile their differences with the colonies and other Indians. Southern New England's Indians and the English had, after all, a history of relative cultural compatibility. Many rebels had, in the past, seen enough similarity between English political culture and their own that they could submit to colonists without wholesale changes in their lives. In the future, however, this would prove difficult and often impossible. The war had dramatically changed the New England political landscape. The Indians who had lost their will to fight were more or less matched by the English who had lost what little willingness they had to accept Indians as members of their society.

7

LEGACIES

KING PHILIP'S War might have ended in August 1676, but its legacies dogged Indians and colonists alike for years to come. Both sides suffered tremendous loss of life and property. Contemporary estimates of casualties varied widely. Royal agent Edmund Randolph reported that 600 English men and 3,000 Indian men, women, and children had died. Nathaniel Saltonstall estimated that more than 800 English had perished. And the anonymous author of *News from New England* guessed with an air of precision that 444 English and 910 Indians had lost their lives. Statements concerning the value of English property losses also covered a wide spectrum—no one bothered committing those of the rebel Indians to writing. On one hand, Randolph stated that the English had lost houses and livestock valued at £150,000, "there having been about twelve hundred houses burnt, eight thousand head of Cattle great and small killed, and many thousand bushels of wheat, pease, and other grain burnt."[1] The United Colonies, on the other hand, claimed that they had spent more than £100,000 just fighting the war, excluding the value of property losses. If the English did indeed suffer £150,000 in property damage and spent £100,000 prosecuting the war, their total cost would have amounted to approximately £21 per household—no mean amount for the time, given that that was the equivalent of the annual salary received by the Connecticut treasurer and the deputy governor in 1676.[2]

None of these contemporary casualty figures can be accepted at face value, since they were affected by the varying motives of different individuals to exaggerate or minimize the casualty estimates. Nevertheless, through a critical and comparative reading of literary sources, demographer Sherburne F. Cook has established some valuable parameters suggestive of the dramatic toll the war took on Indians. Combined with more accurate assessments of the pre- and postwar English population, Cook's work makes it clear that New England's covalent society underwent a dramatic change. He estimated that 60 to 80 percent of Philip's supporters died, were sold into foreign slavery, or fled the region. Indians loyal to the English fared only slightly better. In 1674 Daniel Gookin estimated that Massachusetts had 1,100 praying Indians; by late 1676 he counted 567—a 48 percent decrease. Nonpraying Indians who fought Philip's forces also undoubtedly suffered losses disproportionate to those of their English counterparts. For example, the Mohegans not only contributed a larger portion of their population to putting down the rebellion than did the English of Connecticut, but they also became victims of undiscriminating Mohawk attacks when those Iroquois allied with the English.[3]

Given Cook's estimate that New England lost 60 to 80 percent of the rebel Indians, and postulating based on Gookin's observations that the war resulted in a 48 percent decrease in the population of the region's other Indians, King Philip's War resulted in the removal of between 56 and 69 percent of New England's native inhabitants. As startling as this reduction in the Indian population may be, its significance increases when juxtaposed with the concurrent increase in the number of English people living in New England. Although they lost many hundreds in the war, the victorious English population of New England, unlike their Indian enemy, did not suffer from flight and forced removal. Immunity to these sources of decline, better resistance to disease, and a high fertility rate led to a tremendous natural increase among the English; their population grew between 1670 and 1680 from about 52,000 to 68,000.[4] Against the background of this population jump, the decrease in Indian numbers in New England dramatically changed the character of the society. Whereas in 1670 Indians constituted nearly 25 percent of New England's inhabitants, by 1680 they made up only 8–12 percent.

Although Indians were far from vanishing, their severely reduced physical presence meant that they would play a more meager political role in the postwar New England society. In October 1676, the Massachusetts General Court declared a day of thanksgiving, pronouncing, "Of those severall tribes & parties that have hitherto risen up against us . . . there now scarse remaines a name or family of them in their former habitations but are either slayne, captivated or fled into remote parts of this wilderness."[5] Observers confirmed this change. A visitor to New England in 1687 reported that Indians "were few in Number. The last Wars they had with the English . . . have reduced them to a small Number, and consequently they are incapable of defending themselves."[6] The remaining inhabitants—English as well as Indian—had to adapt to this new context. King Philip's War did not merely bring to an end a generation of coexistence among New England colonists and a large number of Indians. Native Americans had played such a large role in the New England political landscape that their catastrophic decline demanded fundamental changes on the part of the region's remaining inhabitants. Returning to the covalent molecule analogy from chemistry, New England society had consisted of distinct nuclei of Indians and English bonded together. Like the chemical change wherein the oxygen atom's removal from a water molecule leaves behind hydrogen instead of smaller particles of water, the removal of a majority of the Indians from New England meant that the remaining Indians and the English colonies had to substantially transform themselves. In fighting their war, New England's Indians and English had destroyed their society.

History and people, of course, do not follow rigid laws as atoms and molecules do. But King Philip's War certainly left New England's remaining Algonquians struggling to recast their identities while either segregated into weak, scattered enclaves or isolated as individuals laboring among the English. They now faced subordination to the Mohawks of New York in a series of alliances known as the Covenant Chain. Those Algonquians who sought refuge from the war outside of New England frequently helped to form multiethnic communities with other Indians, often under the guidance of French missionaries. The English had to undergo parallel adaptations, even though they were ostensibly on the winning side. Ironically, the reduction of Indian political power in New England did not make the orthodoxy of Puritans in Massachusetts more dominant; rather, the postwar Puritans eventually became like a minority ethnic group themselves as the Crown intervened politically. The years after King Philip's War witnessed the Anglicization of the New England colonies and their greater incorporation within London's imperial system. Strategically accommodating these imperial pressures, the most prominent Puritans, such as Increase Mather and Fitz-John Winthrop, like the Indian sachems on the eve of the war, were reduced to working as brokers in a strategy of cultural self-preservation, mediating between the Crown and the New England colonies.

HISTORIANS HAVE often noted that the end of King Philip's War in 1676 seemed to correspond with the intensification of English royal efforts to rein in the New England colonies' independence. Less clear has been the role of the war in encouraging London's imperial pressures.[7] To be sure, the twenty-five years following King Philip's War witnessed repeated crises for the New England colonies. But other English colonies felt their share of royal intervention and international conflict. How, then, did King Philip's War intensify these problems or shape the quarter-century after its end?

For Massachusetts, historian Timothy Breen has argued that King Philip's War "set off a chain of events that profoundly altered the colony's political culture." He points to the extraordinary levies raised by colonial governments as a source of strained relations between previously more locally oriented communities. Whereas before the war the majority of an inhabitant's taxes went to the town, after the war taxes paid to the colony far exceeded those paid locally. The financial burdens of the war also spurred a dramatic reorganization of New England's political relations. The new tax structure challenged the status of those Englishmen who had served as "brokers" between local and centralized polities. Brokers, much like Indian sachems before the war, mediated between various polities and levels of authority. Their position and social status depended upon their "justifying to members of local communities external policies and demands, while at the same time protecting village clients from outside pressures that threaten customary patterns of life."[8] Many brokers failed to meet the challenge of the new centralized authority, leading local inhabitants to seek new men to mediate for them.

Breen has aptly characterized the complex layers of political relationships in pre- and postwar New England. Undoubtedly the increase in levies and their shift in weight from local to centralized authority strained relations within the region. This in turn led inhabitants to cast a critical eye at those who had served as brokers between their polity and others. Yet increased taxation was responsible for only part of the internal tensions. Breen's argument fails to recognize the strains on political culture caused by the severely reduced Indian presence in the region. Indians played a central role in the political structure of New England during the generation preceding the war; they could not suffer demographic catastrophe without causing sharp repercussions among those who remained.

Before the war, New England's Indian polities functioned as a stabilizing force in the relations among factions of English colonists. Many English polities legitimated their existence before the Crown and competing English factions by reference to their relationship with local Indians. Rhode Islanders, for example, could point to the Narragansetts' submission to them and the Crown to assert their right to exist as an autonomous polity. Some colonists referred to land deeds to prove that they had legally received title from Indians in return for goods or as a gift. Others relied on Indian groups as a military counterweight to those English who threatened them. Without having powerful or populous Indian groups either submit politically, deed their land, or ally with them militarily, the security and autonomy of various factions of English colonists often rested on tenuous grounds.

The war dramatically upset this balance by rendering virtually negligible the political and military power of previously potent native groups. The large, predominantly rebel groups such as the Wampanoags, the Narragansetts, and the Nipmucks lost most of their significance in shaping the political landscape among New England's English polities. On average, the region lost 60 to 80 percent of the population of these Indian groups. The natives who supported the English lost nearly 50 percent. For all of these Indians, adaptation was the key to communal survival, demonstrating that cultural change and cultural persistence were two sides of the same coin. Not only did they have to cope with their own reduced numbers, but they also had to adapt to a heightened ideological estrangement they faced at the hands of the English. Although not as politically useful to the English as they once were, many of these groups successfully struggled to survive in segregated enclaves where they recast their communal identity.[9]

King Philip's War changed the political environment within which such Indians operated. The war precipitated a tremendous shift in the attitudes of the English toward Indians, leading to greater ostracization of native peoples than ever before. Even the dean of American frontier studies, Frederick Jackson Turner, conceded that prior to King Philip's War, interaction among colonists and native inhabitants in Massachusetts did not neatly follow the stages enumerated in his frontier thesis.[10] Nor did

Turner find that a frontier even existed in the sense of a shifting border between settled territory and "free" land. Although Massachusetts towns had been designated "frontier" towns and ordered by the General Court to defend themselves militarily at times before the war, the Massachusetts government did not view them as being on the frontier in the sense that they formed the edge of settlement. Instead, the English and the Indians intermingled. After the war, however, Turner found that this had changed: the colonists came to view frontier towns as forming the single edge of a westward expanding society. He wrote, "In American thought and speech the term 'frontier' has come to mean the edge of settlement, rather than, as in Europe, the military boundary. By 1690 it was already evident that the frontier of settlement and the frontier of military defence were coinciding."[11] According to Turner, Massachusetts developed a frontier only after the conflict. The English in Massachusetts no longer viewed themselves as living or settling among the Indians to the same degree; instead, they frequently perceived a military border demarcating English settlement from wilderness and Indians.

Corroborating Turner's observance of a new frontier that segregated English from Indian settlements, historian Harry Stout has documented a profound transformation in New England Puritanism resulting from the war. The changes that Stout demonstrated served to estrange Indians ideologically in New England. In his study of ministers' unpublished sermons, Stout found that the war resulted in a "renewed corporate solidarity" among Puritans. The war confirmed ministerial predictions of divine punishment for a degenerate people, and the eventual victory validated the Puritans' perceived covenantal relationship with God as his chosen people. The war thus served to reinforce traditional beliefs and renew dedication to the New England Way.[12]

In addition to fortifying traditional beliefs, King Philip's War "had the extremely important effect of establishing New England's identity as a people of war," Stout argued. Artillery election sermons, delivered annually to local militias and their newly elected officers, took on a new tone after 1675, when ministers started encouraging their people to "chop and hack their way to the new Jerusalem over the bodies of diabolical audiences." Instead of relying on fear and guilt, ministers tried to raise the ire and confidence of their congregations. Instead of urging their audiences to look inward at their sins, they encouraged them to look outward at their enemies with an eye toward destroying them.[13]

The changes observed by Turner in the definition of the frontier and by Stout in the tone of Puritan sermons also corroborate the observations made in chapter 6 concerning English behavior. A latent cultural infrastructure became more manifest and widened the gulf between Indian and colonist during the war. Differences as great as those between Roger Williams and the Massachusetts leadership appeared smaller to the parties involved as the successes of their shared enemy grew. Despite frequent colonial efforts to differentiate among Indians according to their involvement with the rebellion, many of the English began to presume that all Indians had associated with the enemy. Debates among English leaders in spring 1676 had foreshadowed this shift in attitude. In March of that year, when the rebellion was at its zenith, the Massachusetts leadership considered building an eight-foot-high wall stretching twelve miles from the head of the Charles River north to the town of Billerica. The establishment of this wall, in addition to being costly, would have meant conceding a number of towns in central Massachusetts to the rebel forces. Although colonial officials never implemented the plan, largely because of objections from those English who would have ended up on the rebel Indian side of the wall, its contemplation reveals the seeds of a new frontier mentality among the English. Indians and the English would in the future have a starker mental border between them. This racial ostracization of Indians, combined with their physically reduced presence, meant that, even if they had not vanished, native groups had lost their prominent political role in the society.[14] The demographic collapse of Indians and their estrangement by the English forced both them and the English to adapt to a new world.

THE INDIANS took multiple and diverse paths after the war, and no single one qualifies as typical. Yet the experiences of most, if put within several categories and subcategories, are traceable with broad brush strokes. On one hand were Indians who remained within the bounds of New England after the war. This first category can be further broken down into groups of nonpraying and praying Indians, as well as individuals working among the English. On the other hand were Indians who either left or remained outside of New England after the war. These included Algonquian refugees and slaves and the relatively powerful groups of Iroquois.

Of the Algonquians who chose to stay within New England, those few nonpraying Indians who continued to live on their own near the English found their actions more tightly restricted. Some found themselves judged according to English norms and values; others had to sacrifice valuable land resources just to maintain what meager autonomy they had. Whereas praying Indians had long lived under the censorious eye of colonial officials, nonpraying Indians had had a large measure of independence before the war. The war resulted in the loss of much of this independence. Even the prominent Indian sachem Awashunkes, who wielded enough power during the war that the English allowed her to switch sides with impunity, had to answer to English authorities for violating their norms in her interpersonal relations with other Indians. In 1683, for example, Plymouth court called Awashunkes to answer the charge of helping her daughter commit infanticide. Awashunkes avoided indictment, but her appearance before the court in 1683 signals her final appearance in the historical record, suggesting that she had lost most of her influence before the English on behalf of Indians.[15]

Awashunkes' fate was only one of many signs that nonpraying Indians within New England had lost much of their autonomy. Other prominent groups, such as the Mohegans under Uncas and the Eastern Niantics under Ninigret, also had their actions severely circumscribed in the postwar environment. Uncas had made a career of spreading fears among the English of other Indians, especially the powerful Narragansetts, in order to consolidate his position among the Mohegans and their tributaries.[16] Because the Narragansett population had suffered at least as much decline as any other group in New England, Uncas lost one of his most powerful tools in the preservation of his group. No longer did the conquered Narragansetts pose the clear threat to the English that they did before and during the war. Uncas could no longer play them off the English.

Facing this predicament, Uncas and his heirs fell back on a policy of granting land to the English in order to enforce their claims to leadership over the Indians living on it. On February 29, 1676, Uncas's son Joshua willed a tract of land to a number of Connecticut English settlers. As part of the agreement, he stipulated that "those Indians that have lately lived or Planted some part of this Land should not Plant there any more but that they should live under my father Uncas."[17] In the short run, such a policy worked to preserve the depleted Mohegans as a political unit. In the long run, however, their land—and their bargaining power—was eventually exhausted.

Another group of non-Christian Indians, under the Eastern Niantic sachem Ninigret, resided near the present-day towns of Charlestown and Westerly, Rhode Island.[18] This Indian community, which was composed of the remnants of previously autonomous groups, contained primarily Eastern Niantics and Narragansetts, but it also had some Wampanoag, Nipmuck, and Pequot refugees. It managed to survive for two main reasons. First, the Eastern Niantic sachem Ninigret, under whose leadership these Indians coalesced, had only moderately supported the colonies during the war, sparing his people much of the devastation that others had faced. Second, the community occupied land that the English competed for among themselves. For this reason they found a temporary respite from the pressures of expanding English settlements. Rhode Island, Connecticut, and the private Atherton Company of Massachusetts all claimed title to this land, and in their squabbles, no one of them was willing to let another occupy it. Within this context the Indians near Charlestown and Westerly held onto the land into the eighteenth century.

Although these Indians had found a temporary "oasis" from English expansion, the process of cultural adaptation to the postwar world was still a dramatic and tumultuous one. The primary problem facing them was how to define their disparate community. Bonds of kinship—biological or metaphorical—linked many of these Indians, but their wartime history threatened to disunite them. Some members of the community belonged to the Wampanoags, who were at the forefront of the war effort; some were Narragansetts, who had to be prodded to join it; and others, such as the Eastern Niantics, had tended to favor the colonies and their Indian allies. Reconciling these differences required significant adjustment. One step in this direction seems to have been their gradual adoption of the label "Narragansetts" in their dealing with others. Although Eastern Niantics formed the main foundation of the community, "Narragansett," for reasons to be illuminated later in this chapter, provided a more effective collective ancestry in their struggle to preserve their weakened yet still semiseparate existence as Indians. It is these Indians whose descendants today are called Narragansetts.[19]

The power wielded by these Narragansetts bore little resemblance to that of the prewar entity. By 1709 they had quitclaimed their land to the Rhode Island government, and more than ever their internal affairs came to be controlled by the colonial legislature. By 1713 the English missionary Experience Mayhew found many of these Indians impoverished and relying on wages from English employers to pay their debts and survive. In

1723 their leader, Ninigret II, died, reportedly of an alcohol overdose. That same year, another missionary estimated that only two hundred Indians lived in Narragansett country. Under these circumstances, English missionaries began to have their first major successes in converting the Indians living within Rhode Island.[20] Weakened and desperately seeking rejuvenation, the Narragansetts proved a receptive audience.

EVEN THE praying Indians, most of whom had opposed the rebellion, were adversely affected by the war. The largest share of them were left devastated and largely alienated as groups from English politics. After the conflict, most of the Christian Indians from Hassanemesit, Salem, Groton, and Wamesit settled with the Indian community at Natick. Despite this consolidation, a census taken by two English ministers in 1698 showed Natick as having roughly the same number of Indian inhabitants as it did in 1674. The consolidation that had barely plateaued the number of Indians living at Natick probably served to weaken that community's political resolve. Made up of diverse Indians, Natick had, in the words of one historian, "too many groups, with conflicting allegiances, and no traditional connection to the lands on which they settled." The heterogeneity of the community allowed it to survive, but it also left it drifting aimlessly.[21]

Not only had the population and political unity of Massachusetts's praying Indians dropped substantially, but they also lost many of their ties to the English communities. John Eliot's missionary work ground to a virtual halt after the war. In his absence, the Natick community's church declined. Any successes that the English missionaries had had in encouraging these Indians to adopt English agrarian ways had apparently faded. Eliot, who had in the past contended that Natick Indians had adopted English agricultural methods, noted in 1684 the use of "places of fishing, hunting, gathering chestnuts, in their seasons." Under these circumstances, in the words of one historian, "alone with little provincial attention or assistance," the praying Indians became "a separate community."[22] They had actually become more autonomous after the war.

Praying and nonpraying Indian communities shared similar problems. In the postwar world, both often consisted of a mixture of individuals who had previously fought against one another. Just as the Indians under Eastern Niantic leadership in Rhode Island had to reconcile their various memories of the war in order to reconstitute their identity, so, too, did the

Indians living in praying communities. The praying towns now contained members who, although perhaps united by either biological or metaphorical kinship, did not share the same wartime history. At the outbreak of the conflict, some praying Indians had fled to participate in the rebellion and then rejoined the Christian Indians once defeated. Other Indians living with the praying Indians after the war had been with Philip's forces from the outset, only to seek refuge among relatives as the tide of the war turned against them. Reconciling differences among these various Indians made recasting community identity necessary but difficult. Over time, Indians who had supported both sides coalesced around a newly heightened sense of pan-Indian cultural heritage.

Christian Indians, in particular, faced a major hurdle in their creation of a communal Indian ancestry distinct from that of the English. Before their adoption of Christianity, origin myths had had a pivotal role in grounding group identity. Yet under the guidance of English missionaries, they had largely replaced their "traditional" creation myth in favor of that of Christianity. Unlike nonpraying Indians, praying Indians now believed they shared the same origins as the people from whom they distinguished themselves. Believing in Christianity's creation myth, yet recognizing their distinctness from the English as a group, the praying Indians gradually transformed the way in which they grounded their communal identity. Legend, rather than origin myth, played a more important role in their self-definition. This change required not only a cosmological shift but also a revision of their wartime history.

Anthropologist William Simmons has compiled a collection of New England Indian folklore recorded between 1620 and 1984 with the aim of understanding and conveying these natives' "spirit." In his study he found a preponderance of legend and memorate and a nearly total absence of myth. Myths "are thought to be truthful accounts of what happened in the earliest possible time; they account for basic creation, are sacred, and provide the authority for existing social institutions, religious beliefs, and ritual. . . . One dominant interpretation is that myth reinforces the solidarity and identity of the group." Myths differ from both legend and memorate. Legends "are set in real places in the recent or more distant past and pertain to culture heroes, ghosts, witches, and fairies as well as to real people." In a similar vein, memorates are personal descriptions of encounters with the supernatural.[23] Both legend and memorate are historically based and adaptable. Simmons's discovery of a preponderance of surviving legend and memorate and a near absence of myth leads him to conclude that "although early Europeans recorded bits of indigenous mythology, Christianity swept this genre away, or rather, replaced it with Christianity's own biblical equivalents."[24]

The legend and memorate of the surviving Indians within New England often posit an oppositional relationship between Indians and the English. Most notably, the Indians, even when they are most directly descended from English allies, trace their ancestry back to those who fought against the English. They believe that Philip's ghost roams the land and that they encounter him frequently.[25] Their work to put down Philip is absent from these legends. Mashpee Indians, under the influence of missionary Richard Bourne, aided the colonists in 1675, yet an Indian author has recently portrayed the group as "under Philip." That work's description of the seventeenth century pitches the Indians against the English and, like most histories of the war produced by Euramericans, focuses more on English conduct and manipulation of Indians than on native agency.[26]

One of the most famous Native American writers of the nineteenth century, William Apess, revised his people's history, perhaps unintentionally, in the interest of cultural preservation. As noted in the introduction, Apess's work simultaneously displayed loyalty to a Pequot and a pan-Indian cultural heritage. The Pequots, it will be remembered, were one of the Indian groups most hostile to the rebellion. Apess's writing, however, portrayed them as part of a pan-Indian resistance movement. Apess's Philip was "King of the Pequot," not the Wampanoags, and "the greatest man that ever lived upon American shores."[27] In revising the past, Apess helped preserve a distinct Pequot identity. Since Apess was a Christian, he traced the origin of all peoples back to Adam. He could not rely on a precontact origin myth to provide a distinct communal identity for the Pequots and Native Americans as a whole. Instead he looked to a history of his people wherein they actively opposed the English.

The Indian revision of the past in order to reconstitute a communal identity simultaneously represented a resistance to a more dominant English culture and a co-optation of it. Casting themselves in opposition to the English clearly served Indian purposes of rejuvenating a communal self. Yet this opposition almost certainly received sustenance from the newly heightened ideological estrangement that Indians faced at the hands of the English after King Philip's War. Like English writers, these

Indian revisers reconceived the war as one between two incompatible peoples or races, masking any mutual assistance or cultural overlap. The Indians, too, created their own community of inquiry—a race or a people—to interpret their past and define themselves. After the war the Indians, largely excluded from the more dominant English and subsequent Anglo-American culture, found greater resonance in a revised past in which they vigorously opposed the English. Indians could thus co-opt Euramerican exclusionary practices and revisionist histories of the war to redefine themselves. They, like the Euramericans, perceived and used the war differently than its contemporaries.

MANY INDIANS who remained in New England after the war existed outside the realm of these recast praying and nonpraying communities. Most of them had close ties to the English, but their links were as individuals rather than as members of groups that wielded political influence. These individuals usually worked as servants in the homes of English colonists. Complaints from some English inhabitants regarding such Indians led Massachusetts to restrict the practice of hiring or buying Indians. On March 29, 1677, the Massachusetts General Court prohibited inhabitants in its jurisdiction from keeping "strange" Indians above the age of twelve in their homes for more than ten days without "allowance from authority."[28] The court threatened to penalize those holding such Indians with forfeiture of the individual and a £5 fine.

This law was not preventive, having been instituted in reaction to a number of individuals who had hired Indians who, in the words of the General Court, had "been in hostility against us or have lived amongst such." Three months before the court passed the law, for example, the selectmen of Hingham, Massachusetts, had tried to impose a twenty-shilling fine on one of the town's inhabitants, Nathaniel Baker, "for his entertaining a Indian or Indians contrary to a town order." In response, Baker, among others, petitioned the general court, admitting that they had Indian servants, "part of them being captives and part of them apprentices for years." They argued that they would be "of great use and advantage to your petitioners and neighbors" and in "no way prejudicial to the town or a disturbance to the public peace." Finally, they asserted that the town order prohibiting the keeping of Indian servants conflicted with the "liberty granted in every town within the three United Colonies for the inhabitants to keep Indians (Boston excepted)." In response, the

Massachusetts Council ordered the selectmen of Hingham to appear before the court and address the petitioners' complaint. It was in this context that the Massachusetts General Court sought to clarify the issue colonywide and made it illegal to keep Indian servants over the age of twelve without permission.[29]

The Massachusetts law precipitated a number of petitions from English colonists requesting approval to harbor Indians they already had. Some, like Samuel Lynde and Stephen Burton, argued that they had acquired their servants when they were under the legal age and that the Indians had grown to be "serviceable," "obedient," or "helpful." Others, such as George and Elizabeth Danson, said they had become "ancient," had worked hard their entire lives, and wanted to rest; keeping their Indian servants would allow them to live the twilight of their lives more leisurely. In responding to these requests, the Massachusetts leadership had to balance the economic incentives for allowing Indian servants against the growing fear and anti-Indian sentiment among the general populace. More often than not, it seems that they permitted petitioners to keep those Indians that they had, so long as they constituted no obvious threat to the public safety.[30]

Historians know very little about the long-term fate of these Indians, and more research needs to be done on them. In all likelihood, they were predominantly women because the gendered worldview of colonial authorities held females to be less of a military threat than males. If their sex ratio heavily favored women, it seems likely that interracial marriage, especially with African American male servants and slaves, was common. Other servants probably returned to native communities once their period of servitude expired, if they were allowed to do so. Despite the probability of frequent interracial marriage and the efforts of some Indians to return to native communities, a solid number of individuals living within white households managed to retain their Indian heritage. In 1774 an (unfortunately rare) census taken in Rhode Island showed that of the 1,481 individuals identified as Indians living within the colony, 35.5 percent resided in white households.[31]

Even without the sustenance of living in an Indian household or community, these servants apparently maintained ties to their native ancestry. Like those Indians who lived outside the realm of English settlements, they undoubtedly retained their culture by adapting it to the postwar world. Although Indian cultures persisted in New England, they no longer exerted a powerful political influence on English settler society. Their numbers had declined relative to those of the English, and they faced ostracization at the hands of the dominant culture.

OUTSIDE OF New England, various Algonquians had to undergo different kinds of cultural adaptations in the postwar world. Demographer Sherburne Cook estimated that of 11,600 Indian rebels, 2,000 left New England as refugees whereas another 1,000 faced Caribbean slavery after their capture. Of the refugees, many traveled as far as the shores of the Saint Lawrence River to join French missionary communities or to form multiethnic communities with natives displaced from other regions.[32] Many of those who joined French missions found cultural revitalization through a syncretic blend of Catholicism, the religion of other Indians, and their own beliefs.[33] A sizable number of Indians from the middle Connecticut River Valley resettled at Schaghticoke on the Hudson River in New York; some from parts of northern Massachusetts began living with the Western Abenakis in what is now northern Vermont and New Hampshire. For these Indians, merging with natives of other groups constituted a semivoluntary means of survival, analogous to the ethnogenesis in the Southeast documented by James Merrell.[34] Other Algonquian refugees bolstered Iroquois numbers less voluntarily, having been captured and adopted by them.

Some of the various Native American refugees reappeared later, conducting raids against English settlements in the Connecticut River Valley. This was especially true of those who hailed from this region or had grievances stemming from the English conduct of the war. In 1677 Indian refugees returned to the Deerfield area and raided Hatfield and Deerfield, taking prisoners back to Canada. Two historians have rightly interpreted this attack and subsequent ones in the region stretching into the eighteenth century as the outgrowth of King Philip's War. Many of the Indians of the Connecticut River Valley had close ties to the victims of Turner at Peskeompscut. Peskeompscut and the subsequent quarter-century of raiding in the Connecticut Valley were evidence of how wartime atrocity could, as many of the English warned, lead to retribution and the prolongation of hostilities.[35]

The English faced similar long-term repercussions from atrocities they committed near what is now Dover, New Hampshire. In September 1676, after Philip was dead and the English and their Indian allies were trying to mop up straggling rebels, Maj. Richard Waldron arranged to meet with local Pennacooks. Although the sachem of the group, Wanalancet, had converted to Christianity before the war began, he and his followers sought refuge in northern New England to avoid entanglement as it expanded. While they were away from their village, Capt. Samuel Moseley's renegade troops burned the abandoned settlement contrary to orders. Massachusetts's efforts to patch relations with the Pennacooks were successful to the point where, as hostilities decreased, these Indians were willing to reestablish ties with the English and agreed to rendezvous with Waldron under a flag of truce. Four hundred natives—mostly Penacooks, but including a number of Nipmucks and others who took an active part in the rebellion—met Waldron's contingent. With orders to seize all suspected of having fought against the English, but lacking the force to impose their will on such a large number of Indians, Waldron developed a ruse to capture those who had participated in the rebellion. Staging a mock fight with the Indians, Waldron's forces captured all of them after the Indians emptied their weapons in a harmless first volley. The English then "separated the peaceable from the perfidious." About half of the four hundred were sent to Boston as suspected rebels. Of those, seven or eight "known to have had their hand in the blood of the English" were executed, and the rest were sold into slavery or servitude. The remaining Indians, mostly Wanalancet's Pennacooks, were allowed to go free.[36]

Many of these Pennacooks, the victims of Moseley's atrocities and Waldron's trickery, fled to Canada, but others, under a new leader, Kancagamus, settled along the Androscoggin River in the part of Massachusetts that is now Maine. Along with some of those who managed to escape their servitude, these Indians attacked Dover in 1689. In the process they captured Waldron and tortured him to death. Not content with just Waldron's death, the Pennacooks subsequently helped Connecticut River Indians retaliate for the wrongs they had experienced, even participating in the famous 1704 attack on Deerfield.[37]

Although the raids from 1677 to 1704 in the Connecticut River Valley were an outgrowth of King Philip's War, they lacked the civil character of the original conflict. A sizable number of the Indians who originally inhabited the region were gone and could no longer bond to the remaining polities or continue to help stabilize the region. Those who eventually resettled in the region precariously played the French off the English and avoided the covalent ties typical of the prewar period. After 1676, the English considered Indian settlements along the Connecticut River, in the words of one historian, "temporary encampments of foreigners." In short, the conflict after King Philip's War resembled "frontier" warfare.[38]

Some Algonquians removed from New England had lost all power to influence the region's history. As discussed earlier, English soldiers often sold captured Indians into Bermudan and West Indian slavery. The fate of these laborers is even less well understood by historians than that of the household servants in New England. Scholars have found little evidence of overt Indian identity on the islands where these natives lived. It is also unclear how southern New England Algonquian identity, if it was asserted, would manifest itself in these former British Caribbean colonies. Today's pan-Indian culture in the United States draws heavily on elements that in the past were specific to residents of the plains and foreign to New England. There is little reason to expect such manifestations of Indian heritage in Bermuda and the West Indies, since those islands' history followed a unique path with few, if any, ties to the plains. Complicating efforts to understand the fate of Indian slave descendants, the Colonial Records of Bermuda fail to distinguish between Africans and Indians after the seventeenth century. Nevertheless, many Bermudans, especially those living on Saint David Island, hold, at the very least, in the words of historian Ethel Boissevain, "weak or confused ideas of their tribal ancestry."[39]

Not all Indian participants in King Philip's War who found themselves outside of New England after the conflict experienced a reduction of their political power. The Iroquois of New York—especially the Mohawks—had intervened in favor of the English and their Indian allies. Their intervention bolstered their population with Algonquian adoptees, and it also allowed them to rise to prominence in the colony of New York. Historian Daniel K. Richter has argued that the results of King Philip's War "could not have been more favorable to the Iroquois."[40]

During the twilight of the conflict, the Mohawks and New York governor Edmund Andros had forged an alliance that turned out to be the seed of the Covenant Chain, a series of English-Indian alliances that made the Iroquois and New England colonists symbolic equals under the leadership of New York. In 1677 Andros brought the Mohawks and the New England colonies into negotiations under his supervision. At these talks the New England colonies abrogated any rights they had had to treat with the Iroquois independent of New York. Future discussions were to be held at Albany with Andros present. Within the Covenant Chain, southern New England Algonquians lost even more than did the New England colonists. The Covenant Chain hierarchy deprived them of any autonomy and reciprocity that they had previously had in their relations with the Iroquois and the English. From now on they were theoretically subordinate to the New England colonies or to the Mohawks, who were in turn equals under New York. The ascendancy of the Iroquois continued into the 1680s as Andros became the governor of the Dominion of New England.[41]

The rise of the Mohawks exemplifies the diversity of fates that befell Indians following their defeat. It also highlights the need for all groups affected by the war to change after it. These Iroquois had to adapt to a new postwar world by absorbing captives and refugees into their communities and exercising their new power as intermediaries between other Indians and English colonists. The removal of 56–69 percent of the Indians from New England also required more significant cultural adaptation both for those who left and for those who remained. Southern New England Algonquians had to recast their identities, some as members of weak and segregated Algonquian enclaves, others as new residents of non-Algonquian communities. The most remarkable legacy for all of these Indians in the wake of Philip's defeat has been their resiliency and ability to survive. Southern New England Algonquians exist in the region today, demonstrating that cultural persistence and cultural change are two sides of the same coin.[42]

CULTURAL ADAPTATION in the postwar world was also a hallmark of the victorious New England colonies. The English settlers could not face the removal of Indians as a powerful presence within the region without feeling serious repercussions. The nature of a covalent chemical bond dictates that when part of a molecule is removed, the remaining substance must dramatically transform itself. New England society, analogously, had to alter its structure following the demographic changes precipitated by King Philip's War. Before the conflict, Indians had played a prominent role in the region's politics, stabilizing various factions of the English. Their reduced physical presence in the region, combined with racial polarization of English attitudes, meant that they could no longer play this role. The English colonies underwent a dramatic political transformation as a result, culminating in their incorporation within the Dominion of New England. The point here is not that the catastrophic effects of the war on Indians played an exclusive and determinative role in shaping the postwar world of the English. To be sure, personal ambitions and changes in transatlantic commercial and social relationships during the latter part of the seventeenth century, as documented by the likes of Charles M. Andrews, Bernard Bailyn, Thomas C. Barrow, Michael G. Hall, and J. M. Sosin, were also important, if not essential. The changing tax structure documented by Timothy H. Breen also affected social relations among the English.[43] These influences, however, should not mask the tremendous impetus that New England's political transformation received from the demographic collapse of Indians.

Within the power vacuum created by the physical and ideological reduction of the Indian presence from most parts of New England, there arose heightened contests over land and political authority. The remaining English polities argued most often over four regions in particular: the Connecticut–New York boundary, the Narragansett country, Mount Hope, and the southernmost portions of what are now Maine and New Hampshire. Although disagreements over these lands were not new, the scope and frequency of the disputes reached new levels after 1676. A quick glance at the *Calendar of State Papers, Colonial Series, America and West Indies* reveals a dramatic change in how New England must have appeared from London. Between January 1673 and December 1674, thirteen documents deal with New England. During the twenty-four months between January 1677 and December 1678, twenty-seven items relate to the region. The frequency with which the Crown or its agents had their attention draw to New England more than doubled after the war.[44]

More important than the quantitative increase, however, is the change in tone and substance. During the two-year period before the war, only five of the eleven documents address disputes within New England over land or politics. Those remaining consist of fairly innocuous items such as a catalog of Harvard's graduates and narratives of the brief war with the Dutch in 1674. In contrast, the twenty-seven postwar items deal entirely with internal disputes. Moreover, the protagonists in these disputes drew on new weapons—self-inflating boasts of heroism and allegations of misconduct on the part of others in King Philip's War. Whereas previous disputes on boundaries and land tended to center around abstruse, legalistic arguments concerning titles and charters, arguments after the war hinged largely on morality plays, issues of physical and financial sacrifice, and rights of conquest.

The arguments presented to the Crown concerning New England's internal disputes immediately preceding the war rarely had their desired impact. For example, Ferdinando Gorges and Robert Mason made repeated efforts in the early 1670s for royal intervention to protect their claims to portions of what is now Maine and New Hampshire. Yet as late as February 4, 1676, the Lords of Trade and Plantations, although they conceded it "necessary to have New England more in Dependence upon his majesty," decided that they "do not suppose that to Consider New England so as to bring Them under Taxes and Impositions or to send thither a Governor to raise a fortune from Them can be of any use or service to his Majesty."[45] In the royal view, there was little benefit in making the sacrifice required to mediate disputes surrounding imaginary lines over rocky, often frozen soil of relatively little value. Rather than inserting its authority into every quarrel that arose, the Crown followed a pragmatic, largely profit-driven strategy that weighed costs against benefits when deciding whether or not to intervene.

Historian Richard Johnson has confirmed the view that imperial pressures on New England were not simply part of a grand scheme by the Crown to increase its authority—militarily or commercially—over all of its colonies. Royal authorities "might fulminate against Boston's 'Common-wealth-like' ways but their hostility could not be translated into action without more substantial incentives." Indeed, the Crown exhibited tremendous reluctance to impose its will on New England. New England, from London's perspective, had relatively little potential value compared to the colonies that produced lucrative cash crops. The English colonies in the Caribbean, meanwhile, attracted tremendous royal attention during the early 1670s. These colonies had confirmed English beliefs that the colonization of tropical climes provided the key to combating Spanish colonialism and bolstering the English economy.[46] The prosperity of the Jamaican sugar planter far outweighed that of the New England merchant. By 1700 sugar accounted for 70 percent of the value of New World exports to England. Accordingly,"the plantation office hounded Massachusetts less tenaciously than Jamaica, because Massachusetts was considered to be a less valuable colony."[47] Indeed, it is questionable whether the Crown would have intervened in New England affairs at all in the absence of the tremendous internal dissension that characterized the years immediately following King Philip's War.

New England's internal changes resulting from the war affected its ability to function. The relative political decline of Indians struck a serious blow to the region's mechanisms of land distribution and the security of title. These changes had significant repercussions for representative government and the toleration of religious dissent from Massachusetts orthodoxy. As historian Karen Ordahl Kupperman has demonstrated, where there was no basic institution of private property in land, efforts to establish English colonies in the seventeenth century failed. Furthermore, in the absence of land ownership and the economic security it fostered, religious dissent could not survive. The events in postwar New England bolster Kupperman's observations. The New England colonies were probably well enough established after the war that they did not run the risk of extinction, as Providence Island did, passing out of existence in 1641; nonetheless, they could not survive fundamental changes in the basis of land ownership without serious political and social adjustment. In the postwar years, when this basic institution, upon which colonial success depended, experienced a period of tumult and fragility, the inevitable adjustment occurred in the form of increased royal attention. Drawing again on the observations of historian Richard Johnson: "Though other issues contributed to bringing New England affairs to London's attention, none were as fundamental and persistent as those concerning the title and possession of land."[48] The Crown recognized a dysfunctional tone in the region's land disputes that signaled deep political problems and thus grudgingly acted to remedy the situation.

If royal authorities saw much less value in the land of the New England colonies than in that of the Caribbean, and since they had also failed to act upon the handful of land disputes that had been brought to their attention in the first half of the 1670s, why did they begin to assert their authority to mediate such disputes in New England following the war? Historians have recognized that the health of the mechanisms for distributing property in land affected the well-being of English colonies in the seventeenth century. They have also noted that New England's land issues eventually attracted the notice of officials in the home country. They have not, however, sufficiently recognized the changing role of the Indians within debates over land. Issues surrounding the treatment of Indians and social and political relationships with them constituted new ammunition in the salvos that the New England colonists launched at one another. Not just a new literary trope or rhetorical device designed to demonize one's opponent, the increased discussion of past relations with Indians involved a sincere debate over the previous nature of New England society and its impact on the future of the region. To the eyes of royal officials, more than cheap land was at stake; doubts about the morality of past actions and social relations among a number of the king's subjects had raised to the fore questions concerning their subservience to the Crown.

THE REDISTRIBUTION of political power resulting from the war awakened slumbering intercolonial tensions in New England. As Randall Holden and John Greene noted in their petition to the Crown in 1678, "open hostilities scarce ended but civil dissentions arose betwixt the colonies."[49] Prominent among these were contests between Rhode Island and its neighbors. Rhode Island's religious dissenters felt that their economic security, and thus their ability to worship freely, was threatened when other colonies challenged their claim to the Narragansett country. With the Narragansetts severely weakened both militarily and politically, the balance of power between Rhode Island and the United Colonies had shifted heavily in favor of the latter. Following that shift, the English Crown became Rhode Island's major source of hope in preserving its role as a refuge for religious dissenters. Rhode Islanders' claims to the Narragansett territory became tenuous as the Indians who had sold them their land and submitted to them politically lost their potency. Not only had the colonies and their Indian allies virtually destroyed the Narragansetts militarily, but in doing so they had also developed a legal claim to their territory that might resonate with the Crown. In accordance with a common interpretation of the English rules of war, the United Colonies could claim the Narragansett territory by right of conquest.

For this reason the end of the war sparked zeal on the part of those trying to get a piece of the Narragansett territory within the royally recognized boundaries of Rhode Island. As one Rhode Island historian has observed, the "destruction of the native inhabitants opened the door to English settlers in the interior west of the [Narragansett] bay, so rivalry over claims grew hotter than ever." Land-seekers from outside of Rhode Island could not make any progress dealing directly with the colony's government, so they "sought royal intervention on their behalf by every conceivable means and so began forcing the colony into frequent dealings with London."[50]

Rhode Island became involved with London because the colonies of

Connecticut, Massachusetts, and Plymouth made their own appeals to
the Crown, attempting to justify their claim to the Narragansett territory.
Connecticut, for example, made a pitch to the Crown claiming that it was
entitled to the Narragansett country by right of conquest, having assisted
in putting down Narragansett rebels. Important in this claim was the
assertion that Rhode Island's behavior before and during the war invali-
dated any rights that colony might have had to the land. The Connecticut
Council claimed on August 22, 1676, that

> sundry of the sayd people there [Rhode Island] inhabiting lived dishonor-
> able both to God, our King and nation, and more unsafe for themselves,
> rather minding gain than Godliness, whereby both his Majesty, ourselves
> and the people have been abused, and the tract or territory more exposed
> to devastation, and so is now become a *vacuum domicilium;* but this late
> merciful recovery being obtained by conquest and success of war unto
> ourselves of this Colony and our confederates,—the Council sees cause to
> declare unto all such person or persons, both English and Indians that have
> or shall pretend to any right or possession there, upon the said deserted or
> vanquished lands in that country, that all such shall make their application
> to the government of this colony.[51]

Before receiving royal approval, the Connecticut Council, in response to a
petition from some Pequots who had allied with the colonies, had already
allowed these "Indian friends liberty to hunt in the conquered lands in
the Narrogancett Country."[52]

In a message sent to the Crown in September 1677, the Connecticut
Council elaborated on the grounds for a transfer of the Narragansett country from Rhode Island to Connecticut hands. Here the colony pointed
again to perceived improprieties on the part of Rhode Island, claiming
that Rhode Island "was planted [by Englishmen] in such a dissolute, for-
lorn and heathenish manner as was both to the dishonor of God, our king
and nation, and so forlornly scituate as exposed it to ruin by the heathen."
Moreover, Rhode Island "refused or neglected to assist in the war to re-
cover it" once the Narragansetts joined Philip's forces.[53]

Rhode Island countered the claims of those colonies trying to get a
piece of the Narragansett country. A common strategy was to turn the
arguments of the land-grabbing colony on their head. When Massachusetts claimed that Rhode Island did not deserve its charter rights to the
Narragansett country because it had not played an active enough role in
putting down the rebellion, Rhode Island countered by portraying Massa-

chusetts's prosecution of the war as unjust. Two petitioners in particular, Holden and Greene of Warwick, Rhode Island, placed blame for the entire war on Massachusetts's poor treatment of Indians within its jurisdiction. According to these two men, Massachusetts had acted so egregiously that not only should their claims to Narragansett land be nullified, but the colony should also be forced to pay for the damages within Rhode Island resulting from the war.[54] In another letter, the two men constructed a syllogism in which they portrayed Connecticut as trying to "take those lands [the Narragansett country] by force from his Majesty, under pretext of conquest from those Indians."[55] By accusing their neighbors of unjustly starting the war and trying to take land directly from the king, these Rhode Islanders brought their morality and subservience to the Crown into question. In reaction to this exchange, the Lords of Trade and Plantations made one of their earliest references to the need for a general governor to mediate and prevent internal dissension in the region.[56]

Another disputed region that involved Rhode Island and vanquished Indians was the small peninsula of land jutting out into the east side of Narragansett Bay that Philip had occupied prior to the war, commonly known as Mount Hope. Rhode Island and Plymouth contested the ownership of the land. Arguments over this land did not hinge entirely upon whether or not any colony had a right to the land by virtue of conquest. Both Rhode Island and Plymouth conceded that Mount Hope had belonged to Philip, and each of them also claimed that the land lay within the bounds delineated by its patent. Thus, the debate centered around whether Philip had forfeited his claim to the land by waging an unjust war and committing treason. The commissioners of the United Colonies made this argument explicit on behalf of Plymouth when they noted that Philip had been a subject of Plymouth and had lost title to the land when he broke his covenant with the colony and rose in war against it.[57] Plymouth pinned blame for the war on Philip and maintained the justness of the colony's actions during the conflict on the grounds that Philip had committed treason.[58]

Plymouth bolstered its claim by also making a need-based appeal. The colony argued that it had suffered disproportionately during the war and had exerted greater effort in fighting it than had Rhode Island. Plymouth pointed out that the disparity between its and Rhode Island's efforts to suppress Philip appeared even greater in view of Rhode Island's greater relative wealth. Plymouth petitioners observed that Rhode Island had more fertile land and a harbor superior to anything Plymouth could claim.

Rhode Island defended its claim to Mount Hope by emphasizing its belief that the territory lay within the bounds of the colony. Moreover, in a letter from Governor Cranston to the king, Rhode Island defended its part in the war. The governor claimed that the war was between Philip and the other colonies, and thus it did not concern Rhode Islanders to a great extent. Nevertheless, Rhode Islanders contributed significantly to the war effort. In support of that claim, the governor pointed out that it was an Indian from Rhode Island who shot Philip. Finally, he pleaded for royal intervention in New England affairs to protect his colony from the tyranny of the United Colonies.[59]

Not all disputes involved the outcast colony of Rhode Island. Even in Connecticut, where most of the Indians had supported the colonies and where Indians maintained the most solid presence in the region after the conflict, long-simmering land disputes flared up with the fuel of alleged misconduct during the war. Friction quickly arose between New York on one side and Massachusetts and Connecticut on the other over the prosecution of the war. New York and these two colonies had a history of disputes, mostly over the borders separating them. With the war, however, the debate shifted to issues of mutual assistance and the justness of wartime conduct. News in London, whether accurate or not, reported that the New England leadership had mismanaged the war and allowed petty rivalries with New York to affect military decisions. One narrative published in London, in particular, questioned the wisdom of the New England leadership in not accepting the assistance of the Mohawks. The author of this account, Nathaniel Saltonstall, wrote that the "Governour of New York, would, upon request, and reasonable Proposals, freely make use of his Interest amongst that People [Mohawks]." A leading Pequot who had actively supported the colonies "seemed much to wonder that we did not carry it on; affirming that the said Mohucks were the only Persons likely to put an End to the War." This advice, "for I know not what good Reasons," was ignored by the New England colonial leadership. Saltonstall's narrative went on to inform its London audience of the pivotal role the Mohawks had played in damaging many of Philip's forces when they sought refuge in New York during the winter of 1676.[60]

After the war, New York officials more explicitly accused the New England colonies of refusing their military assistance in putting down the rebellion. In spring 1678, New York governor Edmund Andros wrote the Lords of Trade and Plantations that "Connecticut & Massachusetts [had] not accepted nor admitted proffered supplies & assistances (from New York) during their Indian War." This denial of aid appeared especially galling to Andros because "[m]utual helps in case of danger ought to be according to the exigence & each collnyes capacity to their power as one people and country." Carried to its logical end, Andros's view threatened New England's autonomy by implying the need for "His Maties asserting & regulating the militia or force of the several colonies; wch regulacion and orders to be indifferently obeyed by all for the future." In response, Connecticut and Massachusetts alleged that New Yorkers had illicitly supplied enemy Indians with arms and powder. Cast in this new framework, the disputes between New York and the New England colonies acquired greater gravity than they had when they had centered merely around the border between them. Allegations concerning relations with Indians as well as with neighboring colonies raised doubts about the ability and righteousness of those in power. Such doubts demanded closer attention on the part of royal authorities.[61]

The war and the morality of its participants even became pivotal issues outside of southern New England in contests over what are now Maine and New Hampshire. The debate over entitlement to this land had steadily smoldered since the early 1670s, with Ferdinando Gorges and Robert Mason petitioning royal authorities and regularly claiming that Massachusetts had usurped their patent rights to the region. Their arguments fell on deaf ears, however, until they bolstered their petitions with allegations that the fighting among the English and the Indians in the region could be attributed directly to the treacherous dealings of Bostonians. The Massachusetts leadership countered these allegations by putting a more positive spin on their involvement in the war. To this end they insisted that their expenditure of eight thousand pounds and numerous lives had prevented the region from coming completely under Indian control.[62] For this favor, Massachusetts argued that it deserved at least the right to the region's patent.

With the debate over Maine and New Hampshire escalating beyond the location of fence lines and into the realm of blame for a bloody war, the Lords of Trade and Plantations opened their eyes and began to act. On January 4, 1679, the royal agent investigating allegations against Massachusetts cited the immediate need for the establishment of a council comprising leading figures from all of the colonies to mediate appeals and rule on accusations of injustice. Even with the establishment of such a body, the peace obtained would be short-lived. The only way to assure long-term comity among the colonists was for the king to establish a general governor for all of New England.[63] Acquiring greater gravity, the bickering over Maine and New Hampshire now not only deserved royal mediation but also required direct royal rule. Like the disputes over the New York–New England boundary, Mount Hope, and the Narragansett country, the debates over northern New England were concerned increasingly with issues of morality, social relationships, and the subservience of subjects to the king. Accordingly, London began to act.

WHAT IS important here is not the details and outcome of every dispute but the new gestalt as it appeared from London. Protagonists in disputes over land seemed intractable, and their weapons were allegations of immoral conduct and blame for a bloody war. More serious than earlier ones, these arguments warranted royal intervention, and it soon came. By 1680 the Crown had separated New Hampshire from Massachusetts and appointed a royal governor as its head. In 1684 the Crown annulled Massachusetts's charter and followed this shortly after with the abrogation of those of Connecticut, Rhode Island, and Plymouth. And, of course, in 1686 James II established the Dominion of New England, wherein all of the New England colonies came under the rule of New York governor Edmund Andros.

Andros's policies threatened Puritans throughout the region. He took measures to promote the toleration of religious dissent and initiated Anglican church services right in the heart of Boston. Perhaps most threatening to many, Andros had all town lands regranted in the king's name and subjected these lands to quitrents. Finally, Andros continued collecting the levies assessed by the colonies' general courts while limiting the powers of town meetings to electing individuals to help collect taxes.[64]

Historian Richard Johnson correctly argues that this royal intervention "sprang in large part from the peculiar obduracy of Massachusetts."[65] That colony's stubbornness in turn derived from its experience of the war and the accusations of others that it was to blame for the horrors of the war. King Philip's War renewed the corporate solidarity of Massachusetts Puritans and infused their culture with a new militarism. This new attitude coincided with the removal of a majority of Indians from New England and efforts by many to defend and acquire land with appeals to the Crown, which included claims that Massachusetts had immorally prosecuted the war. Unwilling to concede this point, Massachusetts vigorously defended its honor. With the protagonists in the various disputes refusing to budge, the Crown intervened to address the failures in the region's mechanisms for self-government and distribution of land.

Herein lay one of the great ironies of King Philip's War. The reduction of the Indian presence in New England did not catapult the orthodox Puritans of Massachusetts who had prosecuted the war so vigorously into a position of greater dominance. Instead, their political status became more like that of most Indian groups before the war. Under the Crown's scrutiny, and eventually under direct royal rule, Puritans lost much of their autonomy. In the words of one historian, "The New England Way ... was obliged to become the New England identity; a common religious profession and a distinctive code of conduct would have to form the basis of, in effect, an ethnic collectivity."[66] Like the Indian sachems before 1675, leading Puritans after the war earned status and respect through their ability to preserve their group's culture in the face of outside encroachment. Sometimes they would accommodate royal authority and try to use the imperial legal system to their advantage; sometimes they would stridently speak out against royal leaders.

Fitz-John Winthrop and Increase Mather provide two examples of leaders—the former primarily political, the latter religious—who fluctuated between policies of accommodation and resistance to carve out a measure of autonomy for Puritans. Fitz-John Winthrop, who succeeded his father to the governorship of Connecticut in 1676, initially took a conciliatory approach to the English imperial system as it seeped into New England. He worked within the system to defend Connecticut's royal charter when it came under attack and abided by Charles II's laws in order to maintain a measure of autonomy for Connecticut. This policy of accommodation stemmed from pragmatism rather than principle. Though he participated in James II's Dominion of New England during its early years, he supported its overthrow when the opportunity presented itself in 1688. In his participation in the revolt against the Dominion, Winthrop reasserted his latent loyalty to the local region at the expense of the imperial community.[67]

Unlike Winthrop, Boston minister Increase Mather initially resisted the encroachment of Dominion government vehemently, and he chastised members of the moderate faction who urged reconciliation with royal authorities. In 1683 Mather openly encouraged New Englanders not to allow London to alter their existing charter and urged them to defend it in court. Nine years later, however, Mather took the lead in negotiating a new charter for Massachusets that included major concessions to the Crown. Despite his religious conservatism, Mather accommodated royal authorities by allowing a charter that based voting rights on property ownership rather than church membership and allowed direct supervision of the colony from London. Mather claimed victory in this compromise charter, citing the empowerment of the Massachusetts General Court to protect congregational churches.[68] Like Philip, whose star rose by virtue of his followers' perception that he had successfully dealt with English encroachment and preserved a measure of autonomy for his group, Increase Mather reached the pinnacle of his influence and power among New England Puritans in 1692 when he worked within the royal framework to guarantee their protection.

PHILIP'S DEFEAT alone did not precipitate the royal intervention in the region's affairs that led up to the establishment of the Dominion of New England. Nor did King Philip's War exclusively and determinatively shape cultural change among the Indians. As others have documented, the rise of imperial government in New England depended, in part, upon a new tax structure, the ambitions of individuals, and broad, transatlantic changes in commercial and social relationships that took place in the latter part of the seventeenth century. But these changes alone were not sufficient to provoke royal intervention. By 1675 Indian and English polities had so intermeshed that in killing one another in King Philip's War they destroyed a part of themselves. When southern New England Algonquians lost most of their ability to play a prominent political role among the English, it triggered a necessary reconfiguration among all of the society's various components. This adjustment to Indian demographic collapse transformed the nature of the society, drew censure from the Crown, and contributed to the end of the New England Way.

CONCLUSION

As a history of a civil war and a society's violent collapse, this has been a study of failure. Yet it was born out of hope, an aspiration to render a distant past meaningful to diverse inhabitants of a contentious present. The result is a history of the Indians and the English in seventeenth-century New England that challenges the core of the national origin myth accepted by most Americans and offers a new way to think about our national ancestry and collective self. It both reacts against an invidious aspect of ethnic history, a tendency to foster divisive identity politics, and builds upon the solid foundation laid by others in recovering the past of Native Americans who left few written records.

In addition to rendering events in seventeenth-century New England comprehensible to modern sensibilities, I am attempting to create new "habits of the mind" for twentieth-century Americans. The argument that King Philip's War was a civil war is, in a sense, a foray into a long-standing dispute over the conflict's name. In the last thirty years this debate has been especially contentious. Gary B. Nash and Francis Jennings broke with the dominant tradition of calling the 1675 conflict King Philip's War in the mid-1970s. In an effort to present Indian culture on its own terms, Nash used Philip's native name and arrived at "Metacom's War." Jennings, in a diatribe against the Puritans, referred to the conflict as "The Second Puritan Conquest." Both authors recognized the inadequacies of previous histories; they also believed strongly in the power of a name. Yet neither name stuck.[1]

In the 1980s Philip Ranlet dismissed such attempts to rename King Philip's War as being of "dubious value." He was partially correct; recent attempts to rename the war have merely substituted another name for King Philip in the title of the war or portrayed the Puritans as the sole determinants of the conflict. As Ranlet noted, Indians often willingly changed their names, and King Philip, originally Metacom, also appears in the record as Philip Keitasscot and Wewasowannett. Thus, according to Ranlet, renaming the conflict "Metacom's War" or "Wewasowannett's War" does not necessarily provide a more "Indian-centered" title, since Metacom willingly used the title King Philip when his relations with the English colonists were still friendly. Similarly, naming the war the "Second Puritan Conquest" relegates Indians to the role of merely reacting to or resisting the actions of English settlers. In the end, efforts to rename the war in the 1970s and 1980s did little to fundamentally alter conceptualizations of the war or to steer historians away from the dominant paradigm in which Indians and English are posited as two opposed and distinct societies.[2]

More recently, Jill Lepore's outstanding study of the conflict's language, *The Name of War,* defiantly clung to the traditional "King Philip's War." Lepore dismissed the term "Indian civil war" because it would lessen the importance of the English-Indian component of the conflict in favor of its Indian-Indian aspects. She is right. But King Philip's War was obviously not just a civil war pitting Indian against Indian. The English and the Indians, as part of the same society with their polities interwoven, fought a civil war by fighting one another. Looking closely at the political culture of the Indians and the English, we see that Philip sought to preserve his people's sovereignty by incorporating them into the English political system. The English, in turn, viewed Philip and his followers as subjects, traitorous ones after they waged war in 1675. Thus King Philip's War was not just an "Indian civil war" but, more broadly, a civil war.[3]

Changing the name is, of course, irrelevant if the way we conceive of the event remains stagnant. Recognizing the extent to which King Philip's War approximated a civil war demands abandoning the dichotomous tone set by most narratives of the conflict and conceptualizing seventeenth-century New England as a single society. For this reason, several objections may be raised to viewing it as a civil war. The first is that, on the surface, doing so fails to serve the purpose of emphasizing the uniqueness of Indian cultures. Instead, one might argue, it is just another step in the colonization and assimilation of Indian peoples. Seeing the conflict as a civil war, in this view, merely makes Indians part of an alien society, when all that Indian peoples have wanted, as Vine Deloria, Jr., argues, is to be left alone.[4]

As for the claim that highlighting the civil aspects of the conflict masks cultural differences among the groups fighting the war, nothing could be further from the truth. The recent historiography on the origins of the American Civil War has demonstrated that, for a conflict of such magnitude to be fought, the combatants must have fundamentally different worldviews. The works of Eric Foner and Eugene Genovese outlining the ideologies of the North and the South, for example, portray the two sides as coming to conflict because of the fundamental incompatibilities of their cultures, especially their contrasting economies and their differences on the issue of slavery.[5] Thus, if a war is a civil war and the scope and scale of its conflict is as great as the name implies, a full understanding of the conflict can be reached only through a thorough comprehension of the differences among the various cultures involved.

Another objection that might possibly be raised is that the Indians and the English settlers never constituted a single society, and thus the war could not have shared the defining features of other civil wars. Admittedly, the definition of society can be ambiguous. In asserting that the Indians and the English had a single, multicultural society, it would be futile to pretend that fissures did not exist. To argue that the Indians and the English occupied the same mental world—that they shared the same ideology and epistemology—would probably cause both Metacom and Mather to roll in their graves, as well as make a total war difficult to explain. Nevertheless, in the years preceding the 1675 conflict, the Indians and the English in New England led a mutually interdependent existence in several important respects. Calling their society covalent is a recognition of how they could be simultaneously united and culturally different.

Some may argue that the use of the term *civil war* in this context lies outside of the traditional application of that term to the breakdown of a unified political community. Yet those who insist on seeing political links to warrant a civil war conceptualization need not look far. Although the Indians and the English may not have primarily constructed their identity in terms of their political community as did the Northerners and the Southerners in the 1850s, the two groups did share a politically defined world. The term *civil war* does not lose all of its traditional political connotations when applied to the conflict in 1675–76. The Algonquians and the English who inhabited Connecticut, Plymouth, Rhode Island, and

Massachusetts had common enemies in the form of a New York–Iroquois alliance to the west and in the form of a French-Abenaki alliance to the north. Francis Jennings has skillfully noted how Connecticut's long-standing border dispute with New York prevented the colony from requesting New York or Iroquois aid. Likewise, fear of the French and their Abenaki allies kept Massachusetts or its Indians from looking north for help.[6] Bounded by hostile peoples to the north and west, the ethnically mixed society living within Connecticut, Plymouth, Rhode Island, and Massachusetts was politically defined.

Furthermore, the English political landscape included Indians as more than allies. Narragansetts and various praying Indians portrayed themselves to the Puritans as subjects of King Charles II with the hope of getting better treatment at the hands of English colonists or protection from the Crown. Similarly, many Wampanoags, some of whom became pivotal figures in the 1675 uprising, took numerous oaths of fidelity to Plymouth Colony in an effort to receive protection under English law. The strategy of political submission allowed the Indians to utilize the English political system to their advantage. By submitting to a colony and the king, Indians expected, and often received, aid and assistance. This strategy is analogous to the way in which tribes today rely on their treaty relationships with the federal government of the United States and file suits in its courts to assert their immunity from state jurisdictions. At the same time such tribes often maintain a measured independence from the federal government.

Sovereignty claims notwithstanding, Indians are a part of today's society. Beyond presenting a viable account of the past based on standards of logic and evidence, the job of the historian is also to provide a meaningful way of looking at the present. The indigenous peoples were not merely supplanted by another people; New England and the United States are still home to a small percentage of Indians, who legitimately maintain their right to sovereignty within the United States. Relations today between Euramericans and Indians hinge largely upon the myths or histories the two groups construct to define themselves. If the understanding gained from traditional histories, which have painted a picture of polarization between the Indians and the Euramericans in early New England, is replaced by evidence of cooperation and interdependence, this can form a piece in the puzzle of how to foster more acceptance of one another today. This book was written with the belief that people can look at their heritage and refashion their self-image. Recognizing how diverse peoples in New England came together to form a single society, only to have it eventually explode in civil war, can help us to view our current world in a different light. My hope is that although the past is a foreign place, by reconceptualizing it various groups in today's society can find new meaning, and hopefully better relations, in the present.

Notes

Introduction

1. Isaiah Berlin, "Historical Inevitability," in Isaiah Berlin, *Four Essays on Liberty* (London: Oxford University Press, 1969), 41–117, quotation from 45.

2. Douglas Edward Leach, *Flintlock and Tomahawk: New England in King Philip's War* (New York: Macmillan, 1958), 1.

3. Ibid., 1, 241. In another, more recent book on Indian military technology and tactics in New England, Patrick M. Malone concludes that the defeat of Philip's forces was "inevitable" before Philip's death and that "complete defeat of the English was impossible from the beginning of the war." *The Skulking Way of War: Technology and Tactics among the New England Indians* (Baltimore: Johns Hopkins University Press, 1993), 120, 128. This seems especially ironic given Malone's Vietnam veteran status.

4. For more details on the planned wall, see Leach, *Flintlock and Tomahawk*, 165–66; and Massachusetts State Archives, Boston, vol. 68, docs. 169a, 172a, 174, 175b, 176a, 179, 180, 183. Document 179 is published in George Madison Bodge, *Soldiers in King Philip's War*, 3d ed. (1906; reprint, Baltimore: Genealogical Publishing Co., 1976), 214. Edward Randolph, "Extracts from Edward Randolph's Report to the Council of Trade, October 12, 1676," in E. B. O'Callaghan and Berthold Fernow, eds., *Documents Relative to the Colonial History of the State of New York*, 15 vols. (Albany, N.Y.: Weed, Parsons and Co., 1853–87), 3:243–44. The number of households is calculated by dividing the English population, 60,000, by 5. The treasurer and deputy governor each received £20. J. Hammond Trumbull and Charles J. Hoadly, eds., *The Public Records of the Colony of Connecticut*, 15 vols. (Hartford, Conn.: F. A. Brown, 1850–90), 2:293. Daniel Gookin, "An Historical Account of the Doings and Sufferings of the Christian Indians in New England [1677]," in *Collections of the American Antiquarian Society* 2 (1836): 494.

5. Casualty estimates receive extensive discussion in chapter 7.

6. Some examples of the assertion that King Philip's War was the deadliest in American history include: Leach, *Flintlock and Tomahawk*, 243; Neal Salisbury,

introduction to Mary Rowlandson, *The Sovereignty and Goodness of God, Together with the Faithfulness of His Promises Displayed: Being a Narrative of the Captivity and Restoration of Mrs. Mary Rowlandson and Related Documents,* ed. Neal Salisbury (Boston: Bedford Books, 1997), 1; and Jill Lepore, *The Name of War: King Philip's War and the Origins of American Identity* (New York: Knopf, 1998), xi; Gordon S. Wood, "The Bloodiest War," review of *The Name of War: King Philip's War and the Origins of American Identity,* by Jill Lepore, *New York Review of Books,* Apr. 9, 1998, 41. My phrasing parallels that of David A. Hollinger, "How Wide the Circle of the We? American Intellectuals and the Problem of the Ethnos since World War II," *American Historical Review* 98 (Apr. 1993): 317–37. See also Hollinger, *Postethnic America* (New York: Basic Books, 1995).

7. The debate over what constitutes early American history has long been spirited but has especially raged in recent years. See, for example, James A. Hijiya, "Why the West Is Lost," *William and Mary Quarterly,* 3d ser., 51 (Apr. 1994): 276–92.

8. Richard White, *The Middle Ground: Indians, Empires, and Republics in the Great Lakes Region, 1650–1815* (New York: Cambridge University Press, 1991), 1. For more on the Beaver Wars, see Francis Jennings, *The Ambiguous Iroquois Empire: The Covenant Chain Confederation of Indian Tribes with English Colonies from Its Beginnings to the Lancaster Treaty of 1744* (New York: Norton, 1984), 84–112; Daniel K. Richter, *The Ordeal of the Longhouse: The Peoples of the Iroquois League in the Era of European Colonization* (Chapel Hill: University of North Carolina Press, 1992), 50–74; and Bruce Trigger, *The Children of Aataentsic: A History of the Huron People to 1660* (Montreal: McGill–Queens University Press, 1976), 603–64, 725–88. Daniel H. Usner, Jr., *Indians, Settlers, and Slaves in a Frontier Exchange Economy: The Lower Mississippi Valley before 1783* (Chapel Hill: University of North Carolina Press, 1992), 65–76. Andrew L. Knaut, *The Pueblo Revolt of 1680: Conquest and Resistance in Seventeenth-Century New Mexico* (Norman: University of Oklahoma Press, 1995), 14, 132–35.

9. Marc Bloch, *The Historian's Craft* (New York: Knopf, 1953), 32.

10. Lepore, *Name of War,* x.

11. Samuel Gorton to John Winthrop, Jr., Sept. 11, 1675, Winthrop Papers, reel 11, Massachusetts Historical Society, Boston (hereafter, MHS).

12. William Hubbard, *A Narrative of the Troubles with the Indians in New England* [1677], reprinted in Samuel G. Drake, ed., *The History of the Indian Wars in New England,* 2 vols. (1865; reissued in facsimile, Bowie, Md.: Heritage Books, 1990), 1:59.

13. Roger Williams to Robert Williams, Apr. 1, 1676, in Glenn W. LaFantasie, ed., *The Correspondence of Roger Williams,* 2 vols. (Hanover: University Press of New England, 1988), 2:720.

14. John Mason wrote that the Mohegans "seem not to be willing to fight with the upland Indians unless they understand the ground of the English warring with them." John Mason to Fitz-John Winthrop, Sept. 6, 1675, Winthrop Papers, reel 11, MHS.

15. Increase Mather, *A Brief History of the War with the Indians in New-England*

[1676], reprinted in Samuel G. Drake, ed., *The History of King Philip's War* (Albany, N.Y.: J. Munsell, 1862), 65, emphasis added.

16. Ibid., 145.

17. Hubbard, *Narrative*, 1:278–79.

18. Quoted in Carla Gardina Pestana, "The Quaker Executions as Myth and History," *Journal of American History* 80 (Sept. 1993): 452. For more on Wharton, see E[dward] W[harton], *New England's Present Sufferings under their cruel Neighboring Indians Represented in two Letters, lately Written from Boston to London* (London, 1675).

19. William Apess, *A Son of the Forest* [1831], in Barry O'Connell, ed., *On Our Own Ground: The Complete Writings of William Apess, A Pequot* (Amherst: University of Massachusetts Press, 1992), 3; and William Apess, *Eulogy on King Philip, as Pronounced at the Odeon, in Federal Street, Boston* [1836], in O'Connell, ed., *On Our Own Ground*, 290.

20. William S. Simmons, *Spirit of the New England Tribes: Indian History and Folklore, 1620–1984* (Hanover, N.H.: University Press of New England, 1986), 141. Constance A. Crosby elaborates on this point and bolsters some of the points made by Simmons by reconciling folklore with an interpretation of changing patterns in the Indian burial of grave goods. "From Myth to History, or Why King Philip's Ghost Walks Abroad," in Mark P. Leone and Parker B. Potter, Jr., eds., *The Recovery of Meaning: Historical Archaeology in the Eastern United States* (Washington, D.C.: Smithsonian Institution Press, 1988), 183–209.

21. Russell M. Peters, *The Wampanoags of Mashpee: An Indian Perspective on American History* (n.p.: Indian Spiritual and Cultural Training Council, 1987), 17.

22. Mather, *Brief History*, 84, 96, 71. Leach, *Flintlock and Tomahawk*, 152, 49, 36.

23. Leach, *Flintlock and Tomahawk*, 168, 132, 130.

24. Hollinger, *Postethnic America*, 105–29, passim.

25. David A. Hollinger, "Postethnic America," *Contention* 2 (fall 1992): 79–80. Barbara Fields, "Ideology and Race in American History," in J. Morgan Kousser and James M. McPherson, eds., *Region, Race, and Reconstruction: Essays in Honor of C. Vann Woodward* (New York: Oxford University Press, 1982), 149. Hollinger, "Postethnic America," 84. For the argument that American history needs to be written with greater attention to race mixture, see Gary B. Nash, "The Hidden History of Mestizo America," *Journal of American History* 82 (Dec. 1995): 941–64.

26. Here I paraphrase Alan Taylor, *William Cooper's Town: Power and Persuasion on the Frontier of the Early American Republic* (New York: Vintage, 1995), 9.

27. Richard R. Johnson, "The Search for a Usable Indian: An Aspect of the Defense of Colonial New England," *Journal of American History* 64 (Dec. 1977): 623. Hubbard, *Narrative*, 2:63–64.

28. The phrase is borrowed from David Lowenthal, *The Past Is a Foreign Country* (Cambridge: Cambridge University Press, 1985).

1. Chiefs and Followers

1. Karen Ordahl Kupperman, "Climate and Mastery of the Wilderness in Seventeenth-Century New England," in David D. Hall and David Grayson Allen,

eds., *Seventeenth-Century New England: A Conference Held by the Colonial Society of Massachusetts, June 18 and 19, 1982* (Boston: Colonial Society of Massachusetts, 1984), 3–37. Darrett B. Rutman, *Winthrop's Boston: Portrait of a Puritan Town, 1630–1649* (Chapel Hill: University of North Carolina Press, 1965), 179.

2. Douglas Edward Leach, *Flintlock and Tomahawk: New England in King Philip's War* (New York: Macmillan, 1958), 1.

3. Jill Lepore, *The Name of War: King Philip's War and the Origins of American Identity* (New York: Knopf, 1998), x.

4. Following the conventions of others, throughout the text I try to be as specific as possible when indicating group affiliations. For Indians this can be especially difficult, because the contemporary English, from whom we get much of our information, were themselves often confused. All of the Indians within New England spoke Algonquian languages. Their neighbors in New York spoke Iroquoian languages. Complicating matters, southern New England's Indians had many layers of sovereignty; the tribes mentioned are just some of the largest entities. For example, Philip was the sachem (leader) of the Wampanoags, but he was also a Pokanoket, a subset of the Wampanoags residing near Mount Hope in western Plymouth colony. When a specific affiliation is unknown or unimportant, I use *Indians, Algonquians, natives,* and *indigenous people* interchangeably. An important subset within *Indians* is *Christian Indians* or *praying Indians,* referring to those who ostensibly converted. Most of these were Massachusetts, but not all Massachusetts were praying Indians. For more on seventeenth-century Indian politics and culture, see Kathleen J. Bragdon, *Native People of Southern New England, 1500–1650* (Norman: University of Oklahoma Press, 1996). An invaluable source is also Bert Salwen, "Indians of Southern New England and Long Island: Early Period," in Bruce Trigger, ed., *Northeast,* vol. 15 of William C. Sturtevant, ed., *Handbook of North American Indians* (Washington, D.C.: Smithsonian Institution Press, 1978), 160–76.

5. Karen Ordahl Kupperman argues convincingly that the establishment of localized webs of social relations was critical to the survival of English colonizing ventures. She writes that "Stuart local government rested on a web of loyalty, mutual obligation, and clientage. These networks were forged in small increments over time. They were fragile, resting on the ability of leaders to command respect in the county and in London and on the willingness of local men to give loyalty and support. No colony would succeed until it found a way to replicate these relationships or devised another web to take their place." *Providence Island, 1630–1641: The Other Puritan Colony* (New York: Cambridge University Press, 1993), 50.

6. James Lockhart and Stuart B. Schwartz, *Early Latin America: A History of Colonial Spanish America and Brazil* (New York: Cambridge University Press, 1983), 79–80. For more on the composition of the Spanish who conquered Peru, see James Lockhart, *The Men of Cajamarca: A Social and Biographical Study of the First Conquerors of Peru* (Austin: University of Texas Press, 1972).

7. For Mexico, see Charles Gibson, *The Aztecs under Spanish Rule: A History of the Indians of the Valley of Mexico, 1519–1810.* (Stanford, Calif.: Stanford University

Press, 1964), esp. chaps. 2, 4; and James Lockhart, *The Nahuas after the Conquest: A Social and Cultural History of the Indians of Central Mexico, Sixteenth through Eighteenth Centuries* (Stanford, Calif.: Stanford University Press, 1992), passim. For Peru, see Steve J. Stern, *Peru's Indian Peoples and the Challenge of Spanish Conquest*, 2d ed. (Madison: University of Wisconsin Press, 1993).

8. For the development of a paid soldiery, presidios, and missions, see Philip W. Powell, *Soldiers, Indians, and Silver: The Northward Advance of New Spain, 1550–1600* (Berkeley: University of California Press, 1952). For the inability of Spain, Mexico, and the United States to conclusively conquer Indians of the Southwest, see Edward H. Spicer, *Cycles of Conquest: The Impact of Spain, Mexico, and the United States on the Indians of the Southwest, 1533–1960* (Tucson: University of Arizona Press, 1962).

9. Lockhart and Schwartz, *Early Latin America*, 59. An exception to the rule that sedentary Indians were easily conquered is, of course the Pueblos, who staged the most successful revolt against European colonization in history. It should be noted that the Pueblos, although definitely sedentary, lacked what the Spanish found so appealing in sedentary peoples—wealth that they could use. Coronado explored the region of the Pueblos in the 1540s, but the Spanish did not settle there permanently until the 1590s. Even then, the number of Spanish people who settled near the Pueblos stayed relatively small, facilitating a successful revolt against their rule in 1680. See Andrew L. Knaut, *The Pueblo Revolt of 1680: Conquest and Resistance in Seventeenth-Century New Mexico* (Norman: University of Oklahoma Press, 1995). Lockhart, *Nahuas after the Conquest*, 5.

10. Eve Ball, *Indeh: An Apache Odyssey* (Norman: University of Oklahoma Press, 1980), xx.

11. An exception would be the French fur trade with Indians in what is now Canada. There the French adapted to Indian ways and kept their numbers small, at least initially. Had they initially sought land rather than furs, the story may have been very different. One of the best books on the fur trade is Sylvia Van Kirk, *Many Tender Ties: Women in Fur Trade Society, 1670–1870* (Norman: University of Oklahoma Press, 1980).

12. Bragdon, *Native People*, 55–79. For the precontact era, Bragdon posits a useful "tripartite settlement model" based upon three distinct ecological regions: "maritime/estuarine; riverine; and uplands/lacustrine" (35–36). However, the tripartite model does not diminish the fundamental distinction between the less sedentary south and the more sedentary north. By the time the colonists arrived, Indians throughout southern New England, especially in the marine and riverine zones, were relying heavily on agriculture, so they were more sedentary than the northern Indians. On the subsistence differences between the Indians of southern and northern New England, see Neal Salisbury, *Manitou and Providence: Indians, Europeans, and the Making of New England, 1500–1643* (New York: Oxford University Press, 1982), 55, 22–49.

13. Bragdon, *Native People*, xiv. Lockhart and Schwartz, *Early Latin America*, 55.

14. Bragdon, *Native People*, 100; and Lynn Ceci, "Wampum as a Peripheral Resource in the Seventeenth-Century World System," in Laurence M. Hauptman

and James O. Wherry, eds., *The Pequots in Southern New England: The Fall and Rise of an American Indian Nation* (Norman: University of Oklahoma Press, 1990), 48–63. For a comparative view of the historical development of chiefdoms, see Allen W. Johnson and Timothy Earle, *The Evolution of Human Societies: From Foraging Group to Agrarian State* (Stanford, Calif.: Stanford University Press, 1987).

15. Timothy Earle, "The Evolution of Chiefdoms," in Timothy Earle, ed., *Chiefdoms: Power, Economy, and Ideology* (New York: Cambridge University Press, 1991), 1. See also Johnson and Earle, *Evolution of Human Societies.* Kristian Kristiansen, "Chiefdoms, States, and Systems of Social Evolution," in Earle, *Chiefdoms,* 25.

16. Timothy H. Breen, "Persistent Localism: English Social Change and the Shaping of New England Institutions," in Timothy H. Breen, *Puritans and Adventurers: Change and Persistence in Early America* (New York: Oxford University Press, 1980), 5. Virginia DeJohn Anderson, *New England's Generation: The Great Migration and the Formation of Society and Culture in the Seventeenth Century* (New York: Cambridge University Press, 1991), 93. Breen, "Persistent Localism," 16.

17. On Iroquois relations with New England Indians, see Neal Salisbury, "Toward the Covenant Chain: Iroquois and Southern New England Algonquians, 1637–1684," in Daniel K. Richter and James H. Merrell, eds., *Beyond the Covenant Chain: The Iroquois and Their Neighbors in Indian North America, 1600–1800* (Syracuse, N.Y.: Syracuse University Press, 1987), 61–73.

18. Kupperman, *Providence Island,* 94, 98. Kupperman writes that because of their familiarity with the Black Legend, the Puritans who settled Providence Island figured that Indians "would gladly accept English sovereignty to be freed of Spanish tyranny." This expectation had some confirmation when an Indian leader did subject himself to Charles I, similar to the way in which many Indians in New England submitted themselves to the English. Although the evidence providing a direct link between the Black Legend and behavior in New England is indirect, it seems likely, given the communication among Puritans in New England and the Caribbean, that it must have existed. For the influence of the Black Legend in England, see William Maltby, *The Black Legend in England: The Development of Anti-Spanish Sentiment, 1558–1660* (Durham, N.C.: Duke University Press, 1971). For more on colonization as a form of competition with Spain, see Arthur Percival Newton, *The Colonising Activities of The English Puritans: The Last Phase of the Elizabethan Struggle with Spain* (New Haven, Conn.: Yale University Press, 1914); and Lepore, *Name of War,* 8–12.

19. Quoted in James Muldoon, "The Indian as Irishman," *Essex Institute Historical Collections* 111 (Oct. 1975): 280.

20. Martin H. Quitt, "Trade and Acculturation at Jamestown, 1607–1609: The Limits of Understanding," *William and Mary Quarterly,* 3d ser., 52 (Apr. 1995): 239. Neal Salisbury, "Squanto: Last of the Patuxets," in Gary B. Nash and David Sweet, eds., *Survival and Struggle in Colonial America* (Berkeley: University of California Press, 1981), 241–43. Neal Salisbury has been correct to point out that the treaty of March 1621 favored the English. Nevertheless, the English at this time were in no position to impose it upon Massasoit against his will, and Massasoit perceived

advantage in the agreement as he understood it through the ritual exchange of gifts and speeches. *Manitou and Providence*, 114–15.

21. Carl Bridenbaugh, ed. *The Pynchon Papers*, vol. 1, *Letters of John Pynchon, 1654–1700* (Boston: Colonial Society of Massachusetts, 1982), xxii. Alfred A. Cave has done a wonderful job of synthesizing some of these political developments in *The Pequot War* (Amherst: University of Massachusetts Press, 1996), chap. 2. Also see Eric Johnson, "'Some by Flatteries and Others by Threatenings': Political Strategies among Native Americans of Seventeenth-Century New England," Ph.D. diss., University of Massachusetts, 1993; Salisbury, *Manitou and Providence*, 85–202; and William S. Simmons, "Narragansett," in Trigger, *Northeast*, 190–97.

22. John Foster, "A Map of New England" (1677), in William Hubbard, *A Narrative of the Troubles with the Indians in New England* [1677], reprinted in Samuel G. Drake, ed., *The History of the Indian Wars in New England*, 2 vols. (1865; reissued in facsimile, Bowie, Md.: Heritage Books, 1990).

23. Edwin A. Churchill, "Mid-Seventeenth-Century Maine: A World on the Edge," in Emerson Woods Baker II, Edwin A. Churchill, Richard D'Abate, Kristine L. Jones, Victor A. Konrad, and Harald E. L. Prins, eds., *American Beginnings: Exploration, Culture, and Cartography in the Land of Norumbega* (Lincoln: University of Nebraska Press, 1994), 241–60; and Emerson Woods Baker II, "The World of Thomas Gorges: Life in the Province of Maine in the 1640s," in Baker, *American Beginnings*, 262. Hubbard, *Narrative*, 2:70. Churchill, "Mid-Seventeenth-Century Maine," 246.

24. Quotations from Churchill, "Mid-Seventeenth-Century Maine," 242.

25. John Canup, *Out of the Wilderness: The Emergence of an American Identity in Colonial New England* (Middletown, Conn.: Wesleyan University Press, 1990), 49–51. For evidence that southern New England was comprised of dispersed, one-story farmsteads, see Joseph S. Wood, *The New England Village* (Baltimore: Johns Hopkins University Press, 1997), 1–70. On the difference between northern and southern New England with regard to land speculation and town development, see John Frederick Martin, *Profits in the Wilderness: Entrepreneurship and the Founding of New England Towns in the Seventeenth Century* (Chapel Hill: University of North Carolina Press, 1991), 100–110.

26. Colin G. Calloway, *The Western Abenakis of Vermont, 1600–1800: War, Migration, and the Survival of an Indian People* (Norman: University of Oklahoma Press, 1990), 10–11; Dean R. Snow, "Eastern Abenaki," in Trigger, *Northeast*, 138; Gordon M. Day, "Western Abenaki," in Trigger, *Northeast*, 153–54; Harald E. L. Prins, "Children of Gluskap: Wabanaki Indians on the Eve of the European Invasion," in Baker, *American Beginnings*, 102–5; and Salisbury, *Manitou and Providence*, 22–49.

27. Prins, "Children of Gluskap," 99.

28. Cave, *Pequot War*. Casualty estimates are from 151.

29. Quotations in ibid., 151, 152.

30. Johnson, "'Some by Flatteries,'" 44–53. Bragdon, *Native People*, 152; and Cave, *Pequot War*, 67.

31. Salisbury, *Manitou and Providence*, 226. See also Johnson, "'Some by Flatteries,'" 53–61.

32. Salisbury, *Manitou and Providence,* 232–35; Johnson, "Some by Flatteries," 57.

33. Williams quoted in Salisbury, "Toward the Covenant Chain," 64. This paragraph draws heavily on Gordon M. Day, "The Ouragie War: A Case History in Iroquois–New England Indian Relations," in Michael K. Foster, Jack Campisi, and Marianne Mithun, eds., *Extending the Rafters: Interdisciplinary Approaches to Iroquoian Studies* (Albany: SUNY Press, 1984), 35–50; Richard I. Melvoin, *New England Outpost: War and Society in Colonial Deerfield* (New York: Norton, 1989), 17–18, 33–48; Salisbury, "Toward the Covenant Chain," 62–65; and Peter Allen Thomas, "In the Maelstrom of Change: The Indian Trade and Cultural Process in the Middle Connecticut Valley, 1635–1665," Ph.D. diss., University of Massachusetts, Amherst, 1979.

34. Thomas, "In the Maelstrom of Change," 312–15.

35. This is not to say that the English shunned Indian labor. Far from it, the English relied more and more on Indian labor right up to King Philip's War. See, for example, Joshua Micah Marshall, "Melancholy People: Anglo-Indian Relations in Early Warwick, Rhode Island, 1642–1675," *New England Quarterly* (Sept. 1995): 402–29.

36. Kupperman, *Providence Island.* English colonists in the Chesapeake also made a shift from a failed effort to colonize trade with Indians to colonizing land, in their case to grow the cash crop tobacco. See Quitt, "Trade and Acculturation," 227–58.

37. Martin, *Profits in the Wilderness,* 10–18, 62–63. For the first English chiefdom, and how it functioned as such, see Rutman, *Winthrop's Boston,* esp. chap. 4. Although Rutman does not refer to anyone as a chief, his "gentry" did many of the same things as chiefs. For example, they made sure people were protected by having forts built, allocated resources for schools, and allocated lands. Their community's population was in the thousands. Heredity and access to resources heavily influenced their status. The Boston gentry also struggled and failed to maintain the loyalty of those within their community as many left and established independent towns.

38. Timothy H. Breen and Stephen Foster point to this localism as a factor in explaining the social cohesion of Massachusetts relative to the other English colonies. "The Puritans' Greatest Achievement: A Study of Social Cohesion in Seventeenth-Century Massachusetts," *Journal of American History* 60 (June 1973): 15. Kenneth A. Lockridge, *A New England Town: The First Hundred Years, 1636–1736* (New York: Norton, 1970), 22.

39. Philip F. Gura, *A Glimpse of Sion's Glory: English Radicalism in New England, 1620–1660* (Middletown, Conn.: Wesleyan University Press, 1984). Sydney V. James, *Colonial Rhode Island: A History* (New York: Scribner's, 1975), 17–18.

40. Mary Louise Pratt, *Imperial Eyes: Travel Writing and Transculturation* (London: Routledge, 1992), 30–31. This paragraph summarizes the superb analysis of Laura K. Arnold, "Crossing Cultures: Subversive Encounters and the Invention of New England, 1620–1682," Ph.D. diss., University of California, Los Angeles, 1995, chap. 2.

41. Nathaniel B. Shurtleff, ed., *Records of the Governor and Company of the Massa-*

chusetts Bay in New England, 5 vols. (Boston: William White, 1853–54), 2:40; Samuel Gorton, *Simplicities Defence against Seven-Headed Policy* [1647], reprinted in *Collections of the Rhode-Island Historical Society* 2 (1835): 21–190; and Paul Alden Robinson, "The Struggle Within: The Indian Debate in Seventeenth-Century Narragansett Country," Ph.D. diss., State University of New York, Binghamton, 1990, 118. Nathaniel B. Shurtleff and David Pulsifer, eds., *Records of the Colony of New Plymouth in New England*, 12 vols. (Boston: William White, 1855–61), 1:133, 4:25–26, 5:79. Testimony of Roger Williams, 13 Dec. 1661, in *The Complete Writings of Roger Williams*, 7 vols. (New York: Russell and Russell, 1963), 6:316–17.

2. PEACE

1. Karen Ordahl Kupperman, *Settling with the Indians: The Meeting of English and Indian Cultures in America, 1580–1640* (Totowa, N.J.: Rowman and Littlefield, 1980), viii, 186.

2. Nathaniel B. Shurtleff and David Pulsifer, eds., *Records of the Colony of New Plymouth in New England*, 12 vols. (Boston: William White, 1855–61) (hereafter, *Plymouth Colony Records*), 1:23, 110.

3. Samuel Gorton, *Simplicities Defence against Seven-Headed Policy* [1647], reprinted in *Collections of the Rhode-Island Historical Society* 2 (1835): 20, 21–190, quotation from 20.

4. Karen Ordahl Kupperman, "Presentment of Civility: English Reading of American Self-Presentation in the Early Years of Colonization," *William and Mary Quarterly*, 3d. ser., 54 (Jan. 1997): 193–228, quotation from 226. Kupperman, *Settling with the Indians*, 169–70.

5. Edmund S. Morgan, *The Puritan Dilemma: The Story of John Winthrop* (Boston: Little, Brown, 1958), 86, 185–86.

6. For more on these boundary disputes, see Clarence Winthrop Bowen, *The Boundary Disputes of Connecticut* (Boston, 1882); and Francis Jennings, *The Invasion of America: Indians, Colonialism, and the Cant of Conquest* (New York: Norton, 1975), 33, 188–89, 198, 255–57, 287–88, 291–92, 300–302, 317–18, 325–26.

7. Nathaniel B. Shurtleff, ed., *Records of the Governor and Company of the Massachusetts Bay in New England*, 5 vols. (Boston: William White, 1853–54) (hereafter, *Massachusetts Colonial Records*), 1:17, 384, 386. Philip F. Gura, *A Glimpse of Sion's Glory: English Radicalism in New England, 1620–1660* (Middletown, Conn.: Wesleyan University Press, 1984), 133, 134–36.

8. Yasuhide Kawashima, *English Justice and the Indian: White Man's Law in Massachusetts, 1630–1763* (Middletown, Conn.: Wesleyan University Press, 1986). *Massachusetts Colonial Records*, 1:392; *Plymouth Colony Records*, 11:183.

9. *Massachusetts Colonial Records*, vol. 4, pt. 2, p. 360; pt. 1, p. 390. These different ways of referring to groups cannot be attributed to differences in their perceived sizes. Although population figures supplied by European observers were always at best rough estimates, population estimates for the Mohawks were roughly comparable to those for major groups in southern New England. For a sampling of European population estimates for Iroquois and southern New En-

gland Algonquians, see Bert Salwen, "Indians of Southern New England and Long Island: Early Period," and Elisabeth Tooker, "The League of the Iroquois: Its History, Politics, and Ritual," both in Bruce Trigger, ed., *Northeast*, vol. 15 of William C. Sturtevant, ed., *Handbook of North American Indians* (Washington, D.C.: Smithsonian Institution Press, 1978), 169, 421.

10. Alden T. Vaughan, *New England Frontier: English and Indians, 1620–1675* (Boston: Little, Brown, 1966), 188–90.

11. Carl Bridenbaugh, ed., *The Pynchon Papers*, vol. 1, *Letters of John Pynchon, 1654–1700* (Boston: Colonial Society of Massachusetts, 1982), 37, 55, 57, 58, 59, 65, 69, 81, 93, 102, 104, 106, 113, 124. "Your Indians" on 56, 62. "Mr. Eliot's Indians" on 102.

12. Timothy H. Breen, *The Character of a Good Ruler: A Study of English Political Ideas in New England, 1630–1730* (New Haven, Conn.: Yale University Press, 1970); Richard L. Bushman, *King and People in Provincial Massachusetts* (Chapel Hill: University of North Carolina Press, 1985); and Perry Miller, *The New England Mind: The Seventeenth Century* (Cambridge, Mass.: Harvard University Press, 1939), chap. 14. Quotations from *Massachusetts Colonial Records*, 1:353–54; 2:40, 55.

13. Roger Williams to Gov. John Winthrop, ca. June 14, 1638, in Glenn W. La-Fantasie, ed., *The Correspondence of Roger Williams*, 2 vols. (Hanover, N.H.: University Press of New England, 1988), 1:163. "Letter from sundry inhabitants of Providence to the Governor and assistants of Mass. Bay relative to the insolent behavior of Samuel Gorton and his company," Nov. 17, 1641, Massachusetts State Archives, Boston, vol. 2, items 2–3. The English were seemingly aware of some of the societal dynamics that have only recently been postulated by Kristian Kristiansen. Kristiansen has argued that as one observes societies farther from the center and closer to the periphery in a world systems model, the societies become simpler. For the English, however, this simplicity signaled declension, whereas those who argue for forms of social evolution today tend to dismiss notions of progress. See Kristian Kristiansen, "Chiefdoms, States, and Systems of Social Evolution," in Timothy Earle, ed., *Chiefdoms: Power, Economy, and Ideology* (New York: Cambridge University Press, 1991), 23–26. Bridenbaugh, *Pynchon Papers*, 22, 84, 87.

14. *Massachusetts Colonial Records*, 1:212–13. Thomas Prince, letter to Boston, May 8, 1671, Winslow Papers, item 58, Massachusetts Historical Society, Boston.

15. For examples of secondary literature on the theme of Indian political power stemming from the ability to deal with the English, see Peter Thomas, "Cultural Change on the Southern New England Frontier, 1630–1665," in William Fitzhugh, ed., *Cultures in Contact: The Impact of European Contacts on Native American Cultural Institutions, a.d. 1000–1800* (Washington, D.C.: Smithsonian Institution Press, 1985), 131–61; and Paul Alden Robinson, "The Struggle Within: The Indian Debate in Seventeenth-Century Narragansett Country," Ph.D. diss., State University of New York, Binghamton, 1990. This idea of Indians "controlling" the English in order to enhance their power is discussed more extensively later in this chapter and in chapter 3.

16. Bridenbaugh, *Pynchon Papers*, 88, 91, and 94, quotations from 91.

17. For an elaboration on these population figures, see chapter 4. From an

Indian perspective, the rapid natural increase in the population of English settlers coupled with the stagnation or decline of the native population after 1638 almost certainly made casting one's lot with the English much more attractive. William Wood, *New England's Prospect* (1638; reprint, New York: Burt Franklin, 1967); and Douglas Edward Leach, *Flintlock and Tomahawk: New England in King Philip's War* (New York: Macmillan, 1958). Pynchon frequently made passing reference to Indians who brought him his letters; see Bridenbaugh, *Pynchon Papers*, 11, 18, 22, 35, 61, 64, 71, 91, 92, 107, 118.

18. *Massachusetts Colonial Records*, 3:7, 1:140; and *Plymouth Colony Records*, 11:66, 184.

19. *Massachusetts Colonial Records*, 3:397; 4:86, 257; 2:85, 103, 252; and Don Gleason Hill, ed., *The Early Records of the Town of Dedham, Massachusetts*, 4 vols. (Dedham, Mass., 1894), 4:170, 208, 210, 212. Neal Salisbury, "Social Relationships on a Moving Frontier: Natives and Settlers in Southern New England, 1638–1675," *Man in the Northeast* 33 (1987): 90; and Thomas, "Cultural Change," 142–43. Indian labor is only beginning to receive the attention it should. See Joshua Micah Marshall, "Melancholy People: Anglo-Indian Relations in Early Warwick, Rhode Island, 1642–1675," *New England Quarterly* (Sept. 1995): 402–29. Marshall's forthcoming dissertation from Brown University should prove a welcome addition to the literature.

20. W. Noel Sainsbury, ed., *Calendar of State Papers, Colonial Series, America and the West Indies*, vol. 9 (London, 1893), 317; *Plymouth Colony Records*, 5:174, 201–3; and Sainsbury, *Calendar of State Papers*, 109.

21. Renato Rosaldo, *Culture and Truth: The Remaking of Social Analysis*, 2d ed. (Boston: Beacon, 1993); Richard White, *The Middle Ground: Indians, Empires, and Republics in the Great Lakes Region, 1650–1815* (New York: Cambridge University Press, 1991).

22. Roger Williams, *A Key into the Language of America* (London, 1643), 134; Daniel Gookin, *Historical Collections of the Indians in New England* [1674], reprinted in *Collections of the Massachusetts Historical Society*, 1st ser., 1 (1792): 141–229, quotation from 154; John Josselyn, *An account of Two Voyages to New England* (London, 1675), reprinted in *Collections of the Massachusetts Historical Society*, 3d. ser., 3 (1833): 211–354, quotation from 308. See also Kupperman, *Settling with the Indians*, 48–53. Kupperman also makes the point that many English saw in Indian societies a model for what English society ought to be (141–58); Kupperman, "Presentment of Civility," 195.

23. Williams, *Key*, 134; Gookin, *Historical Collections*, 154.

24. This was especially true around the time of the American Revolution. See Jill Lepore, *The Name of War: King Philip's War and the Origins of American Identity* (New York: Knopf, 1998), 173–90.

25. Bushman, *King and People*, 14, 37.

26. Breen, *Character of a Good Ruler*, 47. *Massachusetts Colonial Records*, 4:25, 26, 129–33, 168–73.

27. Quoted in Sydney V. James, *Colonial Rhode Island: A History* (New York: Scribner's, 1975), 70.

28. Neal Salisbury, *Manitou and Providence: Indians, Europeans, and the Making of New England, 1500–1643* (New York: Oxford University Press, 1982), 10. Salisbury notes that for Indians in the Northeast "the principle of reciprocity . . . underlay the relationship between leader and follower" (43). John Eliot, *The Christian Commonwealth: Or, the Civil Policy of the Rising Kingdom of Jesus Christ* (1660), reprinted in *Collections of the Massachusetts Historical Society*, 3d ser., 9 (1846): 127–64, quotations from 135, 146, 155. Even if Eliot's teachings differed from those of other Englishmen, his were probably the most influential in shaping Indian perceptions of English political culture. Yet Eliot was by no means an exception. The colony's governor, John Winthrop, declared that "[n]o common weale can be founded but by free consent." Quoted in Breen, *Character of a Good Ruler*, 48.

29. The term *parapolitical* is used by F. G. Bailey to describe political structures "which are partly regulated by, and partly independent of, larger encapsulating political structures; and which, so to speak, fight battles with these larger structures in a way which for them seldom ends in victory, rarely in dramatic defeat, but usually in a long drawn stalemate and defeat by attrition." "Parapolitical Systems," in Marc J. Swartz, ed., *Local-Level Politics: Structural and Cultural Perspectives* (Chicago: Aldine, 1968), 281. Bailey's notion of semi-independent political entities encapsulated within a larger polity has been fruitfully used by Loretta Fowler, *Arapahoe Politics, 1851–1978* (Lincoln: University of Nebraska Press, 1982), 6, 350 n. 10.

30. John Russell Bartlett, ed., *Records of the Colony of Rhode Island and Providence Plantation, in New England,* 10 vols. (Providence, R. I., 1856–65), 1:134, 135, emphasis in the original.

31. Ibid., 2:270.

32. E. B. O'Callaghan, ed., *Documents Relative to the Colonial History of the State of New-York,* vol. 3 (Albany, N.Y.: Weed, Parsons, Printers, 1853), 182.

33. For wills using variations of *nanauwunnumooonkan,* see Ives Goddard and Kathleen J. Bragdon, *Native Writings in Massachusett* (Philadelphia: American Philosophical Society, 1988), 30, 34, 38. For the relationship between the noun for *colony* and the verbs *to protect* and *to look after,* see 657. Kathleen J. Bragdon, personal communication, Sept. 30, 1994. Goddard and Bragdon, *Native Writings,* 631. Granted, these wills may not have been produced by "typical Indians." Their authors were missionized, literate natives under the influence of English missionaries. However, other Indians also referred to English leaders as sachems. John Pynchon, when relating to John Winthrop the verbal expressions of nearby Indians, would use the term "English sachems." See Bridenbaugh, *Pynchon Papers,* 27, 92, 105.

34. For a thorough explication of the political connections between the various English colonies and the Mohegans, the Narragansetts, and the Pequots, see Eric Spencer Johnson, "'Some by Flatteries and Others by Threatenings': Political Strategies among Native Americans of Seventeenth-Century Southern New England," Ph.D. diss., University of Massachusetts, Amherst, 1993, passim. *Massachusetts Colonial Records,* 2:40, 55. Indians continued to submit to Massachusetts into the 1650s (2:73, 3:299).

35. *Massachusetts Colonial Records,* 2:72.

36. Patrick M. Malone, *The Skulking Way of War: Technology and Tactics among the New England Indians* (Baltimore: Johns Hopkins University Press, 1993), 90, 97–98, 99–100; *Massachusetts Colonial Records*, 2:72; Lorraine Elise Williams, "Fort Shantok and Fort Corchaug: A Comparative Study of Seventeenth-Century Culture Contact in the Long Island Sound Area," Ph.D. diss., New York University, 1972, 15, 77, 159, 196; and archaeological files, Rhode Island Historical Preservation Commission, Providence, site no. 0696. *Plymouth Colony Records*, 4:24, 151. Gorton, *Simplicities Defence*, 98–103.

37. Timothy H. Breen, "Transfer of Culture: Chance and Design in Shaping Massachusetts Bay, 1630–1660," in Timothy H. Breen, *Puritans and Adventurers: Change and Persistence in Early America* (New York: Oxford University Press, 1980), 79; and Ola Elizabeth Winslow, *Meetinghouse Hill, 1630–1783* (New York: Macmillan, 1952), 65.

38. Winslow, *Meetinghouse Hill*, 56. John Frederick Martin, *Profits in the Wilderness: Entrepreneurship and the Founding of New England Towns in the Seventeenth Century* (Chapel Hill: University of North Carolina Press, 1991).

39. Winslow, *Meetinghouse Hill*, 145. Hill, *Early Records of the Town of Dedham*, 3:115, 130, 136; 4:1, 30, 54, 55, 163, 169, 170, 173. For more on hierarchy within New England towns, see Kenneth A. Lockridge, *A New England Town: The First Hundred Years, 1636–1736* (New York: Norton, 1970), 37–56.

40. Elise M. Brenner, "Sociopolitical Implications of Mortuary Ritual Remains in Seventeenth-Century Native Southern New England," in Mark P. Leone and Parker B. Potter, Jr., eds., *The Recovery of Meaning: Historical Archaeology in the Eastern United States* (Washington, D.C.: Smithsonian Institution Press, 1988), 147–82; Robinson, "The Struggle Within"; Paul A. Robinson, Marc A. Kelley, and Patricia E. Rubertone, "Preliminary Biocultural Interpretations from a Seventeenth-Century Narragansett Indian Cemetery in Rhode Island," in Fitzhugh, *Cultures in Contact;* and William S. Simmons, *Cautantowwit's House: An Indian Burial Ground on the Island of Conanicut in Narragansett Bay* (Providence, R.I.: Brown University Press, 1970). Similarly, Eric Johnson has analyzed a different form of Indian material culture—pottery—to demonstrate a greater awareness of ethnic identity among groups of Mohegans at this time. See Johnson, "'Some by Flatteries,'" chap. 9. Kathleen Bragdon nicely summarizes the literature on mortuary ritual in *Native People of Southern New England, 1500–1650* (Norman: University of Oklahoma Press, 1996), 233–41.

41. The preceding paragraphs owe a heavy debt to the fine work done by archaeologists over the past fifteen years. In addition to those works cited in the previous note, see Elise M. Brenner, "Strategies for Autonomy: An Analysis of Ethnic Mobility in 17th-century New England," Ph.D. diss., University of Massachusetts, Amherst, 1984; Constance A. Crosby, "From Myth to History, or Why King Philip's Ghost Walks Abroad," in Leone and Potter, *Recovery of Meaning*, 183–209; Susan G. Gibson, ed., *Burr's Hill: A 17th Century Wampanoag Burial Ground in Warren, Rhode Island* (Providence, R.I.: Haffenreffer Museum of Anthropology, 1980); and Michael S. Nassaney, "An Epistemological Enquiry into Some Archaeological and Historical Interpretations of 17th-Century Native American Rela-

tions," in Stephen Shennan, ed., *Archaeological Approaches to Cultural Identity* (London: Unwin Hyman, 1989), 76–93. The above works are concerned primarily with burial sites, but the archaeologist Peter Thomas has arrived at similar conclusions about a growing individualistic ethic among the Northeast's Indians through the analysis of midden deposits and documentary evidence. See Thomas, "Cultural Change," 131–62.

42. Victor Turner, *The Forest of Symbols: Aspects of Ndembu Ritual* (Ithaca, N.Y.: Cornell University Press, 1967). My comparison of these two rituals is based on Turner's analysis of the function of ritual, as well as on the analyses of these rituals in the secondary literature.

43. The preceding three paragraphs draw extensively on Gordon M. Day, "The Ouragie War: A Case History in Iroquois–New England Indian Relations," in Michael K. Foster, Jack Campisi, and Marianne Mithun, eds., *Extending the Rafters: Interdisciplinary Approaches to Iroquoian Studies* (Albany, N.Y.: SUNY Press, 1984), 35–50; Richard I. Melvoin, *New England Outpost: War and Society in Colonial Deerfield* (New York: Norton, 1989), 17–48; and Neal Salisbury, "Toward the Covenant Chain: Iroquois and Southern New England Algonquians, 1637–1684," in Daniel K. Richter and James H. Merrell, eds., *Beyond the Covenant Chain: The Iroquois and Their Neighbors in Indian North America, 1600–1800* (Syracuse, N.Y.: Syracuse University Press, 1987), 64–69.

44. Day, "Ouragie War," 43; and Massachusetts State Archives, vol. 30, 128.

45. Gookin, *Historical Collections*, 162.

46. Ibid., 165.

47. For evidence of Indian fear of Mohawk raids on the part of nonmissionized Indians in the Connecticut River Valley and expectations of English assistance, see Bridenbaugh, *Pynchon Papers*, 46, 50, 54, 61, 65, 70, 71, 80, 81, 102. Neal Salisbury has argued that praying Indians became such because of the harsh effects of English colonization. In the Connecticut River Valley it seems that Mohawk violence might have provided an analogous impulse to seek English assistance. Peter Thomas has estimated that the Indian population of this region fell from 2,300 to 1,700 between 1660 and 1665 because of Mohawk raids. Neal Salisbury, "Red Puritans: The 'Praying Indians' of Massachusetts Bay and John Eliot," *William and Mary Quarterly*, 3d ser., 21 (Jan. 1974): 27–54; and Peter Allen Thomas, "In the Maelstrom of Change: The Indian Trade and Cultural Process in the Middle Connecticut River Valley, 1635–1665," Ph.D. diss., University of Massachusetts, Amherst, 1979, 395.

48. Roger Williams to John Winthrop, Jr., June 25, 1675, in LaFantasie, *Correspondence of Roger Williams*, 2:694.

3. SYMBOL OF A FAILED STRATEGY

1. Among the works showing unequal treatment of Indians in the English legal system are Yasuhide Kawashima, *Puritan Justice and the Indian: White Man's Law in Massachusetts, 1630–1763* (Middletown, Conn.: Wesleyan University Press,

1986); Lyle Koehler, "Red-White Power Relations and Justice in the Courts of Seventeenth-Century New England," *American Indian Culture and Research Journal* 3, no. 4 (1979): 1–31; and James P. Ronda, "Red and White at the Bench: Indians and the Law in Plymouth Colony, 1620–1691," *Essex Institute Historical Collections* 110 (July 1974): 200–215. Although these works are admirable in showing from a social scientific point of view that Indians received unequal treatment in New England courts, they do not demonstrate that Indians knew they were treated unfairly.

2. I use the terms *praying Indian* and *nonpraying Indian* fairly loosely to differentiate between two groups: those Indians who were under the influence of English missionaries and usually congregated around towns established with the purpose of converting Indians to Christianity, such as Natick, Massachusetts, and those Indians who eschewed the missionary influence of the English. The latter includes a variety of broad tribal categories such as Narragansett, Wampanoag, and Mohegan.

3. Neal Salisbury, "Red Puritans: The 'Praying Indians' of Massachusetts Bay and John Eliot," *William and Mary Quarterly*, 3d ser., 21 (Jan. 1974): 27–54.

4. Jean Maria O'Brien, *Dispossession by Degrees: Indian Land and Identity in Natick, Massachusetts, 1650–1790* (New York: Cambridge University Press, 1997), 31–65. For a differing view, see Harold Van Lonkhuyzen, "A Reappraisal of the Praying Indians: Acculturation, Conversion, and Identity at Natick, Massachusetts, 1646–1730," *New England Quarterly* 63 (Mar. 1990): 396–428.

5. Salisbury, "Red Puritans." The formation of the praying Indian communities is analogous to the ethnogenesis of the Catawbas from fragments of preexisting groups in North Carolina. See James Merrell, *The Indians' New World: Catawbas and Their Neighbors from European Contact through the Era of Removal* (New York: Norton, 1989).

6. Kathleen J. Bragdon, "'Another Tongue Brought In:' An Ethnohistorical Study of Native Writings in Massachusetts," Ph.D. diss., Brown University, 1981, 61. Roger Williams, *A Key into the Language of America* (London, 1643), 129 (this citation is also referred to in Bragdon, "'Another Tongue Brought In,'" 61). Kathleen J. Bragdon, "Vernacular Literacy and Massachusett World View, 1650–1750," in Peter Benes, ed., *Algonkians of New England: Past and Present* (Boston: Boston University, 1991), 26.

7. Bragdon, "'Another Tongue Brought In,'" 64. Here my analysis departs from that of Jill Lepore, who writes, "Learning to read and write, and especially learning to read and write English, were among the very last steps on the path to cultural conversion." *The Name of War: King Philip's War and the Origins of American Identity* (New York: Knopf, 1998), 42. It is important to recognize that learning to read and write could just as well be steps to avoid cultural conversion and maintain autonomy. Also, literacy did not dissolve the boundaries between literate Indians and literate English colonists.

8. Elise Brenner, "Strategies for Autonomy: An Analysis of Ethnic Mobility in 17th-Century New England," Ph.D. diss., University of Massachusetts, Amherst, 1984, 123–76. In her superb study of Natick, Jean M. O'Brien highlights the

town as a cultural "accommodation" rather than a conversion. "Indian desires shaped the dialogue." Because they made cultural compromises, some Indians could still claim Natick as "my land." *Dispossession by Degrees*, 32, 63.

9. Brenner, "Strategies for Autonomy," 230–31. Daniel Gookin, "An Historical Account of the Doings and Sufferings of the Christian Indians in New England" [1677], in *Collections of the American Antiquarian Society* 2 (1836): 450.

10. Similarly, Indians incorporated elements of the English practice of raising livestock in ways most compatible with their culture. Virginia DeJohn Anderson, "King Philip's Herds: Indians, Colonists, and the Problem of Livestock in Early New England," *William and Mary Quarterly*, 3d ser., 51 (Oct. 1994): 613–14.

11. Laurie Lee Weinstein has compiled quantitative data confirming an increased presence of Wampanoags in Plymouth courts defending land claims. See "Indian vs. Colonist: Competition for Land in Seventeenth-Century Plymouth Colony," Ph.D. diss., Southern Methodist University, 1983, 188–213. On average, the colonial courts experienced about a fivefold increase in the number of Indian claims between 1640 and 1670. Also chronicling increased tensions over land, more specifically the raising of livestock on land, is Anderson, "King Philip's Herds," 601–24. Anderson shows how the Wampanoags not only used the English legal system but tried to incorporate elements of English subsistence patterns, particularly the raising of swine, into their lifestyle. Plymouth Colony attempted to dissuade Philip's band from raising pigs. Whether or not the Wampanoags ceased is uncertain, but the contest over land clearly segued into related disputes over land usage.

12. Daniel Gookin, *Historical Collections of the Indians in New England* [1674], reprinted in *Collections of the Massachusetts Historical Society*, 1st ser., 1 (1792): 141–229, quotation from 179.

13. Massachusetts State Archives, Boston, 30:21.

14. Don Gleason Hill, ed., *The Early Records of the Town of Dedham, Massachusetts, 1659–1673*, 4 vols. (Dedham, Mass., 1894), 4:270.

15. See also Kenneth A. Lockridge, *A New England Town: The First Hundred Years, Dedham, Massachusetts, 1636–1736* (New York: Norton, 1970), 83–84. For more on the establishment of Natick, see O'Brien, *Dispossession by Degrees*, 31–64.

16. Hill, *Early Records of the Town of Dedham*, 4:58, 147.

17. On the resurfacing of this boundary dispute in the 1660s, see Francis Jennings, *Invasion of America: Indians, Colonialism, and the Cant of Conquest* (New York: Norton, 1975), 291–92. I disagree with Jennings's reading of the treaties between Massasoit and Plymouth, and Philip and Plymouth. Jennings does not see them as subordinating the Wampanoags to the colony, but only to the king of England (191). My reading is more in keeping with that of Neal Salisbury, *Manitou and Providence: Indians, Europeans, and the Making of New England, 1500–1643* (New York: Oxford University Press, 1982), 115, and my own interpretation of Indian political culture in chapter 2. For Philip's loyalty to Plymouth, see Nathaniel B. Shurtleff and David Pulsifer, eds., *Records of the Colony of New Plymouth in New England*, 12 vols. (Boston: William White, 1855–61) (hereafter, *Plymouth Colony Records*), 4:25–26.

18. In his dissertation, Eric Johnson posits that Indian sachems might have sold land to enhance their own power by limiting the mobility of their subjects. "'Some by Flatteries and Others by Threatenings': Political Strategies among Native Americans of Seventeenth-Century Southern New England," Ph.D. diss., University of Massachusetts, 1993, 261. This may have been the case in Plymouth; several Indians petitioned Governor Prince in 1667 complaining that their sachem had sold their land without their consent. Indians of Dartmouth, petition to Thomas Prince, Aug. 9, 1667, Winslow Papers, Massachusetts Historical Society, Boston.

On Philip's acquisition of currency, see *Plymouth Colony Records*, 4:154, 173, 176. Philip needed the currency to purchase cloth, metal, and glass goods to use for both ritual and utilitarian purposes. Purchasing these goods became increasingly difficult for Indians as wampum lost its value among the English after 1662 and the supply of furs diminished. Neal Salisbury, "Social Relationships on a Moving Frontier: Natives and Settlers in Southern New England, 1638–1675," *Man in the Northeast* 33 (1987): 91, 93; and Peter A. Thomas, "Cultural Change on the Southern New England Frontier, 1630–1665," in William W. Fitzhugh, ed., *Cultures in Contact: The Impact of European Contacts on Native American Cultural Institutions, A.D. 1000–1800* (Washington, D.C.: Smithsonian Institution Press, 1985), 107–29.

19. Johnson, "'Some by Flatteries,'" 57, 108–10. *Plymouth Colony Records*, 4:24–26.

20. *Plymouth Colony Records*, 4:164–65, quotation from 165.

21. Ibid., 4:169, 176.

22. I base this guess on the fine work in Anderson, "King Philip's Herds," passim.

23. Quotation from John Easton, *A Relacion of the Indyan Warre* [1675], in Charles H. Lincoln, ed., *Narratives of the Indian Wars, 1675–1699* (New York: Scribner's, 1913), 9. *Plymouth Colony Records*, 5:63–64.

24. *Plymouth Colony Records*, 5:78.

25. Ibid., 5:77.

26. Ibid., 5:79.

27. John Cotton's Journal, Massachusetts Historical Society, quoted in George D. Langdon, Jr., *Pilgrim Colony: A History of New Plymouth, 1620–1691* (New Haven, Conn.: Yale University Press, 1966), 158. See, for example, the submissions of Indians on June 7 and July 6, 1671. These differ from other submissions to the colony in that they include quotations of Scripture and affirmations of belief in God. *Plymouth Colony Records*, 5:66–67, 70–71.

28. *Plymouth Colony Records*, 5:63–64.

29. William Hubbard, *A Narrative of the Troubles with the Indians in New England* [1677], reprinted in Samuel G. Drake, ed., *The History of the Indian Wars in New England*, 2 vols. (1865; reissued in facsimile, Bowie, Md.: Heritage Books, 1990), 1:60, quoted in Lepore, *Name of War*, 38. *Plymouth Colony Records*, 4:24–26. Lepore, *Name of War*, 39. Lepore has done an outstanding job of reconstructing Sassamon's life (28–41), and this paragraph is heavily indebted to her efforts.

30. *Plymouth Colony Records*, 12:230. Easton, *Relacion of the Indyan Warre*, 7. It is

entirely possible that Philip requested Sassamon's help in formulating a will to preserve his heirs' rights to the land in English eyes. The first Indian wills appeared in the late 1660s, mostly among missionized Indians. Even by 1675, however, Indian wills were probably a very rare phenomenon. For more on Indian wills see Ives Goddard and Kathleen J. Bragdon, *Native Writings in Massachusett* (Philadelphia: American Philosophical Society, 1988), passim.

31. Lepore, *Name of War*, 33.

32. What follows is a brief outline of the circumstances surrounding the death of John Sassamon and the resulting trial. I have drawn the narrative from the Plymouth Colony's court records and various contemporary accounts of the war, including *Plymouth Colony Records*, 5:159, 167–68; Easton, *Relacion of the Indyan Warre*; Hubbard, *Narrative*; Increase Mather, *A Brief History of the War with the Indians in New-England* [1676], reprinted in Samuel G. Drake, ed., *The History of King Philip's War* (Albany, N.Y.: J. Munsell, 1862); and Nathaniel Saltonstall, *The Present State of New England with Respect to the Indian War* [1675], reprinted in Lincoln, *Narratives of the Indian Wars*, 75–98. There are inconsistencies among these various accounts, and none of them offers an Indian perspective of events. Therefore, I have tried to limit my account to what can be inferred with near certainty by comparing the various narratives. I agree with Douglas E. Leach, who argued that "it is now impossible to tell whether the accused were actually guilty of the crime." *Flintlock and Tomahawk: New England in King Philip's War* (New York: Macmillan, 1958), 32. Although we may never know the exact circumstances of Sassamon's death and the resulting trial, my interpretation does not rely on any presumptions about his death or the guilt or innocence of the accused. For more on the historiography of the event and the difficulty of reconstructing it, see James P. Ronda and Jeanne Ronda, "The Death of John Sassamon: An Exploration in Writing New England Indian History," *American Indian Quarterly* 1 (summer 1974): 91–102. The Rondas offer a fine synthesis of accounts of Sassamon's death and the trial, to which I am heavily indebted for helping me to sort out a confusing array of often contradictory material.

33. Quotation from Increase Mather, *A Relation of the Troubles which have hapned in New-England* (Boston, 1677), 74–75. To help guarantee the Indians' appearance, the colony seized the land of Tobias, Tuspaquin, and Tuspaquin's son William. *Plymouth Colony Records*, 5:159.

34. For a sound exploration of various possibilities, see Lepore, *Name of War*, 23–26.

35. *Plymouth Colony Records*, 5:168.

36. Easton, *Relacion of the Indyan Warre*, 10.

37. Gookin, *Historical Collections*, 191.

38. Ibid., 209, 210.

39. Easton, *Relacion of the Indyan Warre*, 9.

40. Ibid., 10. Like the Wampanoags, another group of nonmissionized Indians, the Narragansetts, seemed willing to look to the king for assistance, even after the Sassamon trial. After the war had begun, Easton explained that he saw "no way lickly but if a sesation from arems might be procured untill it might be

knone what terems King Charels wold propound, for we have gret Case to think the naroganset kings wold trust our king and that thay wold have acsepted him to be umpire" (16).

41. Edmund S. Morgan, *American Slavery—American Freedom: The Ordeal of Colonial Virginia* (New York: Norton, 1975), 269. I am indebted to Kevin Sweeney for directing me to this quotation.

42. Quotation from William S. Simmons, *Spirit of the New England Tribes: Indian History and Folklore, 1620–1984* (Hanover, N.H.: University Press of New England, 1986), 51. John Foster, *An Almanack of Celestial Motions for the Year of the Christian Era* (Cambridge, Mass., 1675). Contemporary accounts of the war also mention the eclipse, but they make relatively little of it. Hubbard elaborates on it the most when he describes how it frightened some members of a militia marching from Boston toward Plymouth: "Some Melancholy Fancies would not be perswaded, but that the Eclipse falling out at that Instant of Time was ominous, conceiving also that in the Centre of the Moon they discerned an unusual black Spot, not a little resembling the Scalp of an *Indian:* As some others not long before, imagined they saw the form of an *Indian Bow,* accounting that likewise ominous." *Narrative,* 1:67. Hubbard's account perhaps offers the greatest insight as to what the average English settler made of the eclipse. Most of the comprehensive written accounts of the war had elite clergy as their authors, which may explain why those works minimize the effects of the eclipse. A recent work on Puritan beliefs suggests the importance of signs such as eclipses to the Puritan belief system but also argues that the elite clergy tried to discourage such ideas. See David D. Hall, *Worlds of Wonder, Days of Judgement: Popular Religious Belief in Early New England* (Cambridge, Mass.: Harvard University Press, 1989), passim.

As to whether or not the Indians knew of the eclipse before it came, a Jesuit missionary among the Oneidas reported that these Indians could not predict eclipses as of 1674. However, given the Wampanoags' and the praying Indians' close contact with English settlers and the latter group's access to written documents, it is not entirely unlikely that they might have suspected it was coming. See Reuben Gold Thwaites, ed., *The Jesuit Relations and Allied Documents: Travels and Explorations of the Jesuit Missionaries in New France, 1610–1791,* 73 vols. (Cleveland, 1896–1901), 58:181–83.

43. Thwaites, *Jesuit Relations,* 6:225.

44. Ibid., 22:295.

45. Hall, *Worlds of Wonder.*

4. FAULT LINES

1. Roger Williams to John Winthrop, Jr., June 25, 1675, in Glenn W. LaFantasie, ed., *The Correspondence of Roger Williams,* 2 vols. (Hanover, N.H.: University Press of New England, 1988), 2:694.

2. Ibid.

3. The population figures given are extrapolations from two sources, and one

should view them as rough estimates rather than precise calculations. The figure for the English comes from a rough average of the figures for New England's non-Indian population in 1670 and 1680 (51,896 and 68,462, respectively) found in U.S. Bureau of the Census, *Historical Statistics of the United States, Colonial Times to 1970*, vol. 2 (Washington, D.C.: Bureau of the Census, 1975), 1168. For the Indian populations, the figure of 18,435 is the sum of Sherburne F. Cook's estimates of local Indian populations in 1674. Since Cook's estimates for the Indian population of New England cover a larger area than that directly affected by King Philip's War, I have omitted some groups from the figure. These omissions included the Mahicans, the Long Island Indians, and the Wappinger Confederacy east of Paugussett. Sherburne F. Cook, *The Indian Population of New England in the Seventeenth Century* (Berkeley: University of California Press, 1976), passim (see esp. map on p. 3). In estimating populations, Cook multiplies contemporary estimates of the number of households by four to arrive at a figure for the population at large. Although Neal Salisbury has argued with merit that the factor of four is too small for arriving at estimates of precontact Indian population, there is little to suggest that it is overly problematic for the 1674 figures. Neal Salisbury, *Manitou and Providence: Indians, Europeans, and the Making of New England, 1500–1643* (New York: Oxford University Press, 1982), 7–8.

4. Even where plentiful documentary evidence exists concerning military decisions, it is extremely difficult for historians to prioritize the motives of the historical actors involved. Witness, for example, the difficulty historians have in determining why U.S. President Harry S. Truman decided to drop the atomic bomb. Given this difficulty it would seem both absurd and presumptuous for a historian of seventeenth-century New England to pinpoint and prioritize exact motives for fighting for the numerous bands inhabiting the region in 1675.

5. Although borrowing from Victor Turner, Norton applies the term *liminal* differently. Turner used it to describe a transitional passage from one identity to another in an individual's life. Norton uses it not for a passage across time, but to denote marginal political status in a polity. See Victor Turner, "Betwixt and Between: The Liminal Period in *Rites de Passage*," in Victor Turner, *The Forest of Symbols: Aspects of Ndembu Ritual* (Ithaca, N.Y.: Cornell University Press, 1967), 93–111. Anne Norton, *Reflections on Political Identity*, (Baltimore: Johns Hopkins University Press, 1988), 4, and chap. 2; see also Anne Norton, *Alternative Americas: A Reading of Antebellum Political Cultures* (Chicago: University of Chicago Press, 1986), passim. Thomas P. Slaughter, in his "Crowds in Eighteenth-Century America: Reflections and New Directions," *Pennsylvania Magazine of History and Biography* 115 (Jan. 1991): 12–15, suggests the utility of Norton's concept of liminality to explain patterns of crowd violence. I am thankful to Tim Arretche for pointing me to this literature.

6. Norton, *Reflections*, 55. Scattered throughout this chapter are narrative summaries that borrow from several standard accounts of the war—supplemented at times with my findings. The works that I referred to most for this purpose are Russell Bourne, *The Red King's Rebellion: Racial Politics in New En-*

gland, 1675–1678 (New York: Atheneum, 1990); Francis Jennings, *The Invasion of America: Indians, Colonialism, and the Cant of Conquest* (New York: Norton, 1975), 282–326; Douglas Edward Leach, *Flintlock and Tomahawk: New England in King Philip's War* (New York: Macmillan, 1958); Jill Lepore, *The Name of War: King Philip's War and the Origins of American Identity* (New York: Knopf, 1998); Jenny Hale Pulsipher, "Massacre at Hurtleberry Hill: Christian Indians and English Authority in Metacom's War," *William and Mary Quarterly*, 3d ser., 53 (July 1996): 459–86; and Ian K. Steele, *Warpaths: Invasions of North America* (New York: Oxford University Press, 1994), 80–109.

7. Daniel Gookin, "An Historical Account of the Doings and Sufferings of the Christian Indians in New England" [1677], in *Collections of the American Antiquarian Society* 2 (1836): 441.

8. Josiah Winslow to the honored gentlemen of Connecticut, July 29, 1675, Winthrop Papers, reel 11, Massachusetts Historical Society, Boston (hereafter, MHS); and Josiah Winslow to Wetamoo and [illegible] her husband, Sachems of Pocasset, June 15, 1675, Winslow Papers, item 89, MHS. Coddington quoted in Jennings, *Invasion of America*, 307.

9. J. Hammond Trumbull and Charles J. Hoadly, eds., *The Public Records of the Colony of Connecticut*, 15 vols. (Hartford, Conn.: F. A. Brown, 1850–90) (hereafter, *Records of the Colony of Connecticut*), 2:261–63, quotation from 262. Fitz-John Winthrop to Wait Winthrop, July 9, 1675; Edmund Andros to John Winthrop, Jr., July 9, 1675; Thomas Stanton to Wait Winthrop, July 11, 1675; John Allyn to Wait Winthrop, July 12, 1675; and Samuel Symonds to John Winthrop, Jr., July 14, 1675, all in Winthrop Papers, reel 11, MHS.

10. Literature on the jeremiad is profuse. The most influential contributions are Perry Miller, *The New England Mind: From Colony to Province* (Cambridge, Mass.: Harvard University Press, 1953), chap. 2, "The Jeremiad"; challenging Miller's view of the self-critical nature of the jeremiad, Sacvan Bercovitch highlights its means of self-justification in *The American Jeremiad* (Madison: University of Wisconsin Press, 1978); for recognition of the partisan nature of the jeremiad, see Philip F. Gura, *A Glimpse of Sion's Glory: Puritan Radicalism in New England, 1620–1660* (Middletown, Conn.: Wesleyan University Press, 1984); and Stephen Foster, *The Long Argument: English Puritanism and the Shaping of New England Culture, 1570–1700* (Chapel Hill: University of North Carolina Press, 1991). Neal Salisbury minimizes the effects of Puritanism in mediating the colonists' actions toward Indians in *Manitou and Providence*, 12, 244 n. 15.

11. Thomas Walley to John Cotton, n.d. and July 25, 1675, Cotton Papers, 37, 39–40, Boston Public Library. Increase Mather, "Typescript of Diary," transcribed by Michael Garibaldi Hall, American Antiquarian Society, Worcester, Mass., June 16, Oct. 14, 18, 1675. Mather mentions beginning his history of the war in his entry for May 1, 1676. For early evidence of Puritans attributing the war to their own sins, see Increase Mather, *A Brief History of the War with the Indians in New-England* [1676], reprinted in Samuel G. Drake, ed., *The History of King Philip's War,* (Albany, N.Y.: J. Munsell, 1862), 83.

12. Nathaniel B. Shurtleff, ed., *Records of the Governor and Company of the Massachusetts Bay in New England*, 5 vols. (Boston: William White, 1853–54) (hereafter, *Massachusetts Colonial Records*), 5:59–63, quotations from 59 and 63.

13. "A Testimony from the Children of the Light," Aug. 24, 1675, Winthrop Papers, reel 11, MHS.

14. John Pynchon to John Winthrop, Jr., July 2, 1675, in Carl Bridenbaugh, ed., *The Pynchon Papers*, vol. 1, *Letters of John Pynchon, 1654–1700* (Boston: Colonial Society of Massachusetts, 1982), 137.

15. John Winthrop, Jr., to officers of the army at or near Narragansett, July 12, 1675, Winthrop Papers, reel 11, MHS.

16. This paragraph draws on Richard I. Melvoin's painstaking reconstruction of what on the surface seems to be chaotic violence to reveal an underlying strategy. *New England Outpost: War and Society in Colonial Deerfield* (New York: Norton, 1989), 107–11; and Richard I. Melvoin, "New England Outpost: War and Society in Colonial Frontier Deerfield, Massachusetts," 2 vols, Ph.D. diss., University of Michigan, 1983, 1:179–86.

17. Bridenbaugh, *Pynchon Papers*, 149.

18. For more on Indian tactics, see Patrick M. Malone, *The Skulking Way of War: Technology and Tactics among the New England Indians* (Baltimore: Johns Hopkins University Press, 1993); and Adam J. Hirsch, "The Collision of Military Cultures in Seventeenth-Century New England," *Journal of American History* 74 (Mar. 1988): 1187–212.

19. James Fitch to John Winthrop, Jr., Aug. 30, 1675; and John Allyn to John Winthrop, Jr., Sept. 10, 1675, Winthrop Papers, reel 11, MHS. Samuel Willys to John Winthrop, Jr., Feb. 18, 1676, Winthrop Papers, reel 12, MHS. Another observer, Thomas Gardner, also attributed the expansion of the rebel war effort to English efforts to disarm nonhostile Indians. Thomas Gardner to [?], Sept. 22, 1675, photostats, MHS.

20. Edmund Brown to [?], Sept. 26, 1675; James Parker to John Leverett, Aug. 25, 1675; and Council of Connecticut to Council of Massachusetts, Oct. 7, 1675, photostats, MHS. The town of Dorchester went so far as to petition the court to have all Indians residing with families within its town limits evicted for fear that they might secretly aid the enemy. Dorchester Committee of Militia, "Petition to Remove Indians," Mar. 23, 1676, photostats, MHS.

21. Samuel Gorton to John Winthrop, Jr., Sept. 11, 1675, Winthrop Papers, reel 11, MHS.

22. Ibid.

23. Jill Lepore, "Dead Men Tell No Tales: John Sassamon and the Fatal Consequences of Literacy," *American Quarterly* 46 (Dec. 1994): 482.

24. The two population figures for the English in Connecticut are the estimates for the years 1670 and 1680, respectively, in U.S. Bureau of the Census, *Historical Statistics*, 1168. For Indians the estimate of fifteen hundred is extrapolated from Cook, *Indian Population of New England*, 52. I offer five thousand as a maximum to account for Neal Salisbury's critique of Cook that his population figures were far too low. For precontact population, Salisbury arrived at numbers

approximately 2.5 times as great as Cook's. Salisbury, *Manitou and Providence*, 7–8, 27.

25. William Hubbard, *A Narrative of the Troubles with the Indians in New England* [1677], reprinted in Samuel G. Drake, ed., *The History of the Indian Wars in New England*, 2 vols. (1865; reissued in facsimile, Bowie, Md.: Heritage Books, 1990), 1:183. Daniel Henchman to John Leverett, July 31, 1675, Massachusetts State Archives, Boston, vol. 67. The letter is reprinted in George Madison Bodge, *Soldiers in King Philip's War*, 3d ed. (1906; reprint, Baltimore: Genealogical Publishing Co., 1976), 49–50. For more on Indians as members of Indian-English companies, see Bodge, *Soldiers in King Philip's War*, 464; and Benjamin Church, *The Entertaining History of King Philip's War* [1716], reprinted in Benjamin Church, *Diary of King Philip's War, 1675–76* (Chester, Conn.: Pequot Press, 1975), 106, 108.

26. Underhill quoted in Charles Orr, ed., *History of the Pequot War* (Cleveland, 1897), 84. Hirsch, "Collision of Military Cultures," 1211–12.

27. William S. Simmons, *Spirit of the New England Tribes: Indian History and Folklore, 1620–1984* (Hanover, N.H.: University Press of New England, 1986), 172. Kenneth M. Morrison, "Mapping Otherness: Myth and the Study of Cultural Encounter," in Emerson Woods Baker II, Edwin A. Churchill, Richard D'Abate, Kristine L. Jones, Victor A. Konrad, and Harald E. L. Prins, eds., *American Beginnings: Exploration, Culture, and Cartography in the Land of Norumbega* (Lincoln: University of Nebraska Press, 1994), 119–29, quotation from 123. Hubbard, *Narrative*, 59.

28. Neal Salisbury, "Social Relationships on a Moving Frontier: Natives and Settlers in Southern New England, 1638–1675," *Man in the Northeast* 33 (1987): 89–99, quotation from 94.

29. The preceding six paragraphs summarize some of the main points of Salisbury, "Social Relationships." The preceding two paragraphs also emphasize the arguments of Peter Allen Thomas, "In the Maelstrom of Change: The Indian Trade and Cultural Process in the Middle Connecticut River Valley, 1635–1665," Ph.D. diss., University of Massachusetts, Amherst, 1979.

30. Ann Marie Plane, "Putting a Face on Colonization: Factionalism and Gender Politics in the Life History of Awashunkes, the 'Squaw Sachem' of Saconet," in Robert S. Grumet, ed., *Northeastern Indian Lives, 1636–1816* (Amherst: University of Massachusetts Press, 1996), 142–44.

31. Church, *Entertaining History*, 69–73, quotations from 70, 72. I am also indebted to Ann Marie Plane's analysis of this episode. It is unclear what role, if any, Awashunkes' gender had in influencing the English decision to allow her to switch sides.

32. Plane, "Putting a Face," 147; and Church, *Entertaining History*, 125–27.

33. Plane, "Putting a Face," 147–49.

34. Josiah Winslow to Wetamoo and Petonowowett, sachems of Pocasset, June 15, 1675, Winslow Papers, item 89; Josiah Winslow to [?] Freeman, June 28, 1675, Winslow Papers, item 90; and Josiah Winslow to John Leverett, July 6, 1675, Davis Papers, MHS.

35. Church, *Diary*, 73. Daniel Gookin, "Doings and Sufferings," 377; Church,

Entertaining History, 136. Another instance of the war splitting prominent kin is that of Ninigret and Quaiapen—brother and sister—who fought on opposite sides and Peter Jethro, who turned in his rebel father to English forces. For more on the latter example, see Pulsipher, "Massacre at Hurtleberry Hill," 483. For more on Wetamoo, see Church, *Entertaining History,* 90–92, 121.

36. Pulsipher suggests that a parallel generational divide separated those English colonists who advocated harsh treatment for praying Indians from those who argued for moderation. "Massacre at Hurtleberry Hill," 477–79. Hubbard, *Narrative,* 1:98. Roger Williams to John Winthrop, Jr., June 27, 1675, in LaFantasie, *The Correspondence of Roger Williams,* 2:698.

37. Hubbard, *Narrative,* 1:277.

38. Kathleen J. Bragdon, *Native People of Southern New England, 1500–1650* (Norman: University of Oklahoma Press, 1996), 55–79.

39. Bridenbaugh, *Pynchon Papers,* 138, 140, 147, comment about Uncas on 152.

40. Mather, *Brief History,* 75; and Bridenbaugh, *Pynchon Papers,* 149. The itemization "Mothers, Brothers, and Cousins" may suggest matrilineality. Neal Salisbury has argued for an earlier period that "[l]oyalty to kin, more often than to band, induced individuals to participate in retributive violence." *Manitou and Providence,* 41–42. Gookin, "Doings and Sufferings," 454. Hubbard, *Narrative,* 1:123. Pulsipher, "Massacre at Hurtleberry Hill," 465; and Nathaniel Saltonstall, *The Present State of New-England with Respect to the Indian War* [1675], reprinted in Charles H. Lincoln, ed., *Narratives of the Indian Wars 1675–1699* (New York: Scribner's, 1913), 47–48.

41. Mather, *Brief History,* 75. The bond that the English felt together constituted a kind of metaphorical kinship as well, because they were all subjects of a patriarchal king. Again, when talking about the war with Roger Williams, some Narragansetts asked him "why the Massachusets and Rode Iland rose, and joynd with Plymmouth agnst Phillip and left not Phillip and Plymmouth to fight it out." Williams responded, "[A]ll the Colonies were Subject to one K. Charls [King Charles] and it was his pleasure and our Dutie and Engagemnt for one English man to stand to the Death by Each other in all parts of the World." Roger Williams to John Winthrop, Jr., June 25, 1675, in LaFantasie, *Correspondence of Roger Williams,* 2:694.

42. Tobias Sanders to Fitz-John Winthrop, July 3, 1675, Winthrop Papers, reel 11, MHS.

43. William Leete to John Winthrop, Jr., Sept. 21, 1675, Winthrop Papers, reel 11, MHS. Much literature treats the importance of gift-giving in establishing metaphorical kinship. For a sampling of it, see Wilbur R. Jacobs, *Diplomacy and Indian Gifts: Anglo French Rivalry along the Ohio and Northwest Frontiers, 1748–1763* (Stanford, Calif.: Stanford University Press, 1950); Marcel Mauss, *The Gift: Forms and Fashions of Exchange in Archaic Societies,* trans. Ian Cunnison (London: Cohen and West, 1954); and Marshall Sahlins, *Stone Age Economics* (Chicago: Aldine-Atherton, 1972).

44. Daniel Gookin devoted the bulk of his "Historical Account of the Doings and Sufferings of the Christian Indians" to applauding the contribution of the

praying Indians to the war effort. However, he could not find a publisher, even though he had been a licensor of the press in Cambridge. The work was not published until 1836. Gookin also lost reelection to the Massachusetts Court of Assistants in May 1676. See Lepore, *The Name of War*, 45; John Canup, *Out of the Wilderness: The Emergence of an American Identity in Colonial New England* (Middletown, Conn.: Wesleyan University Press, 1990), 185–86; and Douglas Edward Leach, *Flintlock and Tomahawk*, 151.

45. Hubbard, *Narrative*, 1:48–49; and Colin G. Calloway, "Wanalancet and Kancagamus: Indian Strategy and Leadership on the New Hampshire Frontier," *Historical New Hampshire* 43 (winter 1988): 273–74.

46. Gookin, "Doings and Sufferings," 450–51. Moseley receives more attention in chapter 5. Gookin, "Doings and Sufferings," 455–61, quotation from 459.

47. By far the best work on Christian Indians during the war is Pulsipher, "Massacre at Hurtleberry Hill." She too sees the attacks on Springfield as pivotal for colonists' attitudes toward praying Indians (465–66). Gookin, "Doings and Sufferings," 472–74. Quotation from *Massachusetts Colonial Records*, 5:64.

48. Anthony and James to the Massachusetts Council, July 19, 1675, Massachusetts Archives, Boston, 67:220. Gookin quotation from "Doings and Sufferings," 485.

49. *Massachusetts Colonial Records*, 5:64.

50. Gookin, "Doings and Sufferings," 485. Mary Pray to Captain Oliver, Dec. 20, 1675, Winthrop Papers, reel 11, MHS.

51. Jill Lepore examines Printer's case with tremendous subtlety. She sees him as having been captured, although she admits that it "is certainly subject to debate." *Name of War*, 136–49, quotation from 137.

52. Monaque Woaoknuns [sp?] the Cowesit sachem, petition to Plymouth General Court, 1675, Davis Papers, MHS.

53. William Coddington, "Testimony of James Sweet," Oct. 10, 1675; and John Paine to Commissioners of the United Colonies, Oct. [?] 1675, photostats, MHS.

54. Tobias Sanders to John Winthrop, Jr., July 3, 1675; and Sanders to Wait Winthrop, July 7, 1675, Winthrop Papers, reel 11, MHS.

55. John Mason to Fitz-John Winthrop, Aug. 15, 17, 1675, Winthrop Papers, reel 11, MHS. Leach, *Flintlock and Tomahawk*, 146.

56. Salisbury, *Manitou and Providence*, 226. See also Eric Johnson, "'Some by Flatteries and Others by Threatenings': Political Strategies among Native Americans of Seventeenth-Century New England," Ph.D. diss., University of Massachusetts, 1993, 53–61.

57. Gookin, "Doings and Sufferings," 445.

58. *Records of the Colony of Connecticut*, 2:336.

59. Salisbury, *Manitou and Providence*, 232–35.

60. John Mason to Fitz-John Winthrop, Sept. 6, 1675, Winthrop Papers, reel 11, MHS.

61. Hubbard, *Narrative*, 1:252.

62. Ibid., 2:63.

63. Ibid., 2:63–64.

64. Ibid., 1:253. For an astute interpretation of what the torture meant to the English, see Lepore, *Name of War,* 3–18.

5. "Barbarous Inhumane Outrages"

1. These estimates were made by Daniel Gookin and William Hubbard, respectively; see Bert Salwen, "Indians of Southern New England and Long Island: Early Period," in Bruce Trigger, ed., *Northeast,* vol. 15 of William C. Sturtevant, ed., *Handbook of North American Indians* (Washington, D.C.: Smithsonian Institution Press, 1978), 169.

2. Roger Williams to John Winthrop, Jr., Dec. 18, 1675, in Glenn W. LaFantasie, ed., *The Correspondence of Roger Williams,* 2 vols. (Hanover, N.H.: University Press of New England, 1988), 2:708. In reconstructing the chronology of events, I have distilled several standard accounts of the war: Russell Bourne, *The Red King's Rebellion: Racial Politics in New England, 1675–1678* (New York: Atheneum, 1990); Francis Jennings, *The Invasion of America: Indians, Colonialism, and the Cant of Conquest* (New York: Norton, 1975), 282–326; Douglas Edward Leach, *Flintlock and Tomahawk: New England in King Philip's War* (New York: Macmillan, 1958); Jill Lepore, *The Name of War: King Philip's War and the Origins of American Identity* (New York: Knopf, 1998); Jenny Hale Pulsipher, "Massacre at Hurtleberry Hill: Christian Indians and English Authority in Metacom's War," *William and Mary Quarterly,* 3d ser., 53 (July 1996): 459–86; and Ian K. Steele, *Warpaths: Invasions of North America* (New York: Oxford University Press, 1994), 80–109.

3. Roger Williams to John Winthrop, Jr., June 13, 1675, in LaFantasie, *Correspondence of Roger Williams,* 2:691.

4. William Bradford, *Of Plymouth Plantation, 1620–1647,* ed. Samuel Eliot Morison (New York: Knopf, 1953), 296. See David Stannard, *American Holocaust* (New York: Oxford University Press, 1992); and Russell Thornton, *American Indian Holocaust and Survival* (Norman: University of Oklahoma Press, 1987). Referring specifically to New England, Neal Salisbury hinted more obliquely at the parallels between the holocaust perpetrated by the Nazis and Puritan policies in New England when he entitled the last chapter of his dissertation "The Final Solution." "Conquest of the Savage," Ph.D. diss., University of California, Los Angeles, 1973; For essays explicitly debating whether or not the Pequot massacre constituted genocide comparable to the Nazi Holocaust, see Steven T. Katz, "The Pequot War Reconsidered," *New England Quarterly* 64 (June 1991): 206–24; and Michael Freeman, "Puritans and Pequots: The Question of Genocide," *New England Quarterly* 68 (June 1995): 278–93. For a superb analysis of violence in the Pequot War, see Ronald Dale Karr, "'Why Should You Be So Furious?': The Violence of the Pequot War," *Journal of American History* 85 (Dec. 1998): 876–909. Capt. John Underhill wrote that the Narragansetts believed that English-style warfare was "too furious and slays too many men." Charles Orr, ed., *History of the Pequot War* (Cleveland, 1897), 84.

5. Barbara Donagan, "Atrocity, War Crime, and Treason in the English Civil War," *American Historical Review* 99 (Oct. 1994): 1137 and passim. This chapter tries

to unveil Indian motives in their conduct as much as possible, but neither I nor others have been able to discover much from the limited sources. However, much of my analysis proceeds from the assumption that the colonists reacted to the conduct of enemy Indians. In this sense Indian behavior is central to the arguments of this chapter, even if the meaning behind the behavior is lost. Jill Lepore offers some interesting musings on how Indian culture might have governed native conduct in King Philip's War, but she provides little in the way of hard conclusions aside from the notion that culture must have mediated their actions. *Name of War,* 116–19.

6. Philip Vincent, *The Lamentations of Germany* (London, 1638), 22, 16; and [Philip Vincent], *A True Relation of the Late Battell Fought in New England, between the English and the Pequot Salvages* (London, 1638), 20, 16. I follow the authority of the *Dictionary of National Biography,* 1899 ed., which states that the two works "bear traces of being by the same author." S. v. "Vincent, Philip."

7. [Vincent], *True Relation,* 5. Vincent's views accord with those Alden T. Vaughan attributes to the English as a whole during this period in "From White Man to Redskin: Changing Anglo-American Perceptions of the American Indian," *American Historical Review* 87 (Oct. 1982): 917–53.

8. For the permeation of notions of right and wrong in war throughout English culture, especially its literature, see Barbara Donagan, "Halcyon Days and the Literature of War: England's Military Education before 1642," *Past and Present* 147 (May 1995): 65–100; and Theodor Meron, *Henry's Wars and Shakespeare's Laws: Perspectives on the Law of War in the Later Middle Ages* (Oxford: Clarendon Press, 1993). Maurice H. Keen, *The Laws of War in the Late Middle Ages* (London: Routledge, 1965), 121; and Donagan, "Atrocity," 1144.

9. Karen Ordahl Kupperman, *Settling with the Indians: The Meeting of English and Indian Cultures in America, 1580–1640* (Totowa, N.J.: Rowman and Littlefield, 1980), 184–85. William Hubbard, *A Narrative of the Troubles with the Indians in New England* [1677], reprinted in Samuel G. Drake, ed., *The History of the Indian Wars in New England,* 2 vols. (1865; reissued in facsimile, Bowie, Md.: Heritage Books, 1990), 2:32. For just one example of a portrayal of Philip as a traitor or rebel, see William Harris, *A Rhode Islander Reports on King Philip's War: The Second William Harris Letter of August, 1676,* ed. Douglas E. Leach (Providence: Rhode Island Historical Society, 1963), 20. Jennings quoted in Alfred A. Cave, *The Pequot War* (Amherst: University of Massachusetts Press, 1996), 70–71, Winthrop quotation from 71; Jennings quotation from 201 n. 4.

10. Kupperman, *Settling with the Indians,* 170–71. Edward Coke, *The Third Part of the Institutes of the Laws of England. Concerning High Treason, and other Pleas of the Crown, and Criminal Causes,* 5th ed. (London, 1671), 211. *The General Laws and Liberties of the Massachusetts Colony* (Cambridge, Mass., 1672), 15.

11. Nathaniel B. Shurtleff, ed., *Records of the Governor and Company of the Massachusetts Bay in New England,* 5 vols. (Boston: William White, 1853–54) (hereafter, *Massachusetts Colonial Records*), 3:101. See also J. Hammond Trumbull and Charles J. Hoadly, eds., *The Public Records of the Colony of Connecticut,* 15 vols. (Hartford, Conn.: F. A. Brown, 1850–90) (hereafter, *Records of the Colony of Connecticut*),

1:78, 515. Edmund S. Morgan has noted that the courts usually would not implement the death penalty, but instead would take the child away from the parents. *The Puritan Family: Essays on Religion and Domestic Relations in Seventeenth-Century New England* (Boston: Trustees of the Boston Public Library, 1944), 38.

12. Donagan, "Atrocity," 1141, 1155–56. Both Harold Selesky and Douglas Edward Leach have noted the harsh treatment accorded Indians during the latter part of the war. Harold E. Selesky, *War and Society in Colonial Connecticut* (New Haven, Conn.: Yale University Press, 1990), 22; and Leach, *Flintlock and Tomahawk*, 224.

13. John Mason to Wait Winthrop, July 6, 1675, Winthrop Papers, reel 11, Massachusetts Historical Society, Boston (hereafter, MHS). John Winthrop, Jr., remembered the Narragansett assistance to the English in the Pequot War fondly when he cautioned the army not to upset the Narragansetts: "[T]he Narragansetts have hitherto continued in amity with the English, and were voluntarily very helpful to them in those wars with the Pequot." John Winthrop, Jr., to officers of the army at or near Narragansett, July 12, 1675, Winthrop Papers, reel 11, MHS. Thomas Stanton and Thomas Minor to the governor and council at Hartford, June 30, 1675; Wait Winthrop to Fitz-John Winthrop, July [?], 1675, Winthrop Papers, reel 11, MHS.

14. Thomas Stanton to Wait Winthrop, July 9, 1675; Richard Smith to John Winthrop, Jr., Sept. 3, 1675; John Allyn to Wait Winthrop, July 12, 1675, Winthrop Papers, reel 11, MHS.

15. Reported in James Cudworth to Josiah Winslow, July 10, 1675, Winslow Papers, item 93, MHS.

16. John Winthrop, Jr., to the officers of the army at or near Narragansett, July 12, 1675, Winthrop Papers, reel 11, MHS. For a copy of the July treaty, see Elisha R. Potter, *The Early History of Narragansett* (Providence, R.I.: Marshall, Brown and Co., 1835), 167–69; for the October treaty, see Nathaniel B. Shurtleff and David Pulsifer, eds., *Records of the Colony of New Plymouth in New England*, 12 vols. (Boston, 1855–61) (hereafter, *Plymouth Colony Records*), 2:360–61.

17. The word *hostage* appears in 2 Kings 14:14 and 2 Chron. 25:24. The Eliot translation uses the words *wanomwaonganehtea ukeg* and *konohtohsimukeg*, respectively. *The Holy Bible. Containing the Old Testament and the New. Translated into the Indian Language . . .,* trans. John Eliot (Cambridge, Mass., 1663). Richard Smith to John Winthrop, Jr., Sept. 12, 1675, Winthrop Papers, reel 11, MHS.

18. Richard Smith to John Winthrop, Jr., Oct. 27, 1675, Winthrop Papers, reel 11, MHS.

19. Paul Alden Robinson, "The Struggle Within: The Indian Debate in Seventeenth-Century Narragansett Country," Ph.D. diss., State University of New York, Binghamton, 1990. Richard Smith to John Winthrop, Jr., Sept. 3, 1675, Winthrop Papers, reel 11, MHS; Roger Williams to John Winthrop, Jr., June 27, 1675, in LaFantasie, *Correspondence of Roger Williams*, 698. For more evidence of factionalism, see Richard Smith to John Winthrop, Jr., Oct. 27, 1675, Winthrop Papers, reel 11, MHS.

20. Thomas Stanton to Wait Winthrop, July 9, 1675, Winthrop Papers, reel

11, MHS. Quotation from Wait Winthrop to Fitz-John Winthrop, July [?], 1675, Winthrop Papers, reel 11, MHS.

21. Richard Smith to John Winthrop, Jr., Sept. 3, 1675; John Winthrop, Jr. to Richard Smith, Aug. [?], 1675, Winthrop Papers, reel 11, MHS. See also John Winthrop, Jr., to officers of the army at or near Narragansett, July 12, 1675; and John Winthrop, Jr., to Wait Winthrop, July 9, 1675, Winthrop Papers, reel 11, MHS.

22. Richard Smith to John Winthrop, Jr., Nov. 27, 1675, Winthrop Papers, reel 11, MHS.

23. *Plymouth Colony Records*, 10:457–58; and *Massachusetts Colonial Records*, 5:66–67.

24. *Plymouth Colony Records*, 2:357–58. Douglas Edward Leach has admirably reconstructed the chronology of events described in the preceding three paragraphs. *Flintlock and Tomahawk*, 117–19; and Douglas Edward Leach, "A New View of the Declaration of War against the Narragansetts, November, 1675," *Rhode Island History* 15 (April 1956): 33–41.

25. Hubbard, *Narrative*, 2:268; and Samuel Gorton to John Winthrop, Jr., Aug. 11, 1675, Winthrop Papers, reel 11, MHS.

26. Casualty estimates from Leach, *Flintlock and Tomahawk*, 132–33. So far as I can tell, Leach arrived at these figures by guessing the rough average of contemporary estimates. My reconstruction of the events of that day draws extensively on Steele, *Warpaths*, 102.

27. George Madison Bodge, *Soldiers in King Philip's War* (1906; reprint, Baltimore: Genealogical Publishing Co., 1976), 205.

28. James Richards to John Winthrop, Jr., Jan. 5, 13, 1676; and John Allyn to John Winthrop, Jr., Jan. 12, 1676, Winthrop Papers, reel 12, MHS.

29. For the connections between those who fought in the English Civil War and the membership of the Ancient and Honorable Artillery Company of Boston, see Louise A. Breen, "Religious Radicalism in the Puritan Officer Corps: Heterodoxy, the Artillery Company, and Cultural Integration in Seventeenth-Century Boston," *New England Quarterly* 68 (Mar. 1995): 3, 19, and passim.

30. Benjamin Church, *The Entertaining History of King Philip's War* [1716], reprinted in Benjamin Church, *Diary of King Philip's War, 1675–76* (Chester, Conn.: Pequot Press, 1975), 92.

31. Hubbard, *Narrative*, 1:220, 2:135. Hubbard was just one of many Puritans who blamed the war to the east on English provocations. For another example, see Increase Mather, *A Brief History of the War with the Indians in New England* [1676], reprinted in Samuel G. Drake, ed., *The History of King Philip's War*, (Albany, N.Y.: J. Munsell, 1862), 141. Recently it has been discovered that victims of two of the war's worst atrocities did indeed continue to seek vengeance against the English into the eighteenth century. See Evan Haefeli and Kevin Sweeney, "Revisiting *The Redeemed Captive*: New Perspectives on the 1704 Attack on Deerfield," *William and Mary Quarterly*, 3d ser., 52 (Jan. 1995): 19, 22–23.

32. Increase Mather, *Brief History*, 207. The role of the Mohawks only began to receive adequate attention in the 1980s. Douglas Edward Leach did not examine the role of the Mohawks in *Flintlock and Tomahawk*, probably because he

viewed English culture, power, and technology as the critical factors in determining the outcome of the war. Subsequent historians have done a much better job of resurrecting the Mohawk influence in the war. See Jennings, *Invasion of America*, 314–16; Richard I. Melvoin, *New England Outpost: War and Society in Colonial Deerfield* (New York: Norton, 1989), 116–20; Daniel K. Richter, *The Ordeal of the Longhouse: The Peoples of the Iroquois League in the Era of European Colonization* (Chapel Hill: University of North Carolina Press, 1992), 135–37; and Neal Salisbury, "Toward the Covenant Chain: Iroquois and Southern New England Algonquians, 1637–1684," in Daniel K. Richter and James H. Merrell, eds., *Beyond the Covenant Chain: The Iroquois and Their Neighbors in Indian North America, 1600–1800* (Syracuse, N.Y.: Syracuse University Press, 1987), 70–72. For evidence of Andros's involvement in lobbying the Mohawks and the reluctance of the New England colonial governments to accept his help, see Carl Bridenbaugh, ed., *The Pynchon Papers*, vol. 1, *Letters of John Pynchon, 1654–1700* (Boston: Colonial Society of Massachusetts, 1982), 150–52; and *Records of the Colony of Connecticut*, 2:377–78, 397–98, 404–5, 406–7. For evidence of Mohawk attacks against New England Indians, see Bodge, *Soldiers in King Philip's War*, 242; *Records of the Colony of Connecticut*, 2:461–62; and Hubbard, *Narrative*, 1:217.

33. For a more comprehensive account of these battles and others from February to May 1676, especially their English participants, tactics, and marches, see Leach, *Flintlock and Tomahawk*, chap. 9.

34. For more on the narrative, see Neal Salisbury's introduction to Mary Rowlandson, *The Sovereignty and Goodness of God, Together with the Faithfulness of His Promises Displayed: Being a Narrative of the Captivity and Restoration of Mrs. Mary Rowlandson and Related Documents*, ed. Neal Salisbury (Boston: Bedford Books, 1997). Quotations from 75, 76.

35. Increase Mather, *Brief History*, 121. Quotation in Daniel Gookin, "An Historical Account of the Doings and Sufferings of the Christian Indians in New England" [1677], in *Collections of the American Antiquarian Society* 2 (1836): 494.

36. For more details on the planned wall, see Leach, *Flintlock and Tomahawk*, 165–66; and Massachusetts State Archives, Boston, vol. 68, docs. 169a, 172a, 174, 175b, 176a, 179, 180, 183. Document 179 is published in Bodge, *Soldiers in King Philip's War*, 214.

37. See Lepore, *Name of War*, 103–4, for a convenient listing of all the fasts and days of humiliation and thanksgiving. Also see Perry Miller, *The New England Mind: From Colony to Province* (Cambridge, Mass.: Harvard University Press, 1953), 114.

38. *Massachusetts Colonial Records*, 5:86–87.

39. Massachusetts Council to Maj. Simon Willard, Aug. 24, 1675, photostats, MHS. Mather, *Brief History*, 206.

40. Hubbard, *Narrative*, 1:87.

41. Rowlandson, *Sovereignty*, ed. Salisbury, 81–82; and Hubbard, *Narrative*, 1:117, 167, 171, 172, 174, 230–31. Gookin, "Doings and Sufferings," 493.

42. Patrick M. Malone, *The Skulking Way of War: Technology and Tactics among the New England Indians* (Baltimore: Johns Hopkins University Press, 1993), 67–87.

43. For gender roles among the Indians of the seventeenth-century Northeast, see James Axtell, ed., *The Indian Peoples of Eastern America: A Documentary History of the Sexes* (New York: Oxford University Press, 1981), 103–40. Malone, *The Skulking Way of War*, 37–46, 67–87, quotation from 87.

44. Bradford quoted in Malone, *The Skulking Way of War*, 93.

45. Quotations from ibid., 99. Jean-Francois Blanchette, "Firearms," in Susan G. Gibson, ed., *Burr's Hill: A Seventeenth-Century Wampanoag Burial Ground in Warren, Rhode Island* (Providence, R.I.: Haffenreffer Museum of Anthropology, 1980), 71; and Lorraine Elise Williams, "Fort Shantok and Fort Corchaug: A Comparative Study of Seventeenth-Century Culture Contact in the Long Island Sound Area," Ph.D. diss., New York University, 1972, 334–35.

46. Malone, *Skulking Way of War*, 96–97.

47. Adam J. Hirsch, "The Collision of Military Cultures in Seventeenth-Century New England," *Journal of American History* 74 (Mar. 1988): 1187–212. Hirsch's idea of military acculturation applies well to changes in tactics. However, it does not seem that Indian conceptions of victory and defeat changed as much, as suggested later in this chapter.

48. *Dictionary of National Biography*, 1890 ed., s. v. "Gookin, Daniel." For more on Gookin, see Frederick William Gookin's filiopietistic *Daniel Gookin, 1612–1687: Assistant and Major General of the Massachusetts Bay Colony, His Life and Letters and Some Account of His Ancestry* (Chicago: privately printed, 1912). Daniel Gookin, "Doings and Sufferings," 459, 462, 472, 449, 466, 503.

49. Bodge, *Soldiers in King Philip's War*, 62–63. Examining Boston tax lists for 1674, Bodge found that a large number of Moseley's soldiers were apprentices or servants. Hubbard labeled Moseley's soldiers "privateers." *Narrative*, 1:70. Perhaps the most striking example of a Moseley war crime can be found in a letter he wrote on October 16, 1675. After describing the interrogation of a captured Indian woman near Hatfield, Massachusetts, Moseley wrote, "This aforesaid Indian was ordered to be torn to peeces by Doggs and she was soe dealt with all." Bodge, *Soldiers in King Philip's War*, 69. I have not been able to find any kind of reaction to this comment on the part of Massachusetts officials.

50. Gookin, "Doings and Sufferings," 462. Bodge, *Soldiers in King Philip's War*, 67.

51. Samuel Moseley to Gov. John Leverett, Oct. 5, 1675, reprinted in Bodge, *Soldiers in King Philip's War*, 68.

52. An issue needing further investigation is the extent to which ordinary English persons felt insulted because Indians worked at the same jobs as they or held a disproportionate share of land. Daniel Gookin noted that a large number of Indians, especially Christian ones, worked for the English. "Doings and Sufferings," 434–35. John Pynchon to John Winthrop, Jr., Aug. 19, 1675, in Bridenbaugh, *Pynchon Papers*, 146. For the suggestion that anti-Indian sentiment had a generational slant, see Pulsipher, "Massacre at Hurtleberry Hill," 477–79.

53. In reconstructing the death of Canonchet, I have found Bourne, *Red King's Rebellion*, 187–88, useful, as well as Hubbard, *Narrative*, 2:57–60. Increase Mather had a slightly different version of Canonchet's death, writing that upon his cap-

ture "the English caused the Pequods and Monhegins, and Ninnegrets Indians to joyn together in shooting Quanonchet, and cutting off his head, which was sent to Hartford. And herein the English dealt wisely, for by this meanes, those three Indian Nations are to become abominable to the other Indians, and it is now their interest to be faithfull to the English, since their own Countrymen will never forgive them, on account of their taking and killing the Sachem mentioned." *Brief History*, 134.

54. Bodge, *Soldiers in King Philip's War*, 232–34.

55. Ibid., 245. Bourne, *Red King's Rebellion*, 189, 192.

56. This is not to say that Indians close to those who died at Peskeompscut ever forgot the incident. Rather, they continued to retaliate well into the future, including in a famous attack against Deerfield in 1704. Haefeli and Sweeney, "Revisiting," 19.

57. Keith J. Lindley, "The Impact of the 1641 Rebellion upon England and Wales, 1641–5," *Irish Historical Studies* 28 (Sept. 1972): 144–46. Lindley provides quantitative data on the proportion of references to Ireland in Thomason's collection of tracts in the British Library. For a sampling of the tracts highlighting atrocities in general and rapes in particular, see August, *A Treacherous Plot of a Confederacie in Ireland* . . . (London, 1641); n.a., *The Happiest Newes from Ireland that Ever Came to England since the First Rebellion. . . .* (London, 1641); n.a., *The Last Newes from Ireland Being a Relation of the Hostile and bloody procedings of the Rebellious Papists there, at this present. . . .* (London, 1641); n.a., *Late and Lamentable News from Ireland, Wherein are truly related, the Rebellious, and cruell proceedings of the Papists there* . . . (London, 1641); n.a., *The Rebels of Irelands Wicked Conspiracie* . . . (London, 1641); n.a., *Worse and Worse Newes from Ireland* . . . (London, 1641); and Witcome, *The Rebels Turkish Tyranny* . . . (London, 1641).

58. Donagan, "Atrocity," 1148; and Lindley, "Impact," 175.

59. Hubbard, *Narrative*, 2:175, 1:167. Hubbard made note of the respect that Indians accorded their captives throughout his history of the war. For more examples, see 1:207, 2:204. Mary Rowlandson also portrayed her treatment at the hands of Indians as decent. *Sovereignty*, ed. Salisbury, 63–112. The issue of Indian treatment of war captives has received much attention. Highlighting Indian benevolence is James Axtell, "The White Indians of Colonial America," in James Axtell, *The European and the Indian: Essays in the Ethnohistory of Colonial North America* (New York: Oxford University Press, 1981), 168–206. Daniel K. Richter, "War and Culture: The Iroquois Experience," *William and Mary Quarterly*, 3d ser., 40 (Oct. 1983): 528–59, arrived at different conclusions when looking specifically at the Iroquois. It is inconclusive whether or not the southern New England Algonquians adopted their captives as did the Iroquois. Nor is their any solid evidence that these Algonquians tortured their captives before killing them.

60. Virginia DeJohn Anderson, "King Philip's Herds: Indians, Colonists, and the Problem of Livestock in Early New England," *William and Mary Quarterly*, 3d. ser., 51 (Oct. 1994): 601–24.

61. Barbara Donagan, personal communication, July 28, 1995.

62. *Records of the Colony of Connecticut*, 2:280, 369, 379. Mary Rowlandson is the

best-known example of a captive required to make clothing. Her captivity narrative includes numerous instances of her making an article of clothing for the Indians who held her. Rowlandson, *Sovereignty,* ed. Salisbury, 83, 84, 89, 97, 104. She also describes her mistaking a party of Indians at a distance for Englishmen, "for they were dressed in English apparel, with hats, white neckcloths, and sashes about their waists, and ribbons upon their shoulders" (94). For a discussion of the beliefs surrounding plunder, see Keen, *Laws of War,* chap. 9, "Gains of War and Their Division." Reading the colonists' polemical accounts of the war makes it difficult to remember that Indians undoubtedly had cultural norms that restrained their conduct. Uncas, for example, was reluctant to expand the Mohegans' war to include a contest against upland Indians. John Mason wrote that the Mohegans "seem not to be willing to fight with the upland Indians unless they understand the ground of the English warring with them." John Mason to Fitz-John Winthrop, Sept. 6, 1675, Winthrop Papers, reel 11, MHS. For Indian cultural restraints on wartime conduct at the time of the Pequot War, including the sparing of women and children, see Hirsch, "Collision of Military Cultures," 1187–212, esp. 1191.

63. See, for example, the sachem John Monoco calling out to Captain Parker in Hubbard, *Narrative,* 1:199. Benjamin Church knew many of the Indians who fought against the English. This familiarity enabled him sometimes to persuade them to surrender and often fight on his side in exchange for lenient treatment. *Entertaining History,* 135, 168. Russell quoted in Mather, *Brief History,* 75. *Records of the Colony of Connecticut,* 486. The petition is reprinted in Gookin, "Doings and Sufferings," 527–28. Church, *Entertaining History,* 91.

64. For the Puritan belief in the Great Chain of Being, see Stephen Innes, *Creating the Commonwealth: The Economic Culture of Puritan New England* (New York: Norton, 1995), 6, 120. John Winthrop reflected this belief in a natural hierarchy in his famous speech aboard the *Arbella,* "A Modell of Christian Charity," when he wrote, "God Almightie in his most holy and wise Providence hath soe disposed of the condicion of mankind, as in all times some must be rich some poore, some highe and eminent in power and dignitie; others mean and in subjeccion." MHS, *Winthrop Papers,* ed. Allyn B. Forbes, 5 vols. (Boston: Massachusetts Historical Society, 1929–47), 2:289.

65. Gookin, "Doings and Sufferings," 431.

66. Obtaining even an approximation of the number of Indian indentured servants and slaves sold during or immediately after the war is nearly impossible. For an attempt to do so for Rhode Island in the eighteenth century, see John A. Sainsbury, "Indian Labor in Early Rhode Island," *New England Quarterly* 48 (Sept. 1975): 378–93. For a discussion of the rules of war as they apply to the obligations and rights of captors and captives, see Keen, *Rules of War,* chap. 10, "The Law of Ransom."

67. Cotton quoted in John Canup, *Out of the Wilderness: The Emergence of an American Identity in Colonial New England* (Middletown, Conn.: Wesleyan University Press, 1990), 135–36. The *Plymouth Colony Records,* for example, defends slavery on the grounds that captured and surrendered Indians had to be removed for

safety's sake. On July 22, 1677, the Plymouth court decided that certain Indian males above the age of fourteen at the time of their capture could not live within the colony on the grounds that "the permition of Indian men that are captives to settle and abide within this collonie may prove prejudiciall to our comon peace and safety" (5:210).

68. Innes, *Creating the Commonwealth*, 107–60, esp. 126ff.

69. Church, *Entertaining History*, 130, 176. In Massachusetts, Samuel Moseley's troops petitioned for the profits from the sale of captives. If the request was granted, this might have provided an incentive for his zeal. However, I do not know of any evidence showing that it was. *Records of the Colony of Connecticut*, 2:385, 474–75, 487.

70. Leach, *Flintlock and Tomahawk*, chap. 6, "Men Matériel, and Money"; Michael J. Puglisi, *Puritans Besieged: The Legacies of King Philip's War in the Massachusetts Bay Colony* (New York: University Press of America, 1991), chap. 4, "The High Cost of War."

71. Hubbard, *Narrative*, 1:15.

6. VICTORY AND DEFEAT

1. I borrow the distinction between "initial" and "sustaining" motivation to fight from John A. Lynn, *The Bayonets of the Republic: Motivation and Tactics in the Army of Revolutionary France, 1791–1794* (Urbana: University of Illinois Press, 1984), 35–36, 177–82. The concept is put to good use in James M. McPherson, *For Cause and Comrades: Why Men Fought in the Civil War* (New York: Oxford University Press, 1997).

2. Roger Williams to John Winthrop, Jr., June 25, 1675, in Glenn W. LaFantasie, ed., *The Correspondence of Roger Williams*, 2 vols. (Hanover, N.H.: University Press of New England), 2:694. In the same letter Williams says he told the Indians that Plymouth pursued Philip because "He broke all Laws and was in Armes of Rebellion agst that Colony his ancient friends and protectours." That Williams explained the conflict to Narragansetts in these terms and expected it to resonate with them can be seen as further evidence that Indians submitted to English colonies sincerely and expected protection in return.

3. James Richards to John Winthrop, Jr., Jan. 5, 13, 1676; and John Allyn to John Winthrop, Jr., Jan. 12, 1676, Winthrop Papers, reel 12, Massachusetts Historical Society, Boston (hereafter, MHS). Highlighting that ethnicity did not predetermine the schisms in the war, the eastern Niantic sachem Ninigret, too, capitalized on the dead Englishmen strewn throughout the battle site. Rather than pillaging them, however, he chose to bury them in order to prove his loyalty to the English, essentially showing more respect for Connecticut's dead than did the English of Massachusetts. Increase Mather, *A Brief History of the War with the Indians in New-England* [1676], reprinted in Samuel G. Drake, ed., *The History of King Philip's War*, (Albany, N.Y.: J. Munsell, 1862), 108–9.

4. [?] Jocelyn [sp?] and Walter Gendall [?] to Joshua Scottow, Aug. 9, 1676, photostats, MHS.

5. Nathaniel B. Shurtleff, ed., *Records of the Governor and Company of the Massachusetts Bay in New England*, 5 vols. (Boston: William White, 1853–54) (hereafter, *Massachusetts Colonial Records*), 5:79. George Madison Bodge, *Soldiers in King Philip's War*, 3d ed. (1906; reprint, Baltimore: Genealogical Publishing Co., 1976), 291. *Massachusetts Colonial Records*, 90.

6. Roger Williams to John Winthrop, Jr., June 25, 1675, in LaFantasie, *Correspondence of Roger Williams*, 2:694.

7. Roger Williams to John Winthrop, Jr., Dec. 18, 1675; and John Winthrop, Jr. to Roger Williams, Jan. 6, 1675, in LaFantasie, *Correspondence of Roger Williams*, 2:708, 710. Interestingly, two years earlier Daniel Gookin said that some praying Indians said the Mohawks "are unto us, as wolves are to your sheep." *Historical Collection of the Indians in New England* [1674], reprinted in *Collections of the Massachusetts Historical Society*, 1st ser., 1 (1792): 165.

8. Feb. 28, 1676, photostats, MHS.

9. Simon Willard, "Deposition of Elizabeth Belcher, Martha Remington, and Mary Mitchell," Mar. 4, 1676, photostats, MHS. For more on the colonial leaders' efforts to restrain those English who attacked loyal Indians, see Jenny Hale Pulsipher, "Massacre at Hurtleberry Hill: Christian Indians and English Authority in Metacom's War," *William and Mary Quarterly*, 3d ser., 53 (July 1996): 459–86.

10. Perry Miller, *The New England Mind: From Colony to Province* (Cambridge, Mass.: Harvard University Press, 1953), 114, 116. Covenant renewal ceremonies occurred throughout New England. Plymouth's congregation and church, for example, voted on July 22, 1676 to stand up and "solemnly renew their Covenant with God and one another" (116). For more on this ceremony in Plymouth, see "Plymouth Church Records," *Collections of the Colonial Society of Massachusetts*, 22 (1920): 148–53. For more on these ceremonies in general, see Sacvan Bercovitch, *The American Jeremiad* (Madison: University of Wisconsin Press, 1978), 80–83.

11. Edward Rawson, *A Letter from the Council of the Colony of Massachusetts Bay to the Council of the Colony of Connecticut* (Providence: Society of Colonial Wars, 1921), 9. James Bate, petition to Massachusetts Council, Sept. [?], 1675; Thomas Eams, petition to Massachusetts Council, Sept. 1, 1675; and Militia of Woburn, petition to Massachusetts Council, Sept. 18, 1675, photostats, MHS.

12. Rawson, *Letter from the Council*, 10.

13. Benjamin Thompson, *New-England's Crisis* (Boston, 1676). Massachusetts State Archives, Boston, 10:233.

14. Daniel Gookin, "An Historical Account of the Doings and Sufferings of the Christian Indians in New England" [1677], in *Collections of the American Antiquarian Society* 2 (1836): 476.

15. James Quannuponkit, testimony before Massachusetts Council, June [?], 1676, photostats, MHS.

16. Mary Rowlandson, *The Sovereignty and Goodness of God*, ed. Neal Salisbury (Boston: Bedford Books, 1997), 107.

17. Gookin, "Doings and Sufferings," 508.

18. Ibid.

19. Ibid., 509.

20. Anthony and James to Massachusetts Council, July 19, 1675; and Peter Ephraim, testimony before Massachusetts Council, June 1, 1676, photostats, MHS.

21. Daniel K. Richter, "War and Culture: The Iroquois Experience," *William and Mary Quarterly*, 3d ser., 40 (Oct. 1983): 528–59. Mather, *Brief History*, 208, 207.

22. These comments about the Peskeompscuts are based on the insights of Ian K. Steele, *Warpaths: Invasions of North America* (New York: Oxford University Press, 1994), 103–6.

23. William Hubbard, *A Narrative of the Troubles with the Indians in New England* [1677], reprinted in Samuel G. Drake, ed., *The History of the Indian Wars in New England*, 2 vols. (1865; reissued in facsimile, Bowie, Md.: Heritage Books, 1990), 1:249.

24. On the distinction between an offer of "quarter" and one of "mercy," see Barbara Donagan, "Atrocity, War Crime, and Treason in the English Civil War," *American Historical Review* 99 (Oct. 1994): 1150.

25. Hubbard, *Narrative*, 1:249, 250. William Wannukhow, Joseph Wannuckhow, and John Appamatahquoon, petition to Massachusetts Court of Assistants, Sept. 5, 1676, photostats, MHS. Unfortunately, I have no way of knowing whether the Indians wrote this themselves or had assistance in preparing it. They heard of the offer of mercy through "tydings thereof sent by James Printer." In another document, Thomas and John Prentice testify that these Indians "left some Indians behind that desired come in and submit but were hindered." Thomas Prentice, John Prentice, et al., testimony to Massachusetts Council, Sept. [?], 1676, photostats, MHS.

26. Benjamin Church, *The Entertaining History of King Philip's War* [1716], reprinted in Benjamin Church, *Diary of King Philip's War, 1675–76* (Chester, Conn.: Pequot Press, 1975), 128.

27. Ibid., 130, 145.

28. Thomas Walley to John Cotton, July 18, 1676, Davis Papers, MHS. John Eliot to Robert Boyle, Oct. 23, 1677, *Collections of the Massachusetts Historical Society*, 1st ser., 3 (1794): 178.

29. Nathaniel B. Shurtleff and David Pulsifer, eds., *Records of the Colony of New Plymouth in New England*, 12 vols. (Boston: William White, 1855–61) (hereafter, *Plymouth Colony Records*), 5:201–3, quotations from 202. Church, *Entertaining History*, 70–72, 115–17. Hubbard, *Narrative*, 1:271. For more on Awashunkes and her loyalties, see Ann Marie Plane, "Putting a Face on Colonization: Factionalism and Gender Politics in the Life History of Awashunkes, the 'Squaw Sachem' of Saconet," in Robert S. Grumet, ed., *Northeastern Indian Lives, 1636–1816* (Amherst: University of Massachusetts Press, 1996). It is possible that the Puritans allowed Awashunkes to live because she was a woman, but it is impossible to find out because she is the only example of a leading female rebel sachem captured alive.

30. Francis Jennings, *The Invasion of America: Indians, Colonialism, and the Cant of Conquest* (New York: Norton, 1975), 320, is especially strong in dealing with the Talcott campaign.

31. Church, *Entertaining History*, 173.

32. Hubbard, *Narrative*, 1:272. Church, *Entertaining History*, 156.

33. Church, *Entertaining History*, 128, 169.

34. Ibid, 173.

35. *Plymouth Colony Records*, 5:205.

36. *Massachusetts Colonial Records*, 5:115.

37. Pulsipher, "Massacre on Hurtleberry Hill," 484.

38. John Russell Bartlett, ed., *Records of the Colony of Rhode Island and Providence Plantation, in New England*, 10 vols. (Providence, 1856–65), 2:549, 586.

39. Horatio Rogers, George M. Carpenter, and Edward Field, eds., *The Early Records of the Town of Providence*, vol. 8 (Providence, R. I., 1895), 13.

40. Ibid., 13–14.

41. J. Hammond Trumbull and Charles J. Hoadly, eds., *The Public Records of the Colony of Connecticut*, 15 vols. (Hartford, Conn.: F. A. Brown, 1850–90) (hereafter, *Records of the Colony of Connecticut*), 2:297–98.

42. Ibid., 474–75, 479–80.

43. James Barker and Joseph Clarke to Plymouth Council, Oct. 7, 1678, Davis papers, MHS. It is unclear how Barker and Clarke knew of the plight of these Indians if they were sold out of the country. It seems likely that they were sold within New England. Other Indians who believed that promises had been broken in their surrender continued to fight. Indians under Wanalancet who were tricked into surrendering held a grudge for years. Connections exist between them and those who attacked Deerfield in 1704. Evan Haefeli and Kevin Sweeney, "Revisiting *The Redeemed Captive:* New Perspectives on the 1704 Attack on Deerfield," *William and Mary Quarterly*, 3d ser., 52 (Jan. 1995): 22–23.

44. John Winthrop, Jr., to [?] Goodale, Feb. 29, 1676, Winthrop papers, reel 12, MHS.

45. *Records of the Colony of Connecticut*, 2:486. Samuel and Jeremy Hide to Massachusetts Council, Aug. 25, 1676, photostats, MHS. For other examples of Indians lobbying for lenient treatment of kin held captive by the English, see Awanhun to Massachusetts Council, [?], 1676; Job Kattenanit to Massachusetts Council, Feb. 14, 1676; and the Massachusetts Council's order concerning Mary Nemasit and Jacob Indian, Nov. 23, 1676, photostats, MHS.

46. Church, *Entertaining History*, 154–56.

47. In one such effort, historian Russell Bourne conceded that the conflict to the north took on a "shape that fits uncomfortably into the total patterns of King Philip's War." *The Red King's Rebellion: Racial Politics in New England, 1675–1678* (New York: Atheneum, 1990), 211.

48. R[ichard] H[utchinson], *The Warr in New-England Visibly Ended* [1677]; reprinted in Charles Henry Lincoln, *Narratives of the Indian Wars, 1675–1699* (New York: Scribner's, 1913), 103–6. Increase Mather, *Brief History*, 199 n. 1. Hubbard, *Narrative*, 2:138, 69 n. 77, quotation on 138.

49. Hubbard, *Narrative*, 2:256–57, 177.

50. Ibid., 2:91–92, 172, 189–92, 218–19, quotation on 91–92; Gordon M. Day,

"Eastern Abenakis," in Bruce Trigger, ed., *Northeast,* vol. 15 of William C. Sturtevant, ed., *Handbook of North American Indians* (Washington, D.C.: Smithsonian Institution Press, 1978), 143.

51. Hubbard, *Narrative,* 2:249–50, 252–55.

52. Ibid., 2:135.

53. Ibid., 2:149, 170–71.

54. Massachusetts Council to Connecticut Council, [?], 1676, photostats, MHS. Plymouth General Court to the Massachusetts General Court, June 8, 1677, Davis Papers, MHS.

55. Richard R. Johnson, "The Search for a Usable Indian: An Aspect of the Defense of Colonial New England," *Journal of American History* 64 (Dec. 1977): 640.

7. LEGACIES

1. Edward Randolph, "Extracts from Edward Randolph's Report to the Council of Trade, October 12, 1676," in E. B. O'Callaghan and Berthold Fernow, eds., *Documents Relative to the Colonial History of the State of New York,* 15 vols. (Albany, N.Y.: Weed, Parsons and Co., 1853–87) (hereafter, *DRCNY*), 3:243–44; N[athaniel] S[altonstall], *A New and Further Narrative of the State of New-England* [1676], reprinted in Charles H. Lincoln, ed., *Narratives of the Indian Wars, 1675–1699* (New York: Scribner's, 1913), 98; and n.a., *News from New England* [1676], reprinted in Samuel G. Drake, ed., *The Old Indian Chronicle* (Boston: Samuel A. Drake, 1867), 310. Randolph, "Extracts," 243–44.

2. John Russell Bartlett, ed., *Records of the Colony of Rhode Island and Providence Plantation, in New England,* 10 vols. (Providence, R. I., 1856–65) (hereafter, *Rhode Island Records*), 3:64. To lend some perspective to these figures, the region affected by the war included about sixty thousand English settlers and just over eighteen thousand Indians. The number of Indian casualties is higher partly because the Indians contributed heavily to both sides of the conflict. It also seems probable that the English combatants whose estimates made it into writing tended to exaggerate boastfully the number of Indian casualties. For more on these population estimates, see chapter 4. The number of households is calculated by dividing the English population, 60,000, by 5. The treasurer and the deputy governor each received £20 per year. J. Hammond Trumbull and Charles J. Hoadly, eds., *The Public Records of the Colony of Connecticut,* 15 vols. (Hartford, Conn.: F. A. Brown, 1850–90) (hereafter, *Records of the Colony of Connecticut*), 2:293.

3. Sherburne F. Cook, "Interracial Warfare and Population Decline among the New England Indians," *Ethnohistory* 20 (winter 1973): 21. Cook estimated that 11,600 Indians joined the rebel cause. Of these, 1,250 died in battle, 625 died of wounds, 3,000 died of exposure and disease, 1,000 were sold as slaves, and 2,000 were permanent refugees. This left in New England only 3,725 of the original 11,600 rebels. Based on Cook's *Indian Population of New England in the Seventeenth Century* (Berkeley: University of California Press, 1976), we can estimate that there were 18,435 Indians living within the region on the eve of the conflict who were directly affected by King Philip's War. For more on this figure, see chapter

4. The fate of those who survived both within and outside of New England is discussed later in this chapter. Daniel Gookin, *Historical Collections of the Indians in New England* [1674], reprinted in *Collections of the Massachusetts Historical Society,* 1st ser., 1 (1792): 141–229, figures from 195. For Gookin's census of the praying Indians in 1676, see his "Historical Account of the Doings and Sufferings of the Christian Indians in New England" [1677], in *Collections of the American Antiquarian Society* 2 (1836): 533. Neal Salisbury, "Toward the Covenant Chain: Iroquois and Southern New England Algonquians, 1637–1684," in Daniel K. Richter and James H. Merrell, eds., *Beyond the Covenant Chain: The Iroquois and Their Neighbors in Indian North America, 1600–1800* (Syracuse, N.Y.: Syracuse University Press, 1987), 71.

4. U.S. Bureau of the Census, *Historical Statistics of the United States, Colonial Times to 1970,* vol. 2 (Washington, D.C.: Bureau of the Census, 1975), 1168. The exact population figures given in this volume are 51,896 and 68,462.

5. Nathaniel B. Shurtleff, ed., *Records of the Governor and Company of the Massachusetts Bay in New England,* 5 vols. (Boston: William White, 1853–54) (hereafter, *Massachusetts Colonial Records*), 5:130; quoted in Jenny Hale Pulsipher, "Massacre at Hurtleberry Hill: Christian Indians and English Authority in Metacom's War," *William and Mary Quarterly,* 3d ser., 53 (July 1996): 484–85.

6. Quoted in Douglas Edward Leach, *Flintlock and Tomahawk: New England in King Philip's War* (New York: Macmillan, 1958), 246.

7. Recently, Michael Puglisi has tried most explicitly to link New Englanders' problems in the final quarter of the seventeenth century to the war. Yet he fails to demonstrate a causal relationship as opposed to a simple correspondence between the timing of these problems and the war. *Puritans Besieged: The Legacies of King Philip's War in the Massachusetts Bay Colony* (Lanham, Md.: University Press of America, 1991). This flaw has been noted in Richard I. Melvoin, review of *Puritans Besieged,* by Michael Puglisi, *William and Mary Quarterly,* 3d ser., 49 (Jan. 1992): 537–39. Stephen Saunders Webb has posited a different relationship between the war and imperial intervention in New England in *1676: The End of American Independence* (New York: Knopf, 1984). Webb sees a systematic, grand scheme on the part of the Crown to more directly rule the colonies. The war fortuitously provided a window of opportunity to intervene. For a sampling of some works that try to explain royal intervention without drawing much on King Philip's War as an explanatory factor, see Bernard Bailyn, *The New England Merchants in the Seventeenth Century* (Cambridge, Mass.: Harvard University Press, 1955); Richard S. Dunn, "Imperial Pressures on Massachusetts and Jamaica, 1675–1700," in Alison Gilbert Olson and Richard Maxwell Brown, eds., *Anglo-American Political Relations, 1675–1775* (New Brunswick, N.J.: Rutgers University Press, 1970), 52–75; Richard R. Johnson, *Adjustment to Empire: The New England Colonies, 1675–1715* (Leicester: Leicester University Press, 1981); and J. M. Sosin, *English America and the Restoration Monarchy of Charles II: Transatlantic Politics, Commerce, and Kinship* (Lincoln: University of Nebraska Press, 1980). For a useful introduction to the debate over the origins of the imperial system in New England, see the testy debate between Johnson and Webb: Richard R. Johnson, "The Imperial Webb:

The Thesis of Garrison Government in Early America Considered," *William and Mary Quarterly*, 3d ser., 43 (July 1986): 408–30; and Stephen Saunders Webb, "The Data and Theory of Restoration Empire," *William and Mary Quarterly*, 3d ser., 43 (July 1986): 431–59.

8. Timothy H. Breen, "War, Taxes, and Political Brokers: The Ordeal of Massachusetts Bay, 1675–1692," in Timothy H. Breen, *Puritans and Adventurers: Change and Persistence in Early America* (New York: Oxford University Press, 1980), 87, 83. In 1672 Dorchester residents payed £50 3s 8d to the town and £28 4s 4d to the colony. In 1678 they paid £13 12s 10d to the town and £111 10s 7d to the colony. The trends in Salem, Dedham, Watertown, Wenham, and Woburn were the same (88). Colonists would sometimes petition colonial officials for relief from taxes imposed by the colony. For instance, see Inhabitants of Sherburne, petition to Massachusetts General Court, Oct. 2, 1678, photostats, Massachusetts Historical Society, Boston (hereafter, MHS). They would also sometimes petition colonial officials for relief from taxes imposed by the town, precipitating bitter disputes between town officials and residents. See, for example, Inhabitants of Cambridge, petition to Massachusetts General Court, May [?], 1678; and Selectmen of Cambridge, response to the petition of some inhabitants, Oct. 23, 1678, photostats, MHS.

For the region's Indian leaders as cultural brokers, see Peter Thomas, "Cultural Change on the Southern New England Frontier, 1630–1665," in William Fitzhugh, ed., *Cultures in Contact: The Impact of European Contacts on Native American Cultural Institutions, a. d. 1000–1800* (Washington, D.C.: Smithsonian Institution Press, 1985), 131–62; and chapters 1 and 2 of this study.

9. By "useful" here I mean as a semiautonomous political entity, not as individual laborers. To be sure, Indians continued to be very useful to the colonists for their labor and as hired soldiers into the next century. See Richard R. Johnson, "The Search for a Usable Indian: An Aspect of the Defense of Colonial New England," *Journal of American History* 64 (Dec. 1977): 623–51.

10. Frederick Jackson Turner, "The First Official Frontier of the Massachusetts Bay," *Publications of the Colonial Society of Massachusetts* 17 (1915): 254. Turner writes that the frontier "stages succeeded rapidly and intermingled" (254).

11. Ibid., 251.

12. Harry S. Stout, *The New England Soul: Preaching and Religious Culture in Colonial New England* (New York: Oxford University Press, 1986), 78–80, quotation from 80.

13. Ibid., 82–93, quotation from 83. The renewal of corporate solidarity and militarization of Massachusetts's orthodoxy contributed to the colony's heightened obstinace in dealing with other colonies and the Crown, as is demonstrated below.

14. For more details on the planned wall, see Leach, *Flintlock and Tomahawk*, 165–66; and Massachusetts State Archives, Boston, vol. 68, docs. 169a, 172a, 174, 175b, 176a, 179, 180, 183. Document 179 is published in George Madison Bodge, *Soldiers in King Philip's War*, 3d ed. (1906; reprint, Baltimore: Genealogical Publishing Co., 1976), 214. Political scientist Anne Norton has aptly characterized the

role of war in shaping societal identity. She writes, "In choosing what they will reject, nations determine what they signify and what they will become. The recognition that polities are defined in difference should teach them to choose their enemies with care. Their enmities define them. They determine the direction of development, the distribution of resources." *Reflections on Political Identity* (Baltimore: Johns Hopkins University Press, 1988), 54–55.

15. Ann Marie Plane, "Putting a Face on Colonization: Factionalism and Gender Politics in the Life History of Awashunkes, the 'Squaw Sachem' of Saconet," in Robert S. Grumet, ed., *Northeastern Indian Lives, 1636–1816* (Amherst: University of Massachusetts Press, 1996). In another case, John Hunter, a praying Indian who had served the colonialist forces during the war, found himself in a Massachusetts prison for "unsuitable carriage and abuse toward his wife." Hunter petitioned the Massachusetts Council to be released, having paid for his actions. He told the council that he would live with Uncas, a leading nonpraying Indian in Connecticut who had actively served the colonialist cause. John Hunter, petition to Massachusetts Council, Mar. 22, 1677, photostats, MHS.

16. Eric Spencer Johnson, "'Some by Flatteries and Others by Threatenings': Political Strategies among Native Americans of Seventeenth-Century New England," Ph.D. diss., University of Massachusetts, 1993, 57.

17. Joshua's will and testament, Feb. 29, 1676, photostats, MHS. Eric Spencer Johnson has also suggested that Uncas sold land in order to command leadership over Indians marginally under his control. See Johnson, "'Some by Flatteries,'" 258–62.

18. The material in this and the following two paragraphs is based on Paul R. Campbell and Glenn W. LaFantasie, "Scattered to the Winds of Heaven: Narragansett Indians 1676–1880," *Rhode Island History* 37 (Aug. 1978): 67–83, esp. 70–72.

19. The word *oasis* is used in ibid., 70. The process here bears some resemblance to the creation of the Catawbas documented by James Merrell in *The Indians' New World: Catawbas and Their Neighbors from European Contact through the Era of Removal* (New York: Norton, 1989).

20. For more on the fledgling state of the Narragansetts during the first quarter of the eighteenth century, see Campbell and LaFantasie, "Scattered to the Winds of Heaven," 72. In many respects the state of the Narragansetts after King Philip's War resembled that of the Senecas after the American Revolution. Anthony F. C. Wallace, in his *Death and Rebirth of the Seneca* (New York: Knopf, 1969), 184–238, described the Senecas as living in "Slums in the Wilderness."

21. Daniel Mandell, "'To Live More like My Christian English Neighbors': Natick Indians in the Eighteenth Century," *William and Mary Quarterly*, 3d ser., 48 (Oct. 1991): 555–56. Kathleen J. Bragdon quoted in ibid., 556. The process of merging the remnants of weakened groups, found among both praying and nonpraying Indians, is analogous to that which James Merrell describes for the Catawbas. Although the process allowed them to survive, oftentimes "[i]nternal divisions further weakened the Catawba." Merrell, *Indians' New World*, 139.

22. John Eliot to Robert Boyle, Apr. 22, 1684, *Collections of the Massachusetts Historical Society*, 1st ser., 3 (1794): 185. Mandell, "'To Live More like,'" 556. Without

ties to the English, the Natick Indians suffered from occasional Mohawk raids. See Jean M. O'Brien, *Dispossession by Degrees: Indian Land and Identity in Natick, Massachusetts, 1650–1790* (New York: Cambridge University Press, 1997), 65. The Christian Indians on Martha's Vineyard fared slightly better. See James P. Ronda, "Generations of Faith: The Christian Indians of Martha's Vineyard," *William and Mary Quarterly* 38 (July 1981): 369–94. I by no means intend to imply that the war uniformly led to a decline in Christian beliefs among New England Indians. For the praying Indians of Martha's Vineyard, Christianity served as a source of communal strength during and after the conflict. See Ronda, "Generations of Faith."

23. William S. Simmons, *Spirit of the New England Tribes: Indian History and Folklore, 1620–1984* (Hanover, N.H.: University Press of New England, 1986), 7, 6.

24. Ibid., 7.

25. Ibid., 141. Constance A. Crosby elaborates on this point and bolsters some of the points made by Simmons by reconciling folklore with an interpretation of changing patterns in the Indian burial of grave goods. "From Myth to History, or Why King Philip's Ghost Walks Abroad," in Mark P. Leone and Parker B. Potter, Jr., eds., *The Recovery of Meaning: Historical Archaeology in the Eastern United States* (Washington, D.C.: Smithsonian Institution Press, 1988), 183–209.

26. Russell M. Peters, *The Wampanoags of Mashpee: An Indian Perspective on American History* (n.p.: Indian Spiritual and Cultural Training Council, 1987), 17.

27. William Apess, *A Son of the Forest* [1831], in Barry O'Connell, ed., *On Our Own Ground: The Complete Writings of William Apess, A Pequot* (Amherst: University of Massachusetts Press, 1992), 3; and William Apess, *Eulogy on King Philip, as Pronounced at the Odeon, in Federal Street, Boston* [1836], in O'Connell, *On Our Own Ground*, 290.

28. Massachusetts Bay Colony, *At a Court Held at Boston in New England the 29th of March 1677. Forbidding the Buying and Keeping of Indians Without Authority* (Cambridge, Mass., 1677).

29. Selectmen of Hingham to constable of Hingham, Dec. 18, 1676, photostats, MHS. Nathaniel Baker, John Jacob, and Mathew Cushing, petition to the Massachusetts Council, Dec. 21, 1676; Massachusetts Council to selectmen of Hingham, Dec. 21, 1676, photostats, MHS. Another resident of Hingham petitioned the Massachusetts Council several weeks later requesting exemption from the town order against keeping Indians. Peter Thaxter, petition to Massachusetts Council, Jan. 11, 1677, photostats, MHS.

30. Samuel Lynde, petition to Massachusetts Council, Apr. [?], 1677; Stephen Burton, petition to Massachusetts Council, May 7, 1677; and George and Elizabeth Danson, petition to Massachusetts General Court, May 25, 1677, photostats, MHS. Another petition similar to these is Henry Crane, petition to Massachusetts Council, May 7, 1677, photostats, MHS. For more on Indian servitude and slavery during this period, see chapter 6; John A. Sainsbury, "Indian Labor in Early Rhode Island," *New England Quarterly* 48 (Sept. 1975): 378–93; and O'Brien, *Dispossession by Degrees*, 89.

31. Statistics extrapolated in Sainsbury, "Indian Labor," 392–93. The census had no mixed-race categories, so we are left with no measure of that dynamic.

32. Cook, "Interracial Warfare," 21. See, for example, the contention that the community of Odanak on the Saint Lawrence was partly comprised of southern New England Algonquians, in Gordon M. Day, *The Identity of the Saint Francis Indians* (Ottawa: National Museums of Canada, 1981), 16–24. For the receptivity of Eastern Abenakis to French missionization efforts and the success and limits of their proselytization efforts, see Kenneth M. Morrison, *The Embattled Northeast: The Elusive Ideal of Alliance in Abenaki-Euramerican Relations* (Berkeley: University of California Press, 1984), 89–93.

33. This seems likely given Kenneth M. Morrison's findings for the Montagnais at Sillery in the 1630s. See "Montagnais Missionization in Early New France: The Syncretic Imperative," *American Indian Culture and Research Journal* 10, no. 3 (1986): 1–23.

34. James Spady, "As If in a Great Darkness: Native American Refugees of the Middle Connecticut River Valley in the Aftermath of King Philip's War," *Historical Journal of Massachusetts* 23 (summer 1995): 183–97; Colin G. Calloway, *The Western Abenakis of Vermont, 1600–1800: War, Migration, and the Survival of an Indian People* (Norman: University of Oklahoma Press, 1990), 76–89. Merrell, *Indians' New World*.

35. Evan Haefeli and Kevin Sweeney, "Revisiting *The Redeemed Captive*: New Perspectives on the 1704 Attack on Deerfield," *William and Mary Quarterly*, 3d ser., 52 (Jan. 1995): 19.

36. Bodge, *Soldiers in King Philip's War*, 67, 305–6; Calloway, "Wanalancet and Kancagamus: Indian Strategy and Leadership on the New Hampshire Frontier," *Historical New Hampshire* 43 (winter 1988): 275–76; Haefeli and Sweeney, "Revisiting," 22–23; and William Hubbard, *A Narrative of the Troubles with the Indians in New England* [1677], reprinted in Samuel G. Drake, ed., *The History of the Indian Wars in New England*, 2 vols. (1865; reissued in facsimile, Bowie, Md.: Heritage Books, 1990), 2:132–33, quotations from 132.

37. Calloway, "Wanalancet and Kancagamus," 281–89; and Haefeli and Sweeney, "Revisiting," 23.

38. See Spady, "As If in a Great Darkness," passim, quotation from 183.

39. Ethel Boissevain, "Whatever Became of the New England Indians Shipped to Bermuda to Be Sold as Slaves?" *Man in the Northeast* 21 (1981): 107. Though Boissevain's work leaves many issues unaddressed, it is the only work I know of that deals with this topic. Clearly, historians need to do more research on this subject.

40. Daniel K. Richter, *The Ordeal of the Longhouse: The Peoples of the Iroquois League in the Era of European Colonization* (Chapel Hill: University of North Carolina Press, 1992), 136.

41. For more on the relationship between King Philip's War and the beginnings of the Covenant Chain, see Richter, *Ordeal of the Longhouse*, 134–42; Salisbury, "Toward the Covenant Chain," 70–73; and Francis Jennings, *The Ambiguous Iroquois Empire: The Covenant Chain Confederation of Indian Tribes with English Colonies from its Beginnings to the Lancaster Treaty of 1744* (New York: Norton, 1984), 145–71. It should be noted here that Andros benefited not only from King Philip's

War but also from events in the concurrent Bacon's Rebellion. Andros established ties with the Susquehannocks residing in Maryland who had become victims of the rebellion's frontier warfare. He invited the Susquehannocks to reside in New York under the Iroquois. The Iroquois benefited, and so did Andros. He now appeared to be more important to London's imperial eyes as a possible intermediary between the various parties in British North America, making him the logical choice for governor upon the establishment of the Dominion of New England. See Richter, *Ordeal of the Longhouse*, 136; and Jennings, *Ambiguous Iroquois Empire*, 149.

42. The best work on the Indians after King Philip's war has been collected in an anthology: Colin G. Calloway, ed., *After King Philip's War: Presence and Persistence in Indian New England* (Hanover, N.H.: University Press of New England, 1997). Especially useful in that volume is Thomas L. Doughton, "Unseen Neighbors: Native Americans of Central Massachusetts, A People Who Had 'Vanished,'" 207–30.

43. Charles M. Andrews, *The Colonial Period of American History*, vol. 4, *England's Commercial and Colonial Policy* (New Haven, Conn.: Yale University Press, 1938); Bailyn, *New England Merchants;* Thomas C. Barrow, *Trade and Empire: The British Customs Service in Colonial America, 1660–1775* (Cambridge, Mass.: Harvard University Press, 1967); Michael Garibaldi Hall, *Edward Randolph and the American Colonies, 1676–1703* (Chapel Hill: University of North Carolina Press, 1960); Sosin, *English America;* and Breen, "War, Taxes, and Political Brokers."

44. W. Noel Sainsbury et al., eds., *Calendar of State Papers, Colonial Series, America and the West Indies* (hereafter, *CSP*), vols. 8, 10 (London, 1890, 1896). Douglas Edward Leach noted that the end of the war precipitated an increase in intercolonial tensions, but he offered little explanation of their root or how they affected relations between New England and London. *Flintlock and Tomahawk*, 248–49.

45. Quoted in Johnson, *Adjustment to Empire*, 28.

46. Ibid., 24. Karen Ordahl Kupperman, *Providence Island, 1630–1641: The Other Puritan Colony* (New York: Cambridge University Press, 1993), 17, 25. Johnson, *Adjustment to Empire*, 25. For more on the desire of England to expand its sugar production, see Sidney W. Mintz, *Sweetness and Power: The Place of Sugar in Modern History* (New York: Penguin, 1985), 36–42.

47. Dunn, "Imperial Pressures," 56, 63, quotation on 63.

48. Karen Ordahl Kupperman, *Providence Island*, 18–22 and passim. Johnson, *Adjustment to Empire*, 22.

49. Petition of Randall Holden and John Greene to the king, Dec. 1678, in *Collections of the Massachusetts Historical Society*, 5th ser., 1 (1871): 505–9, quotation from 507.

50. Sydney V. James, *Colonial Rhode Island: A History* (New York: Scribner's, 1975), 102.

51. *Records of the Colony of Connecticut*, 473–74.

52. Ibid., 289. Ironically, Connecticut made its original claim to the Pequots'

land by virtue of conquest in the Pequot War. Now the Pequots staked a claim to the land of the English and the Narragansetts by virtue of their assistance in the colonial conquest.

53. Ibid., 505.

54. *CSP,* vol. 10, no. 767.

55. Randall Holden and John Greene to the Lords Committees of Trade and Plantations, n.d. (sometime after July 30, 1678), in *Rhode Island Records,* 3:61.

56. *CSP,* vol. 10, no. 768.

57. Ibid., no. 1102.

58. Similarly, the inhabitants of Marlborough, Massachusetts, requested title to some land near them that been held by some Indians on the grounds that "many of which Indians in this our late war have proved very perfidious, [illegible] & treacherous by combining with the common enemy, whereby we humbly conceive the said land now to lie at your honors' disposal." Inhabitants of Marlborough, petition to Massachusetts General Court, May 23, 1677, photostats, MHS.

59. *CSP,* vol. 10, no. 1082.

60. Saltonstall, *New and Further Narrative,* 227, 242–43.

61. *DRCNY,* 3:263. See also 3:257–58, 258–59; and *CSP,* vol. 10, nos. 502, 652, 653, 654, 660, 677, 678. Stephen Saunders Webb also points to the issue of Mohawk intervention in shaping relations with the Crown. *1676,* 240–41. Webb, unlike Richard Johnson and myself, posits that the Crown was eager to intervene in New England affairs before King Philip's War and just needed an excuse to do so.

62. *CSP,* vol. 10, nos. 168, 740. See also *Massachusetts Colonial Records,* 5:106–7.

63. *CSP,* vol. 10, no. 1305. For more on Indian–English relations in Maine in the seventeenth century and the pivotal role of King Philip's War, see Emerson Woods Baker II, "Trouble to the Eastward: The Failure of Anglo–Indian Relations in Early Maine," Ph.D. diss., College of William and Mary, 1986.

64. On Andros's land policy, Wait Winthrop objected that "The Purchasing of the Natives Right, was made nothing of, and next to a Ridicule. The Enjoyment and Improvement of Lands not inclosed, and espcially if lying in common amongst many was denied to be possession." Quoted in Richard S. Dunn, *Puritans and Yankees: The Winthrop Dynasty of New England, 1630–1717* (Princeton, N.J.: Princeton University Press, 1962), 251. Hall, *Edward Randolph,* 107–10; and Johnson, *Adjustment to Empire,* 73–88.

65. Johnson, *Adjustment to Empire,* 64. Johnson also notes that appeals to the Crown from within New England "broadened the focus of London's appeals from the Bay Colony's misdeeds to the condition of New England as a whole: it was after listening to accounts of the violence and bitterness aroused by the Narragansett issue that the Lords of Trade concluded that only a general governor could heal New England's dissensions." He also notes that Pennsylvania received its charter in 1681, and thus the Crown did not have a coherent plan for bringing all American colonies under tighter royal control. Johnson, *Adjustment to Empire,* 44, 32.

66. Stephen Foster, *The Long Argument: English Puritanism and the Shaping of New England Culture, 1570–1700* (Chapel Hill: University of North Carolina Press, 1991), 237.

67. Richard S. Dunn, *Puritans and Yankees,* vii, 118, 187, 230.

68. Michael Garibaldi Hall, *The Last American Puritan: The Life of Increase Mather, 1639–1723* (Middletown, Conn.: Wesleyan University Press, 1988), 184–254, esp. 252; Foster, *Long Argument,* 247–68.

CONCLUSION

1. See Gary B. Nash, *Red, White, and Black: The Peoples of Early North America,* 3d ed. (Englewood Cliffs, N.J.: Prentice-Hall, 1992), 118–23; Francis Jennings, *The Invasion of America: Indians, Colonialism, and the Cant of Conquest* (New York: Norton, 1975), passim.

2. Philip Ranlet, "Another Look at the Causes of King Philip's War," *New England Quarterly* 61 (Mar. 1988): 80 n. 3; Henry W. Bowden and James P. Ronda, *John Eliot's Indian Dialogues: A Study in Cultural Interaction* [1671] (Westport, Conn.: Greenwood Press, 1980), 120; Nathaniel B. Shurtleff and David Pulsifer, eds., *Records of the Colony of New Plymouth in New England,* 12 vols. (Boston: William White, 1855–61), 8:190–91. I believe that the word *Keitasscot* is simply a variation on the Massachusett word *ketahsoot,* meaning king or sachem. See Ives Goddard and Kathleen J. Bragdon, eds., *Native Writings in Massachusett* (Philadelphia: American Philosophical Society, 1988), 631. I suspect that *Wewasowannett* is related to or a corruption of the Algonquian term *werowance* used by the Powhatans of Virginia. If so, it would be a title similar to "keitasscot." See Karen Ordahl Kupperman, *Settling with the Indians: The Meeting of English and Indian Cultures in America, 1580–1640* (Totowa, N.J.: Rowman and Littlefield, 1980), 48.

3. Jill Lepore, *The Name of War: King Philip's War and the Origins of American Identity* (New York: Knopf, 1998), xv–xvi.

4. Vine Deloria, Jr., *Custer Died for Your Sins: An Indian Manifesto* (New York: Macmillan, 1969).

5. Eric Foner, *Free Soil, Free Labor, Free Men: The Ideology of the Republican Party before the Civil War* (New York: Oxford University Press, 1970); Eric Foner, "Politics, Ideology, and the Origins of the American Civil War," in George Fredrickson, ed., *A Nation Divided* (Minneapolis: Burgess, 1975); and Eugene D. Genovese, *The Political Economy of Slavery: Studies in the Economy and Society of the Slave South,* 2d ed. (Hanover, N.H.: University Press of New England, 1989).

6. Jennings, *Invasion of America,* 301–2. For the long history of antagonism between the Iroquois and New England's Indians, see Gordon M. Day, "The Ouragie War: A Case History in Iroquois–New England Indian Relations," in Michael K. Foster, Jack Campisi, and Marianne Mithun, eds., *Extending the Rafters: Interdisciplinary Approaches to Iroquoian Studies* (Albany, N.Y.: SUNY Press, 1984), 35–50. This essay also explores how the French alliance with the Abenakis altered the political boundaries of the Northeast.

ACKNOWLEDGMENTS

THIS BOOK could not have been completed without the help of many institutions and individuals. It originated as a dissertation at the University of California, Los Angeles. There I was fortunate enough to have the patient guidance of James Lockhart and Timothy Earle through some of the basics of Latin American history and anthropology. Melissa Meyer assisted by giving chapters exceptionally detailed readings. Finally, Gary B. Nash made the study possible by at least pretending that I was not crazy when I first suggested that I wanted to argue that King Philip's War should be seen as a civil war. In subsequent years his patient guidance kept the dissertation going forward.

I also benefited from the help of fellow students at UCLA: members of the Early American Thesis Seminar encouraged and challenged me at every step. In particular, I am grateful to Michael Fickes, Tony Iaccarino, Anne Lombard, and Richard Olivas. Alison Sneider and Mark Spence also read portions of the study and provided some of the friendship necessary to complete a dissertation. Mike Latham gave the entire manuscript a close reading.

For the necessary institutional and financial support, I am grateful to the American Indian Studies Center at UCLA, the Huntington Library, the Massachusetts Historical Society, and the UCLA Research Library and History Department. The staff at the Massachusetts Historical Society were especially patient in helping me to navigate through their archives. And the Huntington Library gave more than just funds and access to source material. Many members of its scholarly community provided thought-provoking discussion or constructive criticism of drafts of chapters. For such input, I am indebted to Dan Bauman, Barbara Donagan, Wilbur Jacobs, Karen Kupperman, and Robert Ritchie. At the UCLA library, Cindy Shelton fulfilled my requests with a sense of humor.

As the foundation for a book, the dissertation proved in many places to be made of sand, and it took many individuals to make me aware of this and help me fix it. Karen Kupperman, Jenny Hale Pulsipher, and Neal Salisbury read the original work (Salisbury more than once), and their suggestions started me on the road to revision. Gary Dunham also offered constructive criticism. Jill Lepore on numerous occasions responded to questions that only a King Philip's War expert could answer.

Portions of chapters 2 and 3 appeared earlier in "Symbol of a Failed Strategy: The Sassamon Trial, Political Culture, and the Outbreak of King Philip's War," *American Indian Culture and Research Journal* 19, no. 2 (1995): 111–41, and are reprintd by permission of the American Indian Studies Center, UCLA. © Regents of the University of California. Parts of chapters 5 and 6 originally appeared as "Restraining Atrocity: The Conduct of King Philip's War," *New England Quarterly* 70 (March 1997): 33–56, and are reprinted by permission of *The New England Quarterly*. At that journal I owe a special debt to the editing skills of Linda Smith Rhoads.

For the University of Massachusetts Press, Colin Calloway and Barry O'Connell gave the manuscript close readings and provided valuable encouragement when I most needed it. Kevin Sweeney, in particular, pushed me to do my best. Clark Dougan helped me interpret reader reports. Ella Kusnetz and Carol Betsch guided the manuscript through the publication process. And Lois Crum saved me from many embarrassing errors and made the book read better with her superb editing.

My colleagues at the University of Colorado and especially at Metropolitan State College of Denver have been extremely supportive. In particular, Laura McCall and Ellen Slatkin read portions of the manuscript, and Steve Leonard provided sound advice and encouragement. Andrew Zantos contributed his computer skills to preparing the map that appears at the beginning of the book.

Finally, I could not have completed the book without my family. Bogey does not have much of a way with words, but he has been a good listener throughout the process. And Monique was always there.

INDEX